Mastering OpenCV with Practical Computer Vision Projects

Step-by-step tutorials to solve common real-world computer vision problems for desktop or mobile, from augmented reality and number plate recognition to face recognition and 3D head tracking

Daniel Lélis Baggio
Shervin Emami
David Millán Escrivá
Khvedchenia Ievgen
Naureen Mahmood
Jason Saragih
Roy Shilkrot

BIRMINGHAM - MUMBAI

Mastering OpenCV with Practical Computer Vision Projects

First published: December 2012

Production Reference: 2231112

Published by Packt Publishing Ltd.
Livery Place
35 Livery Street
Birmingham B3 2PB, UK.

ISBN 978-1-84951-782-9

www.packtpub.com

Cover Image by Neha Rajappan (neha.rajappan1@gmail.com)

Credits

Authors
Daniel Lélis Baggio
Shervin Emami
David Millán Escrivá
Khvedchenia Ievgen
Naureen Mahmood
Jason Saragih
Roy Shilkrot

Reviewers
Kirill Kornyakov
Luis Díaz Más
Sebastian Montabone

Acquisition Editor
Usha Iyer

Lead Technical Editor
Ankita Shashi

Technical Editors
Sharvari Baet
Prashant Salvi

Copy Editors
Brandt D'Mello
Aditya Nair
Alfida Paiva

Project Coordinator
Priya Sharma

Proofreaders
Chris Brown
Martin Diver

Indexer
Hemangini Bari
Tejal Soni
Rekha Nair

Graphics
Valentina D'silva
Aditi Gajjar

Production Coordinator
Arvindkumar Gupta

Cover Work
Arvindkumar Gupta

About the Authors

Daniel Lélis Baggio started his work in computer vision through medical image processing at InCor (Instituto do Coração – Heart Institute) in São Paulo, where he worked with intra-vascular ultrasound image segmentation. Since then, he has focused on GPGPU and ported the segmentation algorithm to work with NVIDIA's CUDA. He has also dived into six degrees of freedom head tracking with a natural user interface group through a project called ehci (http://code.google.com/p/ehci/). He now works for the Brazilian Air Force.

I'd like to thank God for the opportunity of working with computer vision. I try to understand the wonderful algorithms He has created for us to see. I also thank my family, and especially my wife, for all their support throughout the development of the book. I'd like to dedicate this book to my son Stefano.

Shervin Emami (born in Iran) taught himself electronics and hobby robotics during his early teens in Australia. While building his first robot at the age of 15, he learned how RAM and CPUs work. He was so amazed by the concept that he soon designed and built a whole Z80 motherboard to control his robot, and wrote all the software purely in binary machine code using two push buttons for 0s and 1s. After learning that computers can be programmed in much easier ways such as assembly language and even high-level compilers, Shervin became hooked to computer programming and has been programming desktops, robots, and smartphones nearly every day since then. During his late teens he created Draw3D (http://draw3d.shervinemami.info/), a 3D modeler with 30,000 lines of optimized C and assembly code that rendered 3D graphics faster than all the commercial alternatives of the time; but he lost interest in graphics programming when 3D hardware acceleration became available.

In University, Shervin took a subject on computer vision and became highly interested in it; so for his first thesis in 2003 he created a real-time face detection program based on Eigenfaces, using OpenCV (beta 3) for camera input. For his master's thesis in 2005 he created a visual navigation system for several mobile robots using OpenCV (v0.96). From 2008, he worked as a freelance Computer Vision Developer in Abu Dhabi and Philippines, using OpenCV for a large number of short-term commercial projects that included:

- Detecting faces using Haar or Eigenfaces
- Recognizing faces using Neural Networks, EHMM, or Eigenfaces
- Detecting the 3D position and orientation of a face from a single photo using AAM and POSIT
- Rotating a face in 3D using only a single photo
- Face preprocessing and artificial lighting using any 3D direction from a single photo
- Gender recognition
- Facial expression recognition
- Skin detection
- Iris detection
- Pupil detection
- Eye-gaze tracking
- Visual-saliency tracking
- Histogram matching
- Body-size detection
- Shirt and bikini detection
- Money recognition
- Video stabilization
- Face recognition on iPhone
- Food recognition on iPhone
- Marker-based augmented reality on iPhone (the second-fastest iPhone augmented reality app at the time).

OpenCV was putting food on the table for Shervin's family, so he began giving back to OpenCV through regular advice on the forums and by posting free OpenCV tutorials on his website (http://www.shervinemami.info/openCV.html). In 2011, he contacted the owners of other free OpenCV websites to write this book. He also began working on computer vision optimization for mobile devices at NVIDIA, working closely with the official OpenCV developers to produce an optimized version of OpenCV for Android. In 2012, he also joined the Khronos OpenVL committee for standardizing the hardware acceleration of computer vision for mobile devices, on which OpenCV will be based in the future.

I thank my wife Gay and my baby Luna for enduring the stress while I juggled my time between this book, working fulltime, and raising a family. I also thank the developers of OpenCV, who worked hard for many years to provide a high-quality product for free.

David Millán Escrivá was eight years old when he wrote his first program on an 8086 PC with Basic language, which enabled the 2D plotting of basic equations. In 2005, he finished his studies in IT through the Universitat Politécnica de Valencia with honors in human-computer interaction supported by computer vision with OpenCV (v0.96). He had a final project based on this subject and published it on HCI Spanish congress. He participated in Blender, an open source, 3D-software project, and worked in his first commercial movie *Plumiferos - Aventuras voladoras* as a Computer Graphics Software Developer.

David now has more than 10 years of experience in IT, with experience in computer vision, computer graphics, and pattern recognition, working on different projects and startups, applying his knowledge of computer vision, optical character recognition, and augmented reality. He is the author of the "DamilesBlog" (http://blog.damiles.com), where he publishes research articles and tutorials about OpenCV, computer vision in general, and Optical Character Recognition algorithms.

David has reviewed the book *gnuPlot Cookbook* by *Lee Phillips* and published by *Packt Publishing*.

Thanks Izaskun and my daughter Eider for their patience and support. Os quiero pequeñas.

I also thank Shervin for giving me this opportunity, the OpenCV team for their work, the support of Artres, and the useful help provided by Augmate.

Khvedchenia Ievgen is a computer vision expert from Ukraine. He started his career with research and development of a camera-based driver assistance system for Harman International. He then began working as a Computer Vision Consultant for ESG. Nowadays, he is a self-employed developer focusing on the development of augmented reality applications. Ievgen is the author of the *Computer Vision Talks* blog (`http://computer-vision-talks.com`), where he publishes research articles and tutorials pertaining to computer vision and augmented reality.

I would like to say thanks to my father who inspired me to learn programming when I was 14. His help can't be overstated. And thanks to my mom, who always supported me in all my undertakings. You always gave me a freedom to choose my own way in this life. Thanks, parents!

Thanks to Kate, a woman who totally changed my life and made it extremely full. I'm happy we're together. Love you.

Naureen Mahmood is a recent graduate from the Visualization department at Texas A&M University. She has experience working in various programming environments, animation software, and microcontroller electronics. Her work involves creating interactive applications using sensor-based electronics and software engineering. She has also worked on creating physics-based simulations and their use in special effects for animation.

I wanted to especially mention the efforts of another student from Texas A&M, whose name you will undoubtedly come across in the code included for this book. Fluid Wall was developed as part of a student project by Austin Hines and myself. Major credit for the project goes to Austin, as he was the creative mind behind it. He was also responsible for the arduous job of implementing the fluid simulation code into our application. However, he wasn't able to participate in writing this book due to a number of work- and study-related preoccupations.

Jason Saragih received his B.Eng degree in mechatronics (with honors) and Ph.D. in computer science from the Australian National University, Canberra, Australia, in 2004 and 2008, respectively. From 2008 to 2010 he was a Postdoctoral fellow at the Robotics Institute of Carnegie Mellon University, Pittsburgh, PA. From 2010 to 2012 he worked at the Commonwealth Scientific and Industrial Research Organization (CSIRO) as a Research Scientist. He is currently a Senior Research Scientist at Visual Features, an Australian tech startup company.

Dr. Saragih has made a number of contributions to the field of computer vision, specifically on the topic of deformable model registration and modeling. He is the author of two non-profit open source libraries that are widely used in the scientific community; DeMoLib and FaceTracker, both of which make use of generic computer vision libraries including OpenCV.

Roy Shilkrot is a researcher and professional in the area of computer vision and computer graphics. He obtained a B.Sc. in Computer Science from Tel-Aviv-Yaffo Academic College, and an M.Sc. from Tel-Aviv University. He is currently a PhD candidate in Media Laboratory of the Massachusetts Institute of Technology (MIT) in Cambridge.

Roy has over seven years of experience as a Software Engineer in start-up companies and enterprises. Before joining the MIT Media Lab as a Research Assistant he worked as a Technology Strategist in the Innovation Laboratory of Comverse, a telecom solutions provider. He also dabbled in consultancy, and worked as an intern for Microsoft research at Redmond.

Thanks go to my wife for her limitless support and patience, my past and present advisors in both academia and industry for their wisdom, and my friends and colleagues for their challenging thoughts.

About the Reviewers

Kirill Kornyakov is a Project Manager at Itseez, where he leads the development of OpenCV library for Android mobile devices. He manages activities for the mobile operating system's support and computer vision applications development, including performance optimization for NVIDIA's Tegra platform. Earlier he worked at Itseez on real-time computer vision systems for open source and commercial products, chief among them being stereo vision on GPU and face detection in complex environments. Kirill has a B.Sc. and an M.Sc. from Nizhniy Novgorod State University, Russia.

I would like to thank my family for their support, my colleagues from Itseez, and Nizhniy Novgorod State University for productive discussions.

Luis Díaz Más considers himself a computer vision researcher and is passionate about open source and open-hardware communities. He has been working with image processing and computer vision algorithms since 2008 and is currently finishing his PhD on 3D reconstructions and action recognition. Currently he is working in CATEC (http://www.catec.com.es/en), a research center for advanced aerospace technologies, where he mainly deals with the sensorial systems of UAVs. He has participated in several national and international projects where he has proven his skills in C/C++ programming, application development for embedded systems with Qt libraries, and his experience with GNU/Linux distribution configuration for embedded systems. Lately he is focusing his interest in ARM and CUDA development.

Sebastian Montabone is a Computer Engineer with a Master of Science degree in computer vision. He is the author of scientific articles pertaining to image processing and has also authored a book, *Beginning Digital Image Processing: Using Free Tools for Photographers*.

Embedded systems have also been of interest to him, especially mobile phones. He created and taught a course about the development of applications for mobile phones, and has been recognized as a Nokia developer champion.

Currently he is a Software Consultant and Entrepreneur. You can visit his blog at www.samontab.com, where he shares his current projects with the world.

www.PacktPub.com

Support files, eBooks, discount offers and more

You might want to visit www.PacktPub.com for support files and downloads related to your book.

Did you know that Packt offers eBook versions of every book published, with PDF and ePub files available? You can upgrade to the eBook version at www.PacktPub.com and as a print book customer, you are entitled to a discount on the eBook copy. Get in touch with us at service@packtpub.com for more details.

At www.PacktPub.com, you can also read a collection of free technical articles, sign up for a range of free newsletters and receive exclusive discounts and offers on Packt books and eBooks.

http://PacktLib.PacktPub.com

Do you need instant solutions to your IT questions? PacktLib is Packt's online digital book library. Here, you can access, read and search across Packt's entire library of books.

Why Subscribe?

- Fully searchable across every book published by Packt
- Copy and paste, print and bookmark content
- On demand and accessible via web browser

Free Access for Packt account holders

If you have an account with Packt at www.PacktPub.com, you can use this to access PacktLib today and view nine entirely free books. Simply use your login credentials for immediate access.

Table of Contents

Preface

Mastering OpenCV with Practical Computer Vision Projects contains nine chapters, where each chapter is a tutorial for an entire project from start to finish, based on OpenCV's C++ interface including full source code. The author of each chapter was chosen for their well-regarded online contributions to the OpenCV community on that topic, and the book was reviewed by one of the main OpenCV developers. Rather than explaining the basics of OpenCV functions, this is the first book that shows how to apply OpenCV to solve whole problems, including several 3D camera projects (augmented reality, 3D Structure from Motion, Kinect interaction) and several facial analysis projects (such as, skin detection, simple face and eye detection, complex facial feature tracking, 3D head orientation estimation, and face recognition), therefore it makes a great companion to existing OpenCV books.

What this book covers

Chapter 1, Cartoonifier and Skin Changer for Android, contains a complete tutorial and source code for both a desktop application and an Android app that automatically generates a cartoon or painting from a real camera image, with several possible types of cartoons including a skin color changer.

Chapter 2, Marker-based Augmented Reality on iPhone or iPad, contains a complete tutorial on how to build a marker-based augmented reality (AR) application for iPad and iPhone devices with an explanation of each step and source code.

Chapter 3, Marker-less Augmented Reality, contains a complete tutorial on how to develop a marker-less augmented reality desktop application with an explanation of what marker-less AR is and source code.

Chapter 4, Exploring Structure from Motion Using OpenCV, contains an introduction to Structure from Motion (SfM) via an implementation of SfM concepts in OpenCV. The reader will learn how to reconstruct 3D geometry from multiple 2D images and estimate camera positions.

Chapter 5, Number Plate Recognition Using SVM and Neural Networks, contains a complete tutorial and source code to build an automatic number plate recognition application using pattern recognition algorithms using a support vector machine and Artificial Neural Networks. The reader will learn how to train and predict pattern-recognition algorithms to decide if an image is a number plate or not. It will also help classify a set of features into a character.

Chapter 6, Non-rigid Face Tracking, contains a complete tutorial and source code to build a dynamic face tracking system that can model and track the many complex parts of a person's face.

Chapter 7, 3D Head Pose Estimation Using AAM and POSIT, contains all the background required to understand what **Active Appearance Models (AAMs)** are and how to create them with OpenCV using a set of face frames with different facial expressions. Besides, this chapter explains how to match a given frame through fitting capabilities offered by AAMs. Then, by applying the POSIT algorithm, one can find the 3D head pose.

Chapter 8, Face Recognition using Eigenfaces or Fisherfaces, contains a complete tutorial and source code for a real-time face-recognition application that includes basic face and eye detection to handle the rotation of faces and varying lighting conditions in the images.

Chapter 9, Developing Fluid Wall Using the Microsoft Kinect, covers the complete development of an interactive fluid simulation called the Fluid Wall, which uses the Kinect sensor. The chapter will explain how to use Kinect data with OpenCV's optical flow methods and integrating it into a fluid solver.

You can download this chapter from: `http://www.packtpub.com/sites/default/files/downloads/7829OS_Chapter9_Developing_Fluid_Wall_Using_the_Microsoft_Kinect.pdf`.

What you need for this book

You don't need to have special knowledge in computer vision to read this book, but you should have good C/C++ programming skills and basic experience with OpenCV before reading this book. Readers without experience in OpenCV may wish to read the book *Learning OpenCV* for an introduction to the OpenCV features, or read *OpenCV 2 Cookbook* for examples on how to use OpenCV with recommended C/C++ patterns, because *Mastering OpenCV with Practical Computer Vision Projects* will show you how to solve real problems, assuming you are already familiar with the basics of OpenCV and C/C++ development.

In addition to C/C++ and OpenCV experience, you will also need a computer, and IDE of your choice (such as Visual Studio, XCode, Eclipse, or QtCreator, running on Windows, Mac or Linux). Some chapters have further requirements, in particular:

- To develop the Android app, you will need an Android device, Android development tools, and basic Android development experience.

- To develop the iOS app, you will need an iPhone, iPad, or iPod Touch device, iOS development tools (including an Apple computer, XCode IDE, and an Apple Developer Certificate), and basic iOS and Objective-C development experience.

- Several desktop projects require a webcam connected to your computer. Any common USB webcam should suffice, but a webcam of at least 1 megapixel may be desirable.

- CMake is used in some projects, including OpenCV itself, to build across operating systems and compilers. A basic understanding of build systems is required, and knowledge of cross-platform building is recommended.

- An understanding of linear algebra is expected, such as basic vector and matrix operations and eigen decomposition.

Who this book is for

Mastering OpenCV with Practical Computer Vision Projects is the perfect book for developers with basic OpenCV knowledge to create practical computer vision projects, as well as for seasoned OpenCV experts who want to add more computer vision topics to their skill set. It is aimed at senior computer science university students, graduates, researchers, and computer vision experts who wish to solve real problems using the OpenCV C++ interface, through practical step-by-step tutorials.

Conventions

In this book, you will find a number of styles of text that distinguish between different kinds of information. Here are some examples of these styles, and an explanation of their meaning.

Code words in text are shown as follows: "You should put most of the code of this chapter into the `cartoonifyImage()` function."

A block of code is set as follows:

```
int cameraNumber = 0;
if (argc > 1)
    cameraNumber = atoi(argv[1]);
// Get access to the camera.
cv::VideoCapture capture;
```

When we wish to draw your attention to a particular part of a code block, the relevant lines or items are set in bold:

```
// Get access to the camera.
cv::VideoCapture capture;
camera.open(cameraNumber);
if (!camera.isOpened()) {
    std::cerr << "ERROR: Could not access the camera or video!" <<
```

New terms and **important words** are shown in bold. Words that you see on the screen, in menus or dialog boxes for example, appear in the text like this: "clicking the **Next** button moves you to the next screen".

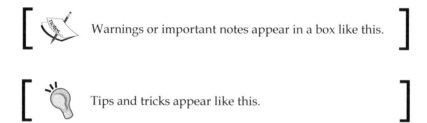

> Warnings or important notes appear in a box like this.

> Tips and tricks appear like this.

Reader feedback

Feedback from our readers is always welcome. Let us know what you think about this book—what you liked or may have disliked. Reader feedback is important for us to develop titles that you really get the most out of.

To send us general feedback, simply send an e-mail to feedback@packtpub.com, and mention the book title via the subject of your message.

If there is a topic that you have expertise in and you are interested in either writing or contributing to a book, see our author guide on www.packtpub.com/authors.

Customer support

Now that you are the proud owner of a Packt book, we have a number of things to help you to get the most from your purchase.

Downloading the example code

You can download the example code files for all Packt books you have purchased from your account at `http://www.PacktPub.com`. If you purchased this book elsewhere, you can visit `http://www.PacktPub.com/support` and register to have the files e-mailed directly to you.

Errata

Although we have taken every care to ensure the accuracy of our content, mistakes do happen. If you find a mistake in one of our books—maybe a mistake in the text or the code—we would be grateful if you would report this to us. By doing so, you can save other readers from frustration and help us improve subsequent versions of this book. If you find any errata, please report them by visiting `http://www.packtpub.com/support`, selecting your book, clicking on the **errata submission form** link, and entering the details of your errata. Once your errata are verified, your submission will be accepted and the errata will be uploaded on our website, or added to any list of existing errata, under the Errata section of that title. Any existing errata can be viewed by selecting your title from `http://www.packtpub.com/support`.

Piracy

Piracy of copyright material on the Internet is an ongoing problem across all media. At Packt, we take the protection of our copyright and licenses very seriously. If you come across any illegal copies of our works, in any form, on the Internet, please provide us with the location address or website name immediately so that we can pursue a remedy.

Please contact us at `copyright@packtpub.com` with a link to the suspected pirated material.

We appreciate your help in protecting our authors, and our ability to bring you valuable content.

Questions

You can contact us at `questions@packtpub.com` if you are having a problem with any aspect of the book, and we will do our best to address it.

1
Cartoonifier and Skin Changer for Android

This chapter will show you how to write some image-processing filters for Android smartphones and tablets, written first for desktop (in C/C++) and then ported to Android (with the same C/C++ code but with a Java GUI), since this is the recommended scenario when developing for mobile devices. This chapter will cover:

- How to convert a real-life image to a sketch drawing
- How to convert to a painting and overlay the sketch to produce a cartoon
- A scary "evil" mode to create bad characters instead of good characters
- A basic skin detector and skin color changer, to give someone green "alien" skin
- How to convert the project from a desktop app to a mobile app

The following screenshot shows the final Cartoonifier app running on an Android tablet:

We want to make the real-world camera frames look like they are genuinely from a cartoon. The basic idea is to fill the flat parts with some color and then draw thick lines on the strong edges. In other words, the flat areas should become much more flat and the edges should become much more distinct. We will detect edges and smooth the flat areas, then draw enhanced edges back on top to produce a cartoon or comic book effect.

When developing mobile computer vision apps, it is a good idea to build a fully working desktop version first before porting it to mobile, since it is much easier to develop and debug a desktop program than a mobile app! This chapter will therefore begin with a complete Cartoonifier desktop program that you can create using your favorite IDE (for example, Visual Studio, XCode, Eclipse, QtCreator, and so on). After it is working properly on the desktop, the last section shows how to port it to Android (or potentially iOS) with Eclipse. Since we will create two different projects that mostly share the same source code with different graphical user interfaces, you could create a library that is linked by both projects, but for simplicity we will put the desktop and Android projects next to each other, and set up the Android project to access some files (`cartoon.cpp` and `cartoon.h`, containing all the image processing code) from the `Desktop` folder. For example:

- `C:\Cartoonifier_Desktop\cartoon.cpp`
- `C:\Cartoonifier_Desktop\cartoon.h`
- `C:\Cartoonifier_Desktop\main_desktop.cpp`
- `C:\Cartoonifier_Android\...`

The desktop app uses an OpenCV GUI window, initializes the camera, and with each camera frame calls the `cartoonifyImage()` function containing most of the code in this chapter. It then displays the processed image on the GUI window. Similarly, the Android app uses an Android GUI window, initializes the camera using Java, and with each camera frame calls the exact same C++ `cartoonifyImage()` function as previously mentioned, but with Android menus and finger-touch input. This chapter will explain how to create the desktop app from scratch, and the Android app from one of the OpenCV Android sample projects. So first you should create a desktop program in your favorite IDE, with a `main_desktop.cpp` file to hold the GUI code given in the following sections, such as the main loop, webcam functionality, and keyboard input, and you should create a `cartoon.cpp` file that will be shared between projects. You should put most of the code of this chapter into `cartoon.cpp` as a function called `cartoonifyImage()`.

Accessing the webcam

To access a computer's webcam or camera device, you can simply call `open()` on a `cv::VideoCapture` object (OpenCV's method of accessing your camera device), and pass 0 as the default camera ID number. Some computers have multiple cameras attached or they do not work as default camera 0; so it is common practice to allow the user to pass the desired camera number as a command-line argument, in case they want to try camera 1, 2, or -1, for example. We will also try to set the camera resolution to 640 x 480 using `cv::VideoCapture::set()`, in order to run faster on high-resolution cameras.

 Depending on your camera model, driver, or system, OpenCV might not change the properties of your camera. It is not important for this project, so don't worry if it does not work with your camera.

You can put this code in the `main()` function of your `main_desktop.cpp`:

```
int cameraNumber = 0;
if (argc > 1)
  cameraNumber = atoi(argv[1]);

// Get access to the camera.
cv::VideoCapture camera;
camera.open(cameraNumber);
if (!camera.isOpened()) {
  std::cerr << "ERROR: Could not access the camera or video!" <<
  std::endl;
  exit(1);
}

// Try to set the camera resolution.
camera.set(cv::CV_CAP_PROP_FRAME_WIDTH, 640);
camera.set(cv::CV_CAP_PROP_FRAME_HEIGHT, 480);
```

After the webcam has been initialized, you can grab the current camera image as a `cv::Mat` object (OpenCV's image container). You can grab each camera frame by using the C++ streaming operator from your `cv::VideoCapture` object into a `cv::Mat` object, just like if you were getting input from a console.

OpenCV makes it very easy to load a video file (such as an AVI or MPG file) and use it instead of a webcam. The only difference to your code would be that you should create the `cv::VideoCapture` object with the video filename, such as `camera.open("my_video.avi")`, rather than the camera number, such as `camera.open(0)`. Both methods create a `cv::VideoCapture` object that can be used in the same way.

Main camera processing loop for a desktop app

If you want to display a GUI window on the screen using OpenCV, you call `cv::imshow()` for each image, but you must also call `cv::waitKey()` once per frame, otherwise your windows will not update at all! Calling `cv::waitKey(0)` waits indefinitely until the user hits a key in the window, but a positive number such as `waitKey(20)` or higher will wait for at least that many milliseconds.

Put this main loop in `main_desktop.cpp`, as the basis for your real-time camera app:

```cpp
while (true) {
  // Grab the next camera frame.
  cv::Mat cameraFrame;
  camera >> cameraFrame;
  if (cameraFrame.empty()) {
    std::cerr << "ERROR: Couldn't grab a camera frame." <<
    std::endl;
    exit(1);
  }
  // Create a blank output image, that we will draw onto.
  cv::Mat displayedFrame(cameraFrame.size(), cv::CV_8UC3);

  // Run the cartoonifier filter on the camera frame.
  cartoonifyImage(cameraFrame, displayedFrame);

  // Display the processed image onto the screen.
  imshow("Cartoonifier", displayedFrame);

  // IMPORTANT: Wait for at least 20 milliseconds,
  // so that the image can be displayed on the screen!
  // Also checks if a key was pressed in the GUI window.
  // Note that it should be a "char" to support Linux.
  char keypress = cv::waitKey(20);  // Need this to see anything!
  if (keypress == 27) {   // Escape Key
```

```
    // Quit the program!
    break;
    }
}//end while
```

Generating a black-and-white sketch

To obtain a sketch (black-and-white drawing) of the camera frame, we will use an edge-detection filter; whereas to obtain a color painting, we will use an edge-preserving filter (bilateral filter) to further smooth the flat regions while keeping the edges intact. By overlaying the sketch drawing on top of the color painting, we obtain a cartoon effect as shown earlier in the screenshot of the final app.

There are many different edge detection filters, such as Sobel, Scharr, Laplacian filters, or Canny-edge detector. We will use a Laplacian edge filter since it produces edges that look most similar to hand sketches compared to Sobel or Scharr, and that are quite consistent compared to a Canny-edge detector, which produces very clean line drawings but is affected more by random noise in the camera frames and the line drawings therefore often change drastically between frames.

Nevertheless, we still need to reduce the noise in the image before we use a Laplacian edge filter. We will use a Median filter because it is good at removing noise while keeping edges sharp; also, it is not as slow as a bilateral filter. Since Laplacian filters use grayscale images, we must convert from OpenCV's default BGR format to Grayscale. In your empty file `cartoon.cpp`, put this code at the top so you can access OpenCV and Standard C++ templates without typing `cv::` and `std::` everywhere:

```cpp
// Include OpenCV's C++ Interface
#include "opencv2/opencv.hpp"

using namespace cv;
using namespace std;
```

Put this and all the remaining code in a `cartoonifyImage()` function in the `cartoon.cpp` file:

```cpp
Mat gray;
cvtColor(srcColor, gray, CV_BGR2GRAY);
const int MEDIAN_BLUR_FILTER_SIZE = 7;
medianBlur(gray, gray, MEDIAN_BLUR_FILTER_SIZE);
Mat edges;
const int LAPLACIAN_FILTER_SIZE = 5;
Laplacian(gray, edges, CV_8U, LAPLACIAN_FILTER_SIZE);
```

The Laplacian filter produces edges with varying brightness, so to make the edges look more like a sketch we apply a binary threshold to make the edges either white or black:

```
Mat mask;
const int EDGES_THRESHOLD = 80;
threshold(edges, mask, EDGES_THRESHOLD, 255, THRESH_BINARY_INV);
```

In the following figure, you can see the original image (left side) and the generated edge mask (right side) that looks similar to a sketch drawing. After we generate a color painting (explained later), we can put this edge mask on top for black line drawings:

Generating a color painting and a cartoon

A strong bilateral filter smoothes flat regions while keeping edges sharp, and is therefore great as an automatic cartoonifier or painting filter, except that it is extremely slow (that is, measured in seconds or even minutes rather than milliseconds!). We will therefore use some tricks to obtain a nice cartoonifier that still runs at an acceptable speed. The most important trick we can use is to perform bilateral filtering at a lower resolution. It will have a similar effect as at full resolution, but will run much faster. Let's reduce the total number of pixels by a factor of four (for example, half width and half height):

```
Size size = srcColor.size();
Size smallSize;
smallSize.width = size.width/2;
smallSize.height = size.height/2;
Mat smallImg = Mat(smallSize, CV_8UC3);
resize(srcColor, smallImg, smallSize, 0,0, INTER_LINEAR);
```

Rather than applying a large bilateral filter, we will apply many small bilateral filters to produce a strong cartoon effect in less time. We will truncate the filter (see the following figure) so that instead of performing a whole filter (for example, a filter size of 21 x 21 when the bell curve is 21 pixels wide), it just uses the minimum filter size needed for a convincing result (for example, with a filter size of just 9 x 9 even if the bell curve is 21 pixels wide). This truncated filter will apply the major part of the filter (the gray area) without wasting time on the minor part of the filter (the white area under the curve), so it will run several times faster:

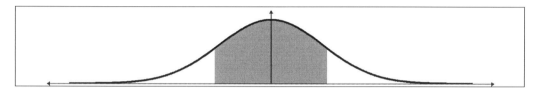

We have four parameters that control the bilateral filter: color strength, positional strength, size, and repetition count. We need a temp Mat since `bilateralFilter()` can't overwrite its input (referred to as "in-place processing"), but we can apply one filter storing a temp Mat and another filter storing back to the input:

```
Mat tmp = Mat(smallSize, CV_8UC3);
int repetitions = 7;  // Repetitions for strong cartoon effect.
for (int i=0; i<repetitions; i++) {
  int ksize = 9;      // Filter size. Has a large effect on speed.
  double sigmaColor = 9;    // Filter color strength.
  double sigmaSpace = 7;    // Spatial strength. Affects speed.
  bilateralFilter(smallImg, tmp, ksize, sigmaColor, sigmaSpace);
  bilateralFilter(tmp, smallImg, ksize, sigmaColor, sigmaSpace);
}
```

Remember that this was applied to the shrunken image, so we need to expand the image back to the original size. Then we can overlay the edge mask that we found earlier. To overlay the edge mask "sketch" onto the bilateral filter "painting" (left-hand side of the following figure), we can start with a black background and copy the "painting" pixels that aren't edges in the "sketch" mask:

```
Mat bigImg;
resize(smallImg, bigImg, size, 0,0, INTER_LINEAR);
dst.setTo(0);
bigImg.copyTo(dst, mask);
```

The result is a cartoon version of the original photo, as shown on the right side of the figure, where the "sketch" mask is overlaid on the "painting":

Generating an "evil" mode using edge filters

Cartoons and comics always have both good and bad characters. With the right combination of edge filters, a scary image can be generated from the most innocent-looking people! The trick is to use a small-edge filter that will find many edges all over the image, then merge the edges using a small Median filter.

We will perform this on a grayscale image with some noise reduction, so the previous code for converting the original image to grayscale and applying a 7 x 7 Median filter should be used again (the first image in the following figure shows the output of the grayscale Median blur). Instead of following it with a Laplacian filter and Binary threshold, we can get a scarier look if we apply a 3 x 3 Scharr gradient filter along x and y (the second image in the figure), and then apply a binary threshold with a very low cutoff (the third image in the figure) and a 3 x 3 Median blur, producing the final "evil" mask (the fourth image in the figure):

```
Mat gray;
cvtColor(srcColor, gray, CV_BGR2GRAY);
const int MEDIAN_BLUR_FILTER_SIZE = 7;
medianBlur(gray, gray, MEDIAN_BLUR_FILTER_SIZE);
Mat edges, edges2;
Scharr(srcGray, edges, CV_8U, 1, 0);
Scharr(srcGray, edges2, CV_8U, 1, 0, -1);
edges += edges2;      // Combine the x & y edges together.
const int EVIL_EDGE_THRESHOLD = 12;
threshold(edges, mask, EVIL_EDGE_THRESHOLD, 255, THRESH_BINARY_INV);
medianBlur(mask, mask, 3);
```

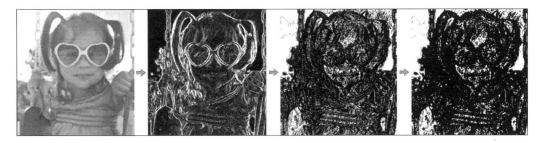

Now that we have an "evil" mask, we can overlay this mask onto the cartoonified "painting" image like we did with the regular "sketch" edge mask. The final result is shown on the right side of the following figure:

Generating an "alien" mode using skin detection

Now that we have a sketch mode, a cartoon mode (painting + sketch mask), and an evil mode (painting + evil mask), for fun let's try something more complex: an "alien" mode, by detecting the skin regions of the face and then changing the skin color to be green.

Skin-detection algorithm

There are many different techniques used for detecting skin regions, from simple color thresholds using **RGB (Red-Green-Blue)** or **HSV (Hue-Saturation-Brightness)** values or color histogram calculation and reprojection, to complex machine-learning algorithms of mixture models that need camera calibration in the CIELab color space and offline training with many sample faces, and so on. But even the complex methods don't necessarily work robustly across various camera and lighting conditions and skin types. Since we want our skin detection to run on a mobile device without any calibration or training, and we are just using skin detection for a "fun" image filter, it is sufficient for us to use a simple skin-detection method. However, the color response from the tiny camera sensors in mobile devices tend to vary significantly, and we want to support skin detection for people of any skin color but without any calibration, so we need something more robust than simple color thresholds.

For example, a simple HSV skin detector can treat any pixel as skin if its hue is fairly red, saturation is fairly high but not extremely high, and its brightness is not too dark or too bright. But mobile cameras often have bad white balancing, and so a person's skin might look slightly blue instead of red, and so on, and this would be a major problem for simple HSV thresholding.

A more robust solution is to perform face detection with a Haar or LBP cascade classifier (shown in *Chapter 8, Face Recognition using Eigenfaces*), and then look at the range of colors for the pixels in the middle of the detected face since you know that those pixels should be skin pixels of the actual person. You could then scan the whole image or the nearby region for pixels of a similar color as the center of the face. This has the advantage that it is very likely to find at least some of the true skin region of any detected person no matter what their skin color is or even if their skin appears somewhat blue or red in the camera image.

Unfortunately, face detection using cascade classifiers is quite slow on current mobile devices, so this method might be less ideal for some real-time mobile applications. On the other hand, we can take advantage of the fact that for mobile apps it can be assumed that the user will be holding the camera directly towards a person's face from close up, and since the user is holding the camera in their hand, which they can easily move, it is quite reasonable to ask the user to place their face at a specific location and distance, rather than try to detect the location and size of their face. This is the basis of many mobile phone apps where the app asks the user to place their face at a certain position or perhaps to manually drag points on the screen to show where the corners of their face are in a photo. So let's simply draw the outline of a face in the center of the screen and ask the user to move their face to the shown position and size.

Showing the user where to put their face

When the alien mode is first started, we will draw the face outline on top of the camera frame so the user knows where to put their face. We will draw a big ellipse covering 70 percent of the image height, with a fixed aspect ratio of 0.72 so that the face will not become too skinny or fat depending on the aspect ratio of the camera:

```
// Draw the color face onto a black background.
Mat faceOutline = Mat::zeros(size, CV_8UC3);
Scalar color = CV_RGB(255,255,0);    // Yellow.
int thickness = 4;
// Use 70% of the screen height as the face height.
int sw = size.width;
int sh = size.height;
int faceH = sh/2 * 70/100;  // "faceH" is the radius of the ellipse.
// Scale the width to be the same shape for any screen width.
int faceW = faceH * 72/100;
// Draw the face outline.
ellipse(faceOutline, Point(sw/2, sh/2), Size(faceW, faceH),
        0, 0, 360, color, thickness, CV_AA);
```

To make it more obvious that it is a face, let's also draw two eye outlines. Rather than drawing an eye as an ellipse, we can make it a bit more realistic (see the following figure) by drawing a truncated ellipse for the top of the eye and a truncated ellipse for the bottom of the eye, since we can specify the start and end angles when drawing with `ellipse()`:

```
// Draw the eye outlines, as 2 arcs per eye.
int eyeW = faceW * 23/100;
int eyeH = faceH * 11/100;
int eyeX = faceW * 48/100;
```

```
int eyeY = faceH * 13/100;
Size eyeSize = Size(eyeW, eyeH);
// Set the angle and shift for the eye half ellipses.
int eyeA = 15; // angle in degrees.
int eyeYshift = 11;
// Draw the top of the right eye.
ellipse(faceOutline, Point(sw/2 - eyeX, sh/2 - eyeY),
        eyeSize, 0, 180+eyeA, 360-eyeA, color, thickness, CV_AA);
// Draw the bottom of the right eye.
ellipse(faceOutline, Point(sw/2 - eyeX, sh/2 - eyeY - eyeYshift),
        eyeSize, 0, 0+eyeA, 180-eyeA, color, thickness, CV_AA);
// Draw the top of the left eye.
ellipse(faceOutline, Point(sw/2 + eyeX, sh/2 - eyeY),
        eyeSize, 0, 180+eyeA, 360-eyeA, color, thickness, CV_AA);
// Draw the bottom of the left eye.
ellipse(faceOutline, Point(sw/2 + eyeX, sh/2 - eyeY - eyeYshift),
        eyeSize, 0, 0+eyeA, 180-eyeA, color, thickness, CV_AA);
```

We can use the same method to draw the bottom lip of the mouth:

```
// Draw the bottom lip of the mouth.
int mouthY = faceH * 48/100;
int mouthW = faceW * 45/100;
int mouthH = faceH * 6/100;
ellipse(faceOutline, Point(sw/2, sh/2 + mouthY), Size(mouthW,
        mouthH), 0, 0, 180, color, thickness, CV_AA);
```

To make it even more obvious that the user should put their face where shown, let's write a message on the screen!

```
// Draw anti-aliased text.
int fontFace = FONT_HERSHEY_COMPLEX;
float fontScale = 1.0f;
int fontThickness = 2;
char *szMsg = "Put your face here";
putText(faceOutline, szMsg, Point(sw * 23/100, sh * 10/100),
        fontFace, fontScale, color, fontThickness, CV_AA);
```

Now that we have the face outline drawn, we can overlay it onto the displayed image by using alpha blending to combine the cartoonified image with this drawn outline:

```
addWeighted(dst, 1.0, faceOutline, 0.7, 0, dst, CV_8UC3);
```

This results in the outline on the following figure, showing the user where to put their face so we don't have to detect the face location:

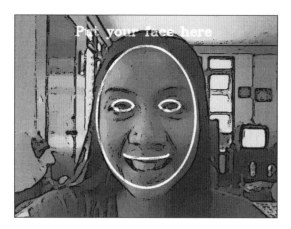

Implementation of the skin-color changer

Rather than detecting the skin color and then the region with that skin color, we can use OpenCV's floodFill(), which is similar to the bucket fill tool in many image editing programs. We know that the regions in the middle of the screen should be skin pixels (since we asked the user to put their face in the middle), so to change the whole face to have green skin, we can just apply a green flood fill on the center pixel, which will always color at least some parts of the face as green. In reality, the color, saturation, and brightness is likely to be different in different parts of the face, so a flood fill will rarely cover all the skin pixels of a face unless the threshold is so low that it also covers unwanted pixels outside the face. So, instead of applying a single flood fill in the center of the image, let's apply a flood fill on six different points around the face that should be skin pixels.

A nice feature of OpenCV's floodFill() function is that it can draw the flood fill into an external image rather than modifying the input image. So this feature can give us a mask image for adjusting the color of the skin pixels without necessarily changing the brightness or saturation, producing a more realistic image than if all skin pixels became an identical green pixel (losing significant face detail as a result).

Skin-color changing does not work so well in the RGB color-space. This is because you want to allow brightness to vary in the face but not allow skin color to vary much, and RGB does not separate brightness from color. One solution is to use the Hue-Saturation-Brightness (HSV) color-space, since it separates brightness from the color (hue) as well as the colorfulness (saturation). Unfortunately, HSV wraps the hue value around red, and since skin is mostly red it means that you need to work both with a hue of less than 10 percent and a hue greater than 90 percent, since these are both red. Accordingly, we will instead use the Y'CrCb color-space (the variant of YUV, which is in OpenCV), since it separates brightness from color, and only has a single range of values for typical skin color rather than two. Note that most cameras, images, and videos actually use some type of YUV as their color-space before conversion to RGB, so in many cases you can get a YUV image without having to convert it yourself.

Since we want our alien mode to look like a cartoon, we will apply the alien filter after the image has already been cartoonified; in other words, we have access to the shrunken color image produced by the bilateral filter, and to the full-sized edge mask. Skin detection often works better at low resolutions, since it is the equivalent of analyzing the average value of each high-resolution pixel's neighbors (or the low-frequency signal instead of the high-frequency noisy signal). So let's work at the same shrunken scale as the bilateral filter (half width and half height). Let's convert the painting image to YUV:

```
Mat yuv = Mat(smallSize, CV_8UC3);
cvtColor(smallImg, yuv, CV_BGR2YCrCb);
```

We also need to shrink the edge mask so it is at the same scale as the painting image. There is a complication with OpenCV's `floodFill()` function when storing to a separate mask image, in that the mask should have a 1-pixel border around the whole image, so if the input image is $W \times H$ pixels in size, the separate mask image should be $(W+2) \times (H+2)$ pixels in size. But `floodFill()` also allows us to initialize the mask with edges that the flood-fill algorithm will ensure it does not cross. Let's use this feature in the hope that it helps prevent the flood fill from extending outside the face. So we need to provide two mask images: the edge mask that measures $W \times H$ in size, and the same edge mask but measuring $(W+2) \times (H+2)$ in size because it should include a border around the image. It is possible to have multiple `cv::Mat` objects (or headers) referencing the same data, or even to have a `cv::Mat` object that references a sub-region of another `cv::Mat` image. So instead of allocating two separate images and copying the edge mask pixels across, let's allocate a single mask image including the border, and create an extra `cv::Mat` header of $W \times H$ (that just references the region of interest in the flood-fill mask without the border). In other words, there is just one array of pixels of size $(W+2) \times (H+2)$ but two `cv::Mat` objects, where one is referencing the whole $(W+2) \times (H+2)$ image and the other is referencing the $W \times H$ region in the middle of that image:

```
int sw = smallSize.width;
int sh = smallSize.height;
Mat mask, maskPlusBorder;
maskPlusBorder = Mat::zeros(sh+2, sw+2, CV_8UC1);
mask = maskPlusBorder(Rect(1,1,sw,sh)); // mask is in maskPlusBorder.
resize(edges, mask, smallSize);        // Put edges in both of them.
```

The edge mask (shown on the left-hand side of the following figure) is full of both strong and weak edges; but we only want strong edges, so we will apply a binary threshold (resulting in the middle image in the following figure). To join some gaps between edges we will then combine the morphological operators `dilate()` and `erode()` to remove some gaps (also referred to as the "close" operator), resulting in the right side of the figure:

```
const int EDGES_THRESHOLD = 80;
threshold(mask, mask, EDGES_THRESHOLD, 255, THRESH_BINARY);
dilate(mask, mask, Mat());
erode(mask, mask, Mat());
```

As mentioned earlier, we want to apply flood fills in numerous points around the face to make sure we include the various colors and shades of the whole face. Let's choose six points around the nose, cheeks, and forehead, as shown on the left side of the next figure. Note that these values are dependent on the face outline drawn earlier:

```
int const NUM_SKIN_POINTS = 6;
Point skinPts[NUM_SKIN_POINTS];
skinPts[0] = Point(sw/2,          sh/2 - sh/6);
skinPts[1] = Point(sw/2 - sw/11,  sh/2 - sh/6);
skinPts[2] = Point(sw/2 + sw/11,  sh/2 - sh/6);
skinPts[3] = Point(sw/2,          sh/2 + sh/16);
skinPts[4] = Point(sw/2 - sw/9,   sh/2 + sh/16);
skinPts[5] = Point(sw/2 + sw/9,   sh/2 + sh/16);
```

Now we just need to find some good lower and upper bounds for the flood fill. Remember that this is being performed in the Y'CrCb color space, so we basically decide how much the brightness, red component, and blue component can vary. We want to allow the brightness to vary a lot, to include shadows as well as highlights and reflections, but we don't want the colors to vary much at all:

```
const int LOWER_Y = 60;
const int UPPER_Y = 80;
const int LOWER_Cr = 25;
const int UPPER_Cr = 15;
const int LOWER_Cb = 20;
const int UPPER_Cb = 15;
Scalar lowerDiff = Scalar(LOWER_Y, LOWER_Cr, LOWER_Cb);
Scalar upperDiff = Scalar(UPPER_Y, UPPER_Cr, UPPER_Cb);
```

We will use `floodFill()` with its default flags, except that we want to store to an external mask, so we must specify `FLOODFILL_MASK_ONLY`:

```
const int CONNECTED_COMPONENTS = 4;  // To fill diagonally, use 8.
const int flags = CONNECTED_COMPONENTS | FLOODFILL_FIXED_RANGE \
    | FLOODFILL_MASK_ONLY;
Mat edgeMask = mask.clone();    // Keep a copy of the edge mask.
// "maskPlusBorder" is initialized with edges to block floodFill().
for (int i=0; i< NUM_SKIN_POINTS; i++) {
  floodFill(yuv, maskPlusBorder, skinPts[i], Scalar(), NULL,
        lowerDiff, upperDiff, flags);
}
```

In the following figure, the left side shows the six flood-fill locations (shown as blue circles), and the right side of the figure shows the external mask that is generated, where skin is shown as gray and edges are shown as white. Note that the right-side image was modified for this book so that skin pixels (of value 1) are clearly visible:

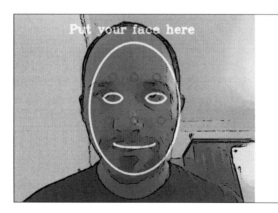

The `mask` image (shown on the right side of the previous figure) now contains:

- pixels of value 255 for the edge pixels
- pixels of value 1 for the skin regions
- pixels of value 0 for the rest

Meanwhile, `edgeMask` just contains edge pixels (as value 255). So to get just the skin pixels, we can remove the edges from it:

```
mask -= edgeMask;
```

The `mask` image now just contains 1s for skin pixels and 0s for non-skin pixels. To change the skin color and brightness of the original image, we can use `cv::add()` with the skin mask to increase the green component in the original BGR image:

```
int Red = 0;
int Green = 70;
int Blue = 0;
add(smallImgBGR, CV_RGB(Red, Green, Blue), smallImgBGR, mask);
```

The following figure shows the original image on the left, and the final alien cartoon image on the right, where at least six parts of the face will now be green!

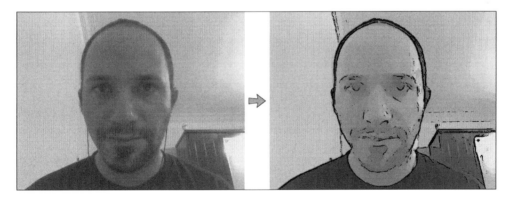

Notice that we have not only made the skin look green but also brighter (to look like an alien that glows in the dark). If you want to just change the skin color without making it brighter, you can use other color-changing methods, such as adding 70 to green while subtracting 70 from red and blue, or convert to HSV color space using `cvtColor(src, dst, "CV_BGR2HSV_FULL")`, and adjust the hue and saturation.

That's all! Run the app in the different modes until you are ready to port it to your mobile.

Porting from desktop to Android

Now that the program works on the desktop, we can make an Android or iOS app from it. The details given here are specific to Android, but also apply when porting to iOS for Apple iPhone and iPad or similar devices. When developing Android apps, OpenCV can be used directly from Java, but the result is unlikely to be as efficient as native C/C++ code and doesn't allow the running of the same code on the desktop as it does for your mobile. So it is recommended to use C/C++ for most OpenCV+Android app development (readers who want to write OpenCV apps purely in Java can use the JavaCV library by Samuel Audet, available at `http://code.google.com/p/javacv/`, to run the same code on the desktop that we run on Android).

 This Android project uses a camera for live input, so it won't work on the Android Emulator. It needs a real Android 2.2 (Froyo) or later device with a camera.

The user interface of an Android app should be written using Java, but for the image processing we will use the same `cartoon.cpp` C++ file that we used for the desktop. To use C/C++ code in an Android app, we must use the **NDK (Native Development Kit)** that is based on **JNI (Java Native Interface)**. We will create a JNI wrapper for our `cartoonifyImage()` function so it can be used from Android with Java.

Setting up an Android project that uses OpenCV

The Android port of OpenCV changes significantly each year, as does Android's method for camera access, so a book is not the best place to describe how it should be set up. Therefore the reader can follow the latest instructions at `http://opencv.org/platforms/android.html` to set up and build a native (NDK) Android app with OpenCV. OpenCV comes with an Android sample project called Sample3Native that accesses the camera using OpenCV and displays the modified image on the screen. This sample project is useful as a base for the Android app developed in this chapter, so readers should familiarize themselves with this sample app (currently available at `http://docs.opencv.org/doc/tutorials/introduction/android_binary_package/android_binary_package_using_with_NDK.html`). We will then modify an Android OpenCV base project so that it can cartoonify the camera's video frames and display the resulting frames on the screen.

If you are stuck with OpenCV development for Android, for example if you are receiving a compile error or the camera always gives blank frames, try searching these websites for solutions:

1. The Android Binary Package NDK tutorial for OpenCV, mentioned previously.
2. The official Android-OpenCV Google group (`https://groups.google.com/forum/?fromgroups#!forum/android-opencv`).
3. OpenCV's Q & A site (`http://answers.opencv.org`).
4. StackOverflow Q & A site (`http://stackoverflow.com/questions/tagged/opencv+android`).
5. The Web (for example `http://www.google.com`).
6. If you still can't fix your problem after trying all of these, you should post a question on the Android-OpenCV Google group with details of the error message, and so on.

Color formats used for image processing on Android

When developing for the desktop, we only have to deal with BGR pixel format because the input (from camera, image, or video file) is in BGR format and so is the output (HighGUI window, image, or video file). But when developing for mobiles, you typically have to convert native color formats yourself.

Input color format from the camera

Looking at the sample code in `jni\jni_part.cpp`, the `myuv` variable is the color image in Android's default camera format: "NV21" `YUV420sp`. The first part of the array is the grayscale pixel array, followed by a half-sized pixel array that alternates between the U and V color channels. So if we just want to access a grayscale image, we can get it directly from the first part of a `YUV420sp` semi-planar image without any conversions. But if we want a color image (for example, BGR or BGRA color format), we must convert the color format using `cvtColor()`.

Output color format for display

Looking at the Sample3Native code from OpenCV, the `mbgra` variable is the color image to be displayed on the Android device, in BGRA format. OpenCV's default format is BGR (the opposite byte order of RGB), and BGRA just adds an unused byte on the end of each pixel, so that each pixel is stored as Blue-Green-Red-Unused. You can either do all your processing in OpenCV's default BGR format and then convert your final output from BGR to BGRA before display on the screen, or you can ensure your image processing code can handle the BGRA format instead of or in addition to BGR format. This can often be simple to allow in OpenCV because many OpenCV functions accept the BGRA, but you must ensure that you create images with the same number of channels as the input, by seeing if the `Mat::channels()` value in your images are 3 or 4. Also, if you directly access pixels in your code, you would need separate code to handle 3-channel BGR and 4-channel BGRA images.

 Some CV operations run faster with BGRA pixels (since it is aligned to 32-bit) while some run faster with BGR (since it requires less memory to read and write), so for maximum efficiency you should support both BGR and BGRA and then find which color format runs fastest overall in your app.

Let's begin with something simple: getting access to the camera frame in OpenCV but not processing it, and instead just displaying it on the screen. This can be done easily with Java code, but it is important to know how to do it using OpenCV too. As mentioned previously, the camera image arrives at our C++ code in `YUV420sp` format and should leave in BGRA format. So if we prepare our `cv::Mat` for input and output, we just need to convert from `YUV420sp` to BGRA using `cvtColor`. To write C/C++ code for an Android Java app, we need to use special JNI function names that match the Java class and package name that will use that JNI function, in the format:

```
JNIEXPORT <Return> JNICALL Java_<Package>_<Class>_<Function>(
        JNIEnv* env, jobject, <Args>)
```

So let's create a `ShowPreview()` C/C++ function that is used from a `CartoonifierView` Java class in a `Cartoonifier` Java package. Add this `ShowPreview()` C/C++ function to `jni\jni_part.cpp`:

```
// Just show the plain camera image without modifying it.
JNIEXPORT void
JNICALL Java_com_Cartoonifier_CartoonifierView_ShowPreview(
  JNIEnv* env, jobject,
  jint width, jint height, jbyteArray yuv, jintArray bgra)
{
  jbyte* _yuv  = env->GetByteArrayElements(yuv, 0);
```

```
    jint*  _bgra = env->GetIntArrayElements(bgra, 0);

    Mat myuv = Mat(height + height/2, width, CV_8UC1, (uchar *)_yuv);
    Mat mbgra = Mat(height, width, CV_8UC4, (uchar *)_bgra);


    // Convert the color format from the camera's
    // NV21 "YUV420sp" format to an Android BGRA color image.
    cvtColor(myuv, mbgra, CV_YUV420sp2BGRA);


    // OpenCV can now access/modify the BGRA image "mbgra" ...


    env->ReleaseIntArrayElements(bgra, _bgra, 0);
    env->ReleaseByteArrayElements(yuv, _yuv, 0);
}
```

While this code looks complex at first, the first two lines of the function just give us native access to the given Java arrays, the next two lines construct `cv::Mat` objects around the given pixel buffers (that is, they don't allocate new images, they make `myuv` access the pixels in the `_yuv` array, and so on), and the last two lines of the function release the native lock we placed on the Java arrays. The only real work we did in the function is to convert from YUV to BGRA format, so this function is the base that we can use for new functions. Now let's extend this to analyze and modify the BGRA `cv::Mat` before display.

> The `jni\jni_part.cpp` sample code in OpenCV v2.4.2 uses this code:
> ```
>     cvtColor(myuv, mbgra, CV_YUV420sp2BGR, 4);
> ```
>
> This looks like it converts to 3-channel BGR format (OpenCV's default format), but due to the "4" parameter it actually converts to 4-channel BGRA (Android's default output format) instead! So it's identical to this code, which is less confusing:
> ```
>     cvtColor(myuv, mbgra, CV_YUV420sp2BGRA);
> ```

Since we now have a BGRA image as input and output instead of OpenCV's default BGR, it leaves us with two options for how to process it:

- Convert from BGRA to BGR before we perform our image processing, do our processing in BGR, and then convert the output to BGRA so it can be displayed by Android

- Modify all our code to handle BGRA format in addition to (or instead of) BGR format, so we don't need to perform slow conversions between BGRA and BGR

For simplicity, we will just apply the color conversions from BGRA to BGR and back, rather than supporting both BGR and BGRA formats. If you are writing a real-time app, you should consider adding 4-channel BGRA support in your code to potentially improve performance. We will do one simple change to make things slightly faster: we are converting the input from YUV420sp to BGRA and then from BGRA to BGR, so we might as well just convert straight from YUV420sp to BGR!

It is a good idea to build and run with the ShowPreview() function (shown previously) on your device so you have something to go back to if you have problems with your C/C++ code later. To call it from Java, we add the Java declaration just next to the Java declaration of CartoonifyImage() near the bottom of CartoonifyView.java:

```
public native void ShowPreview(int width, int height,
byte[] yuv, int[] rgba);
```

We can then call it just like the OpenCV sample code called FindFeatures(). Put this in the middle of the processFrame() function of CartoonifierView.java:

```
ShowPreview(getFrameWidth(), getFrameHeight(), data, rgba);
```

You should build and run it now on your device, just to see the real-time camera preview.

Adding the cartoonifier code to the Android NDK app

We want to add the cartoon.cpp file that we used for the desktop app. The file jni\Android.mk sets the C/C++/Assembly source files, header search paths, native libraries, and GCC compiler settings for your project:

1. Add cartoon.cpp (and ImageUtils_0.7.cpp if you want easier debugging) to LOCAL_SRC_FILES, but remember that they are in the desktop folder instead of the default jni folder. So add this after: LOCAL_SRC_FILES := jni_part.cpp:

    ```
    LOCAL_SRC_FILES += ../../Cartoonifier_Desktop/cartoon.cpp
    LOCAL_SRC_FILES += ../../Cartoonifier_Desktop/ImageUtils_0.7.cpp
    ```

2. Add the header file search path so it can find cartoon.h in the common parent folder:

    ```
    LOCAL_C_INCLUDES += $(LOCAL_PATH)/../../Cartoonifier_Desktop
    ```

3. In the file `jni\jni_part.cpp`, insert this near the top instead of `#include <vector>`:

```
#include "cartoon.h"     // Cartoonifier.
#include "ImageUtils.h"    // (Optional) OpenCV debugging
                          // functions.
```

4. Add a JNI function `CartoonifyImage()` to this file; this will cartoonify the image. We can start by duplicating the function `ShowPreview()` we created previously, which just shows the camera preview without modifying it. Notice that we convert directly from YUV420sp to BGR since we don't want to process BGRA images:

```
// Modify the camera image using the Cartoonifier filter.
JNIEXPORT void
JNICALL Java_com_Cartoonifier_CartoonifierView_CartoonifyImage(
    JNIEnv* env, jobject,
    jint width, jint height, jbyteArray yuv, jintArray bgra)
    {
    // Get native access to the given Java arrays.
    jbyte* _yuv  = env->GetByteArrayElements(yuv, 0);
    jint* _bgra = env->GetIntArrayElements(bgra, 0);

    // Create OpenCV wrappers around the input & output data.
    Mat myuv(height + height/2, width, CV_8UC1, (uchar *)_yuv);
    Mat mbgra(height, width, CV_8UC4, (uchar *)_bgra);

    // Convert the color format from the camera's YUV420sp
    // semi-planar
    // format to OpenCV's default BGR color image.
    Mat mbgr(height, width, CV_8UC3);   // Allocate a new image
buffer.
    cvtColor(myuv, mbgr, CV_YUV420sp2BGR);


    // OpenCV can now access/modify the BGR image "mbgr", and should
    // store the output as the BGR image "displayedFrame".
    Mat displayedFrame(mbgr.size(), CV_8UC3);

    // TEMPORARY: Just show the camera image without modifying it.
    displayedFrame = mbgr;


    // Convert the output from OpenCV's BGR to Android's BGRA
    //format.
```

```
        cvtColor(displayedFrame, mbgra, CV_BGR2BGRA);

        // Release the native lock we placed on the Java arrays.
        env->ReleaseIntArrayElements(bgra, _bgra, 0);
        env->ReleaseByteArrayElements(yuv, _yuv, 0);
    }
```

5. The previous code does not modify the image, but we want to process the image using the cartoonifier we developed earlier in this chapter. So now let's insert a call to our existing `cartoonifyImage()` function that we created in `cartoon.cpp` for the desktop app. Replace the temporary line of code `displayedFrame = mbgr` with this:

   `cartoonifyImage(mbgr, displayedFrame);`

6. That's it! Build the code (Eclipse should compile the C/C++ code for you using `ndk-build`) and run it on your device. You should have a working Cartoonifier Android app (right at the beginning of this chapter there is a sample screenshot showing what you should expect)! If it does not build or run, go back over the steps and fix the problems (look at the code provided with this book if you wish). Continue with the next steps once it is working.

Reviewing the Android app

You will quickly notice four issues with the app that is now running on your device:

- It is extremely slow; many seconds per frame! So we should just display the camera preview and only cartoonify a camera frame when the user has touched the screen to say it is a good photo.

- It needs to handle user input, such as to change modes between sketch, paint, evil, or alien modes. We will add these to the Android menu bar.

- It would be great if we could save the cartoonified result to image files, to share with others. Whenever the user touches the screen for a cartoonified image, we will save the result as an image file on the user's SD card and display it in the Android Gallery.

- There is a lot of random noise in the sketch edge detector. We will create a special "pepper" noise reduction filter to deal with this later.

Cartoonifying the image when the user taps the screen

To show the camera preview (until the user wants to cartoonify the selected camera frame), we can just call the ShowPreview() JNI function we wrote earlier. We will also wait for touch events from the user before cartoonifying the camera image. We only want to cartoonify one image when the user touches the screen; therefore we set a flag to say the next camera frame should be cartoonified and then that flag is reset, so it continues with the camera preview again. But this would mean the cartoonified image is only displayed for a fraction of a second and then the next camera preview will be displayed again. So we will use a second flag to say that the current image should be frozen on the screen for a few seconds before the camera frames overwrite it, to give the user some time to see it:

1. Add the following header imports near the top of the CartoonifierApp.java file in the src\com\Cartoonifier folder:

   ```
   import android.view.View;
   import android.view.View.OnTouchListener;
   import android.view.MotionEvent;
   ```

2. Modify the class definition near the top of CartoonifierApp.java:

   ```
   public class CartoonifierApp
   extends Activity implements OnTouchListener {
   ```

3. Insert this code on the bottom of the onCreate() function:

   ```
   // Call our "onTouch()" callback function whenever the user
   // touches the screen.
   mView.setOnTouchListener(this);
   ```

4. Add the function onTouch() to process the touch event:

   ```
   public boolean onTouch(View v, MotionEvent m) {
       // Ignore finger movement event, we just care about when the
       // finger first touches the screen.
       if (m.getAction() != MotionEvent.ACTION_DOWN) {
           return false; // We didn't use this touch movement event.
       }
       Log.i(TAG, "onTouch down event");
       // Signal that we should cartoonify the next camera frame and save
       // it, instead of just showing the preview.
       mView.nextFrameShouldBeSaved(getBaseContext());
       return true;
   }
   ```

5. Now we need to add the `nextFrameShouldBeSaved()` function to `CartoonifierView.java`:

```
// Cartoonify the next camera frame & save it instead of preview.
protected void nextFrameShouldBeSaved(Context context) {
    bSaveThisFrame = true;
}
```

6. Add these variables near the top of the `CartoonifierView` class:

```
private boolean bSaveThisFrame = false;
private boolean bFreezeOutput = false;
private static final int FREEZE_OUTPUT_MSECS = 3000;
```

7. The `processFrame()` function of `CartoonifierView` can now switch between cartoon and preview, but should also make sure to only display something if it is not trying to show a frozen cartoon image for a few seconds. So replace `processFrame()` with this:

```
@Override
protected Bitmap processFrame(byte[] data) {
    // Store the output image to the RGBA member variable.
    int[] rgba = mRGBA;
    // Only process the camera or update the screen if we aren't
    // supposed to just show the cartoon image.
    if (bFreezeOutputbFreezeOutput) {
        // Only needs to be triggered here once.
        bFreezeOutput = false;
        // Wait for several seconds, doing nothing!
        try {
            wait(FREEZE_OUTPUT_MSECS);
        } catch (InterruptedException e) {
            e.printStackTrace();
        }
        return null;
    }
    if (!bSaveThisFrame) {
        ShowPreview(getFrameWidth(), getFrameHeight(), data,
rgba);
    }
    else {
        // Just do it once, then go back to preview mode.
        bSaveThisFrame = false;
        // Don't update the screen for a while, so the user can
        // see the cartoonifier output.
```

```
bFreezeOutput = true;

CartoonifyImage(getFrameWidth(), getFrameHeight(), data,
        rgba, m_sketchMode, m_alienMode, m_evilMode,
        m_debugMode);
}

// Put the processed image into the Bitmap object that will be
// returned for display on the screen.
Bitmap bmp = mBitmap;
bmp.setPixels(rgba, 0, getFrameWidth(), 0, 0, getFrameWidth(),
        getFrameHeight());

return bmp;
}
```

8. You should be able to build and run it to verify that the app works nicely now.

Saving the image to a file and to the Android picture gallery

We will save the output both as a PNG file and display in the Android picture gallery. The Android Gallery is designed for JPEG files, but JPEG is bad for cartoon images with solid colors and edges, so we'll use a tedious method to add PNG images to the gallery. We will create a Java function savePNGImageToGallery() to perform this for us. At the bottom of the processFrame() function just seen previously, we see that an Android Bitmap object is created with the output data; so we need a way to save the Bitmap object to a PNG file. OpenCV's imwrite() Java function can be used to save to a PNG file, but this would require linking to both OpenCV's Java API and OpenCV's C/C++ API (just like the OpenCV4Android sample project "tutorial-4-mixed" does). Since we don't need the OpenCV Java API for anything else, the following code will just show how to save PNG files using the Android API instead of the OpenCV Java API:

1. Android's Bitmap class can save files to PNG format, so let's use it. Also, we need to choose a filename for the image. Let's use the current date and time, to allow saving many files and making it possible for the user to remember when it was taken. Insert this just before the return bmp statement of processFrame():

```
if (bFreezeOutput) {
// Get the current date & time
SimpleDateFormat s = new SimpleDateFormat("yyyy-MM-dd,HH-mm-ss");
```

```
String timestamp = s.format(new Date());
String baseFilename = "Cartoon" + timestamp + ".png";

// Save the processed image as a PNG file on the SD card and show
// it in the Android Gallery.
savePNGImageToGallery(bmp, mContext, baseFilename);
}
```

2. Add this to the top section of `CartoonifierView.java`:

```
// For saving Bitmaps to file and the Android picture gallery.
import android.graphics.Bitmap.CompressFormat;
import android.net.Uri;
import android.os.Environment;
import android.provider.MediaStore;
import android.provider.MediaStore.Images;
import android.text.format.DateFormat;
import android.util.Log;
import java.io.BufferedOutputStream;
import java.io.File;
import java.io.FileOutputStream;
import java.io.IOException;
import java.io.OutputStream;
import java.text.SimpleDateFormat;
import java.util.Date;
```

3. Insert this inside the `CartoonifierView` class, on the top:

```
private static final String TAG = "CartoonifierView";
private Context mContext;  // So we can access the Android
// Gallery.
```

4. Add this to your `nextFrameShouldBeSaved()` function in `CartoonifierView`:

```
mContext = context;  // Save the Android context, for GUI
// access.
```

5. Add the `savePNGImageToGallery()` function to `CartoonifierView`:

```
// Save the processed image as a PNG file on the SD card
// and shown in the Android Gallery.
protected void savePNGImageToGallery(Bitmap bmp, Context context,
        String baseFilename)
{
    try {
    // Get the file path to the SD card.
    String baseFolder = \
    Environment.getExternalStoragePublicDirectory( \
```

```
        Environment.DIRECTORY_PICTURES).getAbsolutePath() \
        + "/";
        File file = new File(baseFolder + baseFilename);
        Log.i(TAG, "Saving the processed image to file [" + \
        file.getAbsolutePath() + "]");

        // Open the file.
        OutputStream out = new BufferedOutputStream(
        new FileOutputStream(file));
        // Save the image file as PNG.
        bmp.compress(CompressFormat.PNG, 100, out);
        // Make sure it is saved to file soon, because we are about
        // to add it to the Gallery.
        out.flush();
        out.close();

        // Add the PNG file to the Android Gallery.
        ContentValues image = new ContentValues();
        image.put(Images.Media.TITLE, baseFilename);
        image.put(Images.Media.DISPLAY_NAME, baseFilename);
        image.put(Images.Media.DESCRIPTION,
        "Processed by the Cartoonifier App");
        image.put(Images.Media.DATE_TAKEN,
        System.currentTimeMillis()); // msecs since 1970 UTC.
        image.put(Images.Media.MIME_TYPE, "image/png");
        image.put(Images.Media.ORIENTATION, 0);
        image.put(Images.Media.DATA, file.getAbsolutePath());
        Uri result = context.getContentResolver().insert(
        MediaStore.Images.Media.EXTERNAL_CONTENT_URI,image);
        }
    catch (Exception e) {
        e.printStackTrace();
        }
    }
```

6. Android apps need permission from the user during installation if they need
    to store files on the device. So insert this line in AndroidManifest.xml just
    next to the similar line requesting permission for camera access:

```
<uses-permission
android:name="android.permission.WRITE_EXTERNAL_STORAGE"/>
```

7. Build and run the app! When you touch the screen to save a photo, you should eventually see the cartoonified image shown on the screen (perhaps after 5 or 10 seconds of processing). Once it is shown on the screen, it means it should be saved to your SD card and to your photo gallery. Exit the Cartoonifier app, open the Android Gallery app, and view the Pictures album. You should see the cartoon image as a PNG image in your screen's full resolution.

Showing an Android notification message about a saved image

If you want to show a notification message whenever a new image is saved to the SD card and Android Gallery, follow these steps; otherwise feel free to skip this section:

1. Add the following to the top section of `CartoonifierView.java`:

```
// For showing a Notification message when saving a file.
import android.app.Notification;
import android.app.NotificationManager;
import android.app.PendingIntent;
import android.content.ContentValues;
import android.content.Intent;
```

2. Add this near the top section of `CartoonifierView`:

```
private int mNotificationID = 0;

// To show just 1 notification.
```

3. Insert this inside the `if` statement below the call to `savePNGImageToGallery()` in `processFrame()`:

```
showNotificationMessage(mContext, baseFilename);
```

4. Add the `showNotificationMessage()` function to `CartoonifierView`:

```
// Show a notification message, saying we've saved another image.
protected void showNotificationMessage(Context context,
    String filename)
{
// Popup a notification message in the Android status
// bar. To make sure a notification is shown for each
// image but only 1 is kept in the status bar at a time,
// use a different ID each time
// but delete previous messages before creating it.
final NotificationManager mgr = (NotificationManager) \
```

```
context.getSystemService(Context.NOTIFICATION_SERVICE);

// Close the previous popup message, so we only have 1
//at a time, but it still shows a popup message for each
//one.
if (mNotificationID > 0)
  mgr.cancel(mNotificationID);
mNotificationID++;

Notification notification = new Notification(R.drawable.icon,
"Saving to gallery (image " + mNotificationID + ") ...",
System.currentTimeMillis());
Intent intent = new Intent(context, CartoonifierView.class);
// Close it if the user clicks on it.
notification.flags |= Notification.FLAG_AUTO_CANCEL;
PendingIntent pendingIntent = PendingIntent.getActivity(context,
0, intent, 0);
notification.setLatestEventInfo(context, "Cartoonifier saved " +
mNotificationID + " images to Gallery", "Saved as '" +
filename + "'", pendingIntent);
mgr.notify(mNotificationID, notification);
}
```

5. Once again, build and run the app! You should see a notification message pop up whenever you touch the screen for another saved image. If you want the notification message to pop up before the long delay of image processing rather than after, move the call to showNotificationMessage() before the call to cartoonifyImage(), and move the code for generating the date and time string so that the same string is given to the notification message and the actual file is saved.

Changing cartoon modes through the Android menu bar

Let's allow the user to change modes through the menu:

1. Add the following headers near the top of the file src\com\Cartoonifier\ CartoonifierApp.java:

```
import android.view.Menu;
import android.view.MenuItem;
```

2. Insert the following member variables inside the `CartoonifierApp` class:

```
// Items for the Android menu bar.
private MenuItem mMenuAlien;
private MenuItem mMenuEvil;
private MenuItem mMenuSketch;
private MenuItem mMenuDebug;
```

3. Add the following functions to `CartoonifierApp`:

```
/** Called when the menu bar is being created by Android. */
public boolean onCreateOptionsMenu(Menu menu) {
Log.i(TAG, "onCreateOptionsMenu");
mMenuSketch = menu.add("Sketch or Painting");
mMenuAlien = menu.add("Alien or Human");
mMenuEvil = menu.add("Evil or Good");
mMenuDebug = menu.add("[Debug mode]");
return true;
}

/** Called whenever the user pressed a menu item in the menu bar.
*/
public boolean onOptionsItemSelected(MenuItem item) {
Log.i(TAG, "Menu Item selected: " + item);
if (item == mMenuSketch)
mView.toggleSketchMode();
else if (item == mMenuAlien)
mView.toggleAlienMode();
else if (item == mMenuEvil)
mView.toggleEvilMode();
else if (item == mMenuDebug)
mView.toggleDebugMode();
return true;
}
```

4. Insert the following member variables inside the `CartoonifierView` class:

```
private boolean m_sketchMode = false;
private boolean m_alienMode = false;
private boolean m_evilMode = false;
private boolean m_debugMode = false;
```

5. Add the following functions to `CartoonifierView`:

```
protected void toggleSketchMode() {
m_sketchMode = !m_sketchMode;
}
protected void toggleAlienMode() {
```

```
m_alienMode = !m_alienMode;
}
protected void toggleEvilMode() {
m_evilMode = !m_evilMode;
}
protected void toggleDebugMode() {
m_debugMode = !m_debugMode;
}
```

6. We need to pass the mode values to the `cartoonifyImage()` JNI
   code, so let's send them as arguments. Modify the Java declaration of
   `CartoonifyImage()` in `CartoonifierView`:

   ```
   public native void CartoonifyImage(int width, int height,
   byte[] yuv,
   int[] rgba, boolean sketchMode, boolean alienMode,
   boolean evilMode, boolean debugMode);
   ```

7. Now modify the Java code so we pass the current mode values in
   `processFrame()`:

   ```
   CartoonifyImage(getFrameWidth(), getFrameHeight(), data,
   rgba,
   m_sketchMode, m_alienMode, m_evilMode, m_debugMode);
   ```

8. The JNI declaration of `CartoonifyImage()` in `jni\jni_part.cpp` should
   now be:

   ```
   JNIEXPORT void JNICALL Java_com_Cartoonifier_CartoonifierView_
   CartoonifyImage(
       JNIEnv* env, jobject, jint width, jint height,
       jbyteArray yuv, jintArray bgra, jboolean sketchMode,
       jboolean alienMode, jboolean evilMode, jboolean debugMode)
   ```

9. We then need to pass the modes to the C/C++ code in `cartoon.cpp` from
   the JNI function in `jni\jni_part.cpp`. When developing for Android we
   can only show one GUI window at a time, but on a desktop it is handy to
   show extra windows while debugging. So instead of taking a Boolean flag for
   `debugMode`, let's pass a number that would be 0 for non-debug, 1 for debug
   on mobile (where creating a GUI window in OpenCV would cause a crash!),
   and 2 for debug on desktop (where we can create as many extra windows as
   we want):

   ```
   int debugType = 0;
   if (debugMode)
     debugType = 1;

   cartoonifyImage(mbgr, displayedFrame, sketchMode, alienMode,
   evilMode, debugType);
   ```

10. Update the actual C/C++ implementation in `cartoon.cpp`:

```
void cartoonifyImage(Mat srcColor, Mat dst, bool sketchMode,
bool alienMode, bool evilMode, int debugType)
{
```

11. And update the C/C++ declaration in `cartoon.h`:

```
void cartoonifyImage(Mat srcColor, Mat dst, bool sketchMode,
bool alienMode, bool evilMode, int debugType);
```

12. Build and run it; then try pressing the small options-menu button on the bottom of the window. You should find that the sketch mode is real-time, whereas the paint mode has a large delay due to the bilateral filter.

Reducing the random pepper noise from the sketch image

Most of the cameras in current smartphones and tablets have significant image noise. This is normally acceptable, but it has a large effect on our 5 x 5 Laplacian-edge filter. The edge mask (shown as the sketch mode) will often have thousands of small blobs of black pixels called "pepper" noise, made of several black pixels next to each other in a white background. We are already using a Median filter, which is usually strong enough to remove pepper noise, but in our case it may not be strong enough. Our edge mask is mostly a pure white background (value of 255) with some black edges (value of 0) and the dots of noise (also values of 0). We could use a standard closing morphological operator, but it will remove a lot of edges. So, instead, we will apply a custom filter that removes small black regions that are surrounded completely by white pixels. This will remove a lot of noise while having little effect on actual edges.

We will scan the image for black pixels, and at each black pixel we'll check the border of the 5 x 5 square around it to see if all the 5 x 5 border pixels are white. If they are all white we know we have a small island of black noise, so we fill the whole block with white pixels to remove the black island. For simplicity in our 5 x 5 filter, we will ignore the two border pixels around the image and leave them as they are.

The following figure shows the original image from an Android tablet on the left side, with a sketch mode in the center (showing small black dots of pepper noise), and the result of our pepper-noise removal shown on the right side, where the skin looks cleaner:

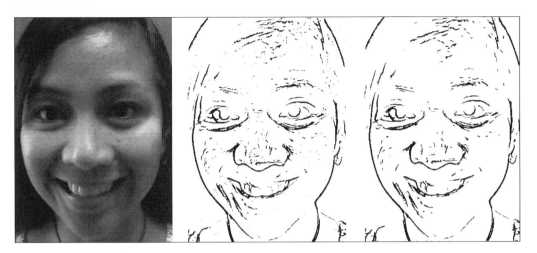

The following code can be named as the function `removePepperNoise()`. This function will edit the image in place for simplicity:

```
void removePepperNoise(Mat &mask)
{
for (int y=2; y<mask.rows-2; y++) {
  // Get access to each of the 5 rows near this pixel.
  uchar *pUp2 = mask.ptr(y-2);
  uchar *pUp1 = mask.ptr(y-1);
  uchar *pThis = mask.ptr(y);
  uchar *pDown1 = mask.ptr(y+1);
  uchar *pDown2 = mask.ptr(y+2);

  // Skip the first (and last) 2 pixels on each row.
  pThis += 2;
  pUp1 += 2;
  pUp2 += 2;
  pDown1 += 2;
  pDown2 += 2;
  for (int x=2; x<mask.cols-2; x++) {
    uchar value = *pThis;  // Get this pixel value (0 or 255).
    // Check if this is a black pixel that is surrounded by
    // white pixels (ie: whether it is an "island" of black).
    if (value == 0) {
```

```
bool above, left, below, right, surroundings;
above = *(pUp2 - 2) && *(pUp2 - 1) && *(pUp2) &&
*(pUp2 + 1) && *(pUp2 + 2);
left = *(pUp1 - 2) && *(pThis - 2) && *(pDown1 - 2);
below = *(pDown2 - 2) && *(pDown2 - 1) && *(pDown2) &&
*(pDown2 + 1) && *(pDown2 + 2);
right = *(pUp1 + 2) && *(pThis + 2) && *(pDown1 + 2);
surroundings = above && left && below && right;
if (surroundings == true) {
    // Fill the whole 5x5 block as white. Since we know
    // the 5x5 borders are already white, we just need to
    // fill the 3x3 inner region.
    *(pUp1 - 1) = 255;
    *(pUp1 + 0) = 255;
    *(pUp1 + 1) = 255;
    *(pThis - 1) = 255;
    *(pThis + 0) = 255;
    *(pThis + 1) = 255;
    *(pDown1 - 1) = 255;
    *(pDown1 + 0) = 255;
    *(pDown1 + 1) = 255;
    // Since we just covered the whole 5x5 block with
    // white, we know the next 2 pixels won't be black,
    // so skip the next 2 pixels on the right.
    pThis += 2;
    pUp1 += 2;
    pUp2 += 2;
    pDown1 += 2;
    pDown2 += 2;
    }
}
// Move to the next pixel on the right.
pThis++;
pUp1++;
pUp2++;
pDown1++;
pDown2++;
    }
  }
}
```

Showing the FPS of the app

If you want to show the frames per second (FPS) speed—which is less important for a slow app such as this, but still useful—on the screen, perform the following steps:

1. Copy the file `src\org\opencv\samples\imagemanipulations\FpsMeter.java` from the ImageManipulations sample folder in OpenCV (for example, `C:\OpenCV-2.4.1\samples\android\image-manipulations`) to your `src\com\Cartoonifier` folder.

2. Replace the package name at the top of `FpsMeter.java` to be `com.Cartoonifier`.

3. In the file `CartoonifierViewBase.java`, declare your `FpsMeter` member variable after `private byte[]  mBuffer;`:

   ```
   private FpsMeter  mFps;
   ```

4. Initialize the `FpsMeter` object in the `CartoonifierViewBase()` constructor, after `mHolder.addCallback(this);`:

   ```
   mFps = new FpsMeter();
   mFps.init();
   ```

5. Measure the FPS of each frame in `run()` after the `try/catch` block:

   ```
   mFps.measure();
   ```

6. Draw the FPS onto the screen for each frame, in `run()` after the `canvas.drawBitmap()` function:

   ```
   mFps.draw(canvas, (canvas.getWidth() - bmp.getWidth()) /2, 0);
   ```

Using a different camera resolution

If you want your app to run faster, knowing that the quality will suffer, you should definitely consider either asking for a smaller camera image from the hardware or shrinking the image once you have it. The sample code that the Cartoonifier is based on uses the closest camera preview resolution to the screen height. So if your device has a 5 megapixel camera and the screen is just 640 x 480, it might use a camera resolution of 720 x 480, and so on. If you want to control which camera resolution is chosen, you can modify the parameters to `setupCamera()` in the `surfaceChanged()` function in `CartoonifierViewBase.java`. For example:

```
public void surfaceChanged(SurfaceHolder _holder, int format,
   int width, int height) {
   Log.i(TAG, "Screen size: " + width + "x" + height);
   // Use a camera resolution of roughly half the screen height.
   setupCamera(width/2, height/2);
}
```

An easy method to obtain the highest preview resolution from a camera is to pass a large size such as 10,000 x 10,000 and it will choose the maximum resolution available (note that it will only give the maximum preview resolution, which is the camera's video resolution and therefore is often much less than the camera's still-image resolution). Or if you want it to run really fast, pass 1 x 1 and it will find the lowest camera preview resolution (for example 160 x 120) for you.

Customizing the app

Now that you have created a whole Android Cartoonifier app, you should know the basics of how it works and which parts do what; you should customize it! Change the GUI, the app behavior and workflow, the cartoonifier filter constants, the skin detector algorithm, or replace the cartoonifier code with your own ideas.

You can improve the skin-detection algorithm in many ways, such as by using a more complex skin-detection algorithm (for example, using trained Gaussian models from many recent CVPR or ICCV conference papers at `http://www.cvpapers.com`) or by adding face detection (see the *Face Detection* section of *Chapter 8, Face Recognition using Eigenfaces*) to the skin detector, so that it detects where the user's face is rather than asking the user to put their face in the center of the screen. Beware that face detection may take many seconds on some devices or high-resolution cameras, so this approach may be limited by the comparatively slow processing speed, but smartphones and tablets are getting significantly faster every year, so this will become less of a problem.

The most significant way to speed up mobile computer vision apps is to reduce the camera resolution as much as possible (for example, 0.5 megapixel instead of 5 megapixel), allocate and free up images as rarely as possible, and do image conversions as rarely as possible (for instance, by supporting BGRA images throughout your code). You can also look for optimized image processing or math libraries from the CPU vendor of your device (for example, NVIDIA Tegra, Texas Instruments OMAP, Samsung Exynos, Apple Ax, or QualComm Snapdragon) or for your CPU family (for example, the ARM Cortex-A9). Remember, there may be an optimized version of OpenCV for your device.

To make customizing NDK and desktop image-processing code easier, this book comes with files `ImageUtils.cpp` and `ImageUtils.h` to help you experiment. It includes functions such as `printMatInfo()`, which prints a lot of information about a `cv::Mat` object, making debugging OpenCV much easier. There are also timing macros to easily add detailed timing statistics to your C/C++ code. For example:

```
DECLARE_TIMING(myFilter);

void myImageFunction(Mat img) {
```

```
    printMatInfo(img, "input");

    START_TIMING(myFilter);
    bilateralFilter(img, …);
    STOP_TIMING(myFilter);
    SHOW_TIMING(myFilter, "My Filter");
}
```

You would then see something like the following printed to your console:

```
input: 800w600h 3ch 8bpp, range[19,255][17,243][47,251]

My Filter: time:   213ms   (ave=215ms min=197ms max=312ms, across 57 runs).
```

This is useful when your OpenCV code is not working as expected; particularly for mobile development where it is often quite difficult to use an IDE debugger, and `printf()` statements generally won't work in Android NDK. However, the functions in `ImageUtils` work on both Android and desktop.

Summary

This chapter has shown several different types of image-processing filters that can be used to generate various cartoon effects: a plain sketch mode that looks like a pencil drawing, a paint mode that looks like a color painting, and a cartoon mode that overlays the sketch mode on top of the paint mode to make the image appear like a cartoon. It also shows that other fun effects can be obtained, such as the evil mode that greatly enhances noisy edges, and the alien mode that changes the skin of the face to appear bright green.

There are many commercial smartphone apps that perform similar fun effects on the user's face, such as cartoon filters and skin-color changers. There are also professional tools using similar concepts, such as skin-smoothing video post-processing tools that attempt to beautify women's faces by smoothing their skin while keeping the edges and non-skin regions sharp, in order to make their faces appear younger.

This chapter shows how to port the app from a desktop application to an Android mobile app, by following the recommended guidelines of developing a working desktop version first, porting it to a mobile app, and creating a user interface that is suitable for the mobile app. The image-processing code is shared between the two projects so that the reader can modify the cartoon filters for the desktop application, and by rebuilding the Android app it should automatically show their modifications in the Android app as well.

The steps required to use OpenCV4Android change regularly, and Android development itself is not static; so this chapter shows how to build the Android app by adding functionality to one of the OpenCV sample projects. It is expected that the reader can add the same functionality to an equivalent project in future versions of OpenCV4Android.

This book includes source code for both the desktop project and the Android project.

2
Marker-based Augmented Reality on iPhone or iPad

Augmented reality (**AR**) is a live view of a real-world environment whose elements are augmented by computer-generated graphics. As a result, the technology functions by enhancing one's current perception of reality. Augmentation is conventionally in real-time and in semantic context with environmental elements. With the help of advanced AR technology (for example, adding computer vision and object recognition) the information about the surrounding real world of the user becomes interactive and can be digitally manipulated. Artificial information about the environment and its objects can be overlaid on the real world.

In this chapter we will create an AR application for iPhone/iPad devices. Starting from scratch, we will create an application that uses markers to draw some artificial objects on the images acquired from the camera. You will learn how to set up a project in XCode IDE and configure it to use OpenCV within your application. Also, aspects such as capturing a video from a built-in camera, 3D scene rendering using OpenGL ES, and building of a common AR application architecture are going to be explained.

Before we start, let me give you a brief list of knowledge and software you will need:

- You will need an Apple computer with XCode IDE installed. Development of applications for iPhone/iPad is possible only with Apple's XCode IDE. This is the only way to build apps for this platform.

- You will need a model of iPhone, iPad, or iPod Touch devices. To run your applications on the device, you will have to purchase the Apple Developer Certificate for USD 99 per year. It's impossible to run developed applications on the device without this certificate.

- You will also need basic knowledge of XCode IDE. We will assume readers have some experience using this IDE.
- Basic knowledge of Objective-C and C++ programming languages is also necessary. However, all complex parts of application source code will be explained in detail.

From this chapter you'll learn more about markers. The full detection routine is explained. After reading this chapter you will be able to write your own marker detection algorithm, estimate the marker pose in 3D world with regards to camera pose, and use this transformation between them to visualize arbitrary 3D objects.

You'll find the example project in this book's media for this chapter. It's a good starting point to create your first mobile Augmented Reality application.

In this chapter, we will cover the following topics:

- Creating an iOS project that uses OpenCV
- Application architecture
- Marker detection
- Marker identification
- Marker code recognition
- Placing a marker in 3D
- Rendering the 3D virtual object

Creating an iOS project that uses OpenCV

In this section we will create a demo application for iPhone/iPad devices that will use the **OpenCV (Open Source Computer Vision)** library to detect markers in the camera frame and render 3D objects on it. This example will show you how to get access to the raw video data stream from the device camera, perform image processing using the OpenCV library, find a marker in an image, and render an AR overlay.

We will start by first creating a new XCode project by choosing the iOS **Single View Application** template, as shown in the following screenshot:

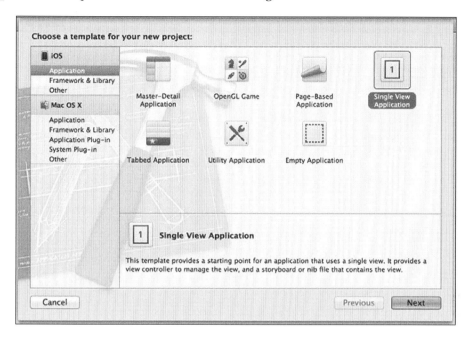

Now we have to add OpenCV to our project. This step is necessary because in this application we will use a lot of functions from this library to detect markers and estimate position position.

OpenCV is a library of programming functions for real-time computer vision. It was originally developed by Intel and is now supported by Willow Garage and Itseez. This library is written in C and C++ languages. It also has an official Python binding and unofficial bindings to Java and .NET languages.

Adding OpenCV framework

Fortunately the library is cross-platform, so it can be used on iOS devices. Starting from version 2.4.2, OpenCV library is officially supported on the iOS platform and you can download the distribution package from the library website at `http://opencv.org/`. The **OpenCV for iOS** link points to the compressed OpenCV framework. Don't worry if you are new to iOS development; a framework is like a bundle of files. Usually each framework package contains a list of header files and list of statically linked libraries. Application frameworks provide an easy way to distribute precompiled libraries to developers.

Of course, you can build your own libraries from scratch. OpenCV documentation explains this process in detail. For simplicity, we follow the recommended way and use the framework for this chapter.

After downloading the file we extract its content to the project folder, as shown in the following screenshot:

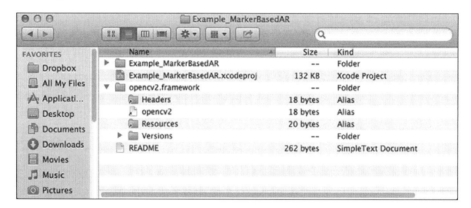

To inform the XCode IDE to use any framework during the build stage, click on **Project options** and locate the **Build phases** tab. From there we can add or remove the list of frameworks involved in the build process. Click on the plus sign to add a new framework, as shown in the following screenshot:

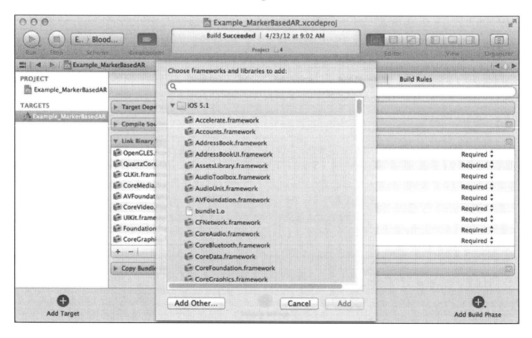

From here we can choose from a list of standard frameworks. But to add a custom framework we should click on the **Add other** button. The open file dialog box will appear. Point it to **opencv2.framework** in the project folder as shown in the following screenshot:

Including OpenCV headers

Now that we have added the OpenCV framework to the project, everything is almost done. One last thing—let's add OpenCV headers to the project's precompiled headers. The precompiled headers are a great feature to speed up compilation time. By adding OpenCV headers to them, all your sources automatically include OpenCV headers as well. Find a .pch file in the project source tree and modify it in the following way.

The following code shows how to modify the .pch file in the project source tree:

```
//
// Prefix header for all source files of the 'Example_MarkerBasedAR'
//

#import <Availability.h>

#ifndef __IPHONE_5_0
```

```
#warning "This project uses features only available in iOS SDK 5.0 and
later."
#endif

#ifdef __cplusplus
#include <opencv2/opencv.hpp>
#endif

#ifdef __OBJC__
  #import <UIKit/UIKit.h>
  #import <Foundation/Foundation.h>
#endif
```

Now you can call any OpenCV function from any place in your project.

That's all. Our project template is configured and we are ready to move further. Free advice: make a copy of this project; this will save you time when you are creating your next one!

Application architecture

Each iOS application contains at least one instance of the `UIViewController` interface that handles all view events and manages the application's business logic. This class provides the fundamental view-management model for all iOS apps. A view controller manages a set of views that make up a portion of your app's user interface. As part of the controller layer of your app, a view controller coordinates its efforts with model objects and other controller objects—including other view controllers—so your app presents a single coherent user interface.

The application that we are going to write will have only one view; that's why we choose a **Single-View Application** template to create one. This view will be used to present the rendered picture. Our `ViewController` class will contain three major components that each AR application should have (see the next diagram):

- Video source
- Processing pipeline
- Visualization engine

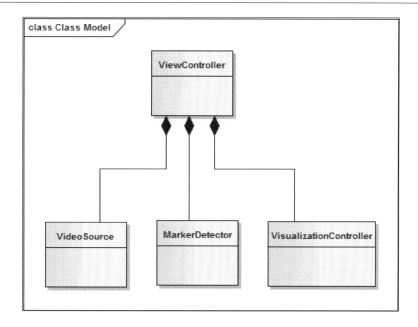

The video source is responsible for providing new frames taken from the built-in camera to the user code. This means that the video source should be capable of choosing a camera device (front- or back-facing camera), adjusting its parameters (such as resolution of the captured video, white balance, and shutter speed), and grabbing frames without freezing the main UI.

The image processing routine will be encapsulated in the MarkerDetector class. This class provides a very thin interface to user code. Usually it's a set of functions like processFrame and getResult. Actually that's all that ViewController should know about. We must not expose low-level data structures and algorithms to the view layer without strong necessity. VisualizationController contains all logic concerned with visualization of the Augmented Reality on our view. VisualizationController is also a facade that hides a particular implementation of the rendering engine. Low code coherence gives us freedom to change these components without the need to rewrite the rest of your code.

Such an approach gives you the freedom to use independent modules on other platforms and compilers as well. For example, you can use the MarkerDetector class easily to develop desktop applications on Mac, Windows, and Linux systems without any changes to the code. Likewise, you can decide to port VisualizationController on the Windows platform and use Direct3D for rendering. In this case you should write only new VisualizationController implementation; other code parts will remain the same.

The main processing routine starts from receiving a new frame from the video source. This triggers video source to inform the user code about this event with a callback. `ViewController` handles this callback and performs the following operations:

1. Sends a new frame to the visualization controller.

2. Performs processing of the new frame using our pipeline.

3. Sends the detected markers to the visualization stage.

4. Renders a scene.

Let's examine this routine in detail. The rendering of an AR scene includes the drawing of a background image that has a content of the last received frame; artificial 3D objects are drawn later on. When we send a new frame for visualization, we are copying image data to internal buffers of the rendering engine. This is not actual rendering yet; we are just updating the text with a new bitmap.

The second step is the processing of new frame and marker detection. We pass our image as input and as a result receive a list of the markers detected. on it. These markers are passed to the visualization controller, which knows how to deal with them. Let's take a look at the following sequence diagram where this routine is shown:

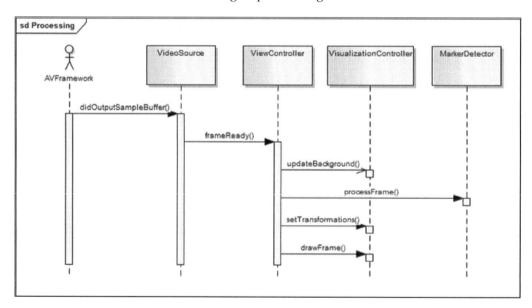

We start development by writing a video capture component. This class will be responsible for all frame grabbing and for sending notifications of captured frames via user callback. Later on we will write a marker detection algorithm. This detection routine is the core of your application. In this part of our program we will use a lot of OpenCV functions to process images, detect contours on them, find marker rectangles, and estimate their position. After that we will concentrate on visualization of our results using Augmented Reality. After bringing all these things together we will complete our first AR application. So let's move on!

Accessing the camera

The Augmented Reality application is impossible to create without two major things: video capturing and AR visualization. The video capture stage consists of receiving frames from the device camera, performing necessary color conversion, and sending it to the processing pipeline. As the single frame processing time is so critical to AR applications, the capture process should be as efficient as possible. The best way to achieve maximum performance is to have direct access to the frames received from the camera. This became possible starting from iOS Version 4. Existing APIs from the AVFoundation framework provide the necessary functionality to read directly from image buffers in memory.

You can find a lot of examples that use the `AVCaptureVideoPreviewLayer` class and the `UIGetScreenImage` function to capture videos from the camera. This technique was used for iOS Version 3 and earlier. It has now become outdated and has two major disadvantages:

- Lack of direct access to frame data. To get a bitmap, you have to create an intermediate instance of `UIImage`, copy an image to it, and get it back. For AR applications this price is too high, because each millisecond matters. Losing a few frames per second (FPS) significantly decreases overall user experience.

- To draw an AR, you have to add a transparent overlay view that will present the AR. Referring to Apple guidelines, you should avoid non-opaque layers because their blending is hard for mobile processors.

Classes `AVCaptureDevice` and `AVCaptureVideoDataOutput` allow you to configure, capture, and specify unprocessed video frames in 32 bpp BGRA format. Also you can set up the desired resolution of output frames. However, it does affect overall performance since the larger the frame the more processing time and memory is required.

There is a good alternative for high-performance video capture. The AVFoundation API offers a much faster and more elegant way to grab frames directly from the camera. But first, let's take a look at the following figure where the capturing process for iOS is shown:

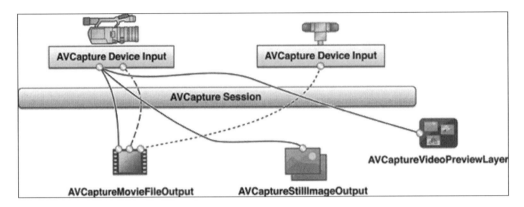

AVCaptureSession is a root capture object that we should create. Capture session requires two components—an input and an output. The input device can either be a physical device (camera) or a video file (not shown in diagram). In our case it's a built-in camera (front or back). The output device can be presented by one of the following interfaces:

- AVCaptureMovieFileOutput
- AVCaptureStillImageOutput
- AVCaptureVideoPreviewLayer
- AVCaptureVideoDataOutput

The AVCaptureMovieFileOutput interface is used to record video to the file, the AVCaptureStillImageOutput interface is used to to make still images, and the AVCaptureVideoPreviewLayer interface is used to play a video preview on the screen. We are interested in the AVCaptureVideoDataOutput interface because it gives you direct access to video data.

The iOS platform is built on top of the Objective-C programming language. So to work with AVFoundation framework, our class also has to be written in Objective-C. In this section all code listings are in the Objective-C++ language.

To encapsulate the video capturing process, we create the `VideoSource` interface as shown by the following code:

```
@protocol VideoSourceDelegate<NSObject>

-(void)frameReady:(BGRAVideoFrame) frame;

@end


@interface VideoSource : NSObject<AVCaptureVideoDataOutputSampleBuffe
rDelegate>
{

}

@property (nonatomic, retain) AVCaptureSession *captureSession;
@property (nonatomic, retain) AVCaptureDeviceInput *deviceInput;
@property (nonatomic, retain) id<VideoSourceDelegate> delegate;

- (bool) startWithDevicePosition:(AVCaptureDevicePosition)
devicePosition;
- (CameraCalibration) getCalibration;
- (CGSize) getFrameSize;

@end
```

In this callback we lock the image buffer to prevent modifications by any new frames, obtain a pointer to the image data and frame dimensions. Then we construct temporary BGRAVideoFrame object that is passed to outside via special delegate. This delegate has following prototype:

```
@protocol VideoSourceDelegate<NSObject>
-(void)frameReady:(BGRAVideoFrame) frame;

@end
```

Within `VideoSourceDelegate`, the `VideoSource` interface informs the user code that a new frame is available.

The step-by-step guide for the initialization of video capture is listed as follows:

1. Create an instance of AVCaptureSession and set the capture session quality preset.

2. Choose and create AVCaptureDevice. You can choose the front- or back-facing camera or use the default one.

3. Initialize AVCaptureDeviceInput using the created capture device and add it to the capture session.

4. Create an instance of AVCaptureVideoDataOutput and initialize it with format of video frame, callback delegate, and dispatch the queue.

5. Add the capture output to the capture session object.

6. Start the capture session.

Let's explain some of these steps in more detail. After creating the capture session, we can specify the desired quality preset to ensure that we will obtain optimal performance. We don't need to process HD-quality video, so 640 x 480 or an even lesser frame resolution is a good choice:

```
- (id)init
{
  if ((self = [super init]))
  {
    AVCaptureSession * capSession = [[AVCaptureSession alloc] init];

    if ([capSession canSetSessionPreset:AVCaptureSessionPreset64
0x480])
    {
      [capSession setSessionPreset:AVCaptureSessionPreset640x480];
      NSLog(@"Set capture session preset
AVCaptureSessionPreset640x480");
    }
    else if ([capSession canSetSessionPreset:AVCaptureSessionPresetL
ow])
    {
      [capSession setSessionPreset:AVCaptureSessionPresetLow];
      NSLog(@"Set capture session preset AVCaptureSessionPresetLow");
    }

    self.captureSession = capSession;
  }
  return self;
}
```

Always check hardware capabilities using the appropriate API; there is no guarantee that every camera will be capable of setting a particular session preset.

After creating the capture session, we should add the capture input—the instance of AVCaptureDeviceInput will represent a physical camera device. The cameraWithPosition function is a helper function that returns the camera device for the requested position (front, back, or default):

```
- (bool) startWithDevicePosition:(AVCaptureDevicePosition)
devicePosition
{
  AVCaptureDevice *videoDevice = [self cameraWithPosition:devicePosit
ion];

  if (!videoDevice)
    return FALSE;


  {
  NSError *error;

  AVCaptureDeviceInput *videoIn = [AVCaptureDeviceInput
  deviceInputWithDevice:videoDevice error:&error];
  self.deviceInput = videoIn;

  if (!error)
  {
    if ([[self captureSession] canAddInput:videoIn])
    {
      [[self captureSession] addInput:videoIn];
    }
    else
    {
      NSLog(@"Couldn't add video input");
      return FALSE;
    }
  }
  else
  {
    NSLog(@"Couldn't create video input");
    return FALSE;
  }
```

```
    }

    [self addRawViewOutput];
    [captureSession startRunning];
    return TRUE;
}
```

Please notice the error handling code. Take care of return values for such an important thing as working with hardware setup is a good practice. Without this, your code can crash in unexpected cases without informing the user what has happened.

We created a capture session and added a source of the video frames. Now it's time to add a receiver—an object that will receive actual frame data. The AVCaptureVideoDataOutput class is used to process uncompressed frames from the video stream. The camera can provide frames in BGRA, CMYK, or simple grayscale color models. For our purposes the BGRA color model fits best of all, as we will use this frame for visualization and image processing. The following code shows the addRawViewOutput function:

```
- (void) addRawViewOutput
{
  /*We setup the output*/
  AVCaptureVideoDataOutput *captureOutput = [[AVCaptureVideoDataOutput
alloc] init];

    /*While a frame is processes in -captureOutput:didOutputSampleBuff
er:fromConnection: delegate methods no other frames are added in the
queue.
        If you don't want this behaviour set the property to NO */
    captureOutput.alwaysDiscardsLateVideoFrames = YES;

    /*We create a serial queue to handle the processing of our frames*/
    dispatch_queue_t queue;
    queue = dispatch_queue_create("com.Example_MarkerBasedAR.
cameraQueue",
    NULL);
    [captureOutput setSampleBufferDelegate:self queue:queue];
    dispatch_release(queue);

    // Set the video output to store frame in BGRA (It is supposed to be
faster)
    NSString* key = (NSString*)kCVPixelBufferPixelFormatTypeKey;
    NSNumber* value = [NSNumber
```

```
    numberWithUnsignedInt:kCVPixelFormatType_32BGRA];

    NSDictionary* videoSettings = [NSDictionary
  dictionaryWithObject:value
    forKey:key];
    [captureOutput setVideoSettings:videoSettings];

    // Register an output
    [self.captureSession addOutput:captureOutput];
  }
```

Now the capture session is finally configured. When started, it will capture frames from the camera and send it to user code. When the new frame is available, an `AVCaptureSession` object performs a `captureOutput: didOutputSampleBuffer: fromConnection` callback. In this function, we will perform a minor data conversion operation to get the image data in a more usable format and pass it to user code:

```
  - (void)captureOutput:(AVCaptureOutput *)captureOutput
  didOutputSampleBuffer:(CMSampleBufferRef)sampleBuffer
         fromConnection:(AVCaptureConnection *)connection
  {
    // Get a image buffer holding video frame
    CVImageBufferRef imageBuffer = CMSampleBufferGetImageBuffer(sampleB
  uffer);

    // Lock the image buffer
    CVPixelBufferLockBaseAddress(imageBuffer,0);

    // Get information about the image
    uint8_t *baseAddress = (uint8_t *)CVPixelBufferGetBaseAddress(image
  Buffer);
    size_t width = CVPixelBufferGetWidth(imageBuffer);
    size_t height = CVPixelBufferGetHeight(imageBuffer);
    size_t stride = CVPixelBufferGetBytesPerRow(imageBuffer);

    BGRAVideoFrame frame = {width, height, stride, baseAddress};
    [delegate frameReady:frame];

    /*We unlock the  image buffer*/
    CVPixelBufferUnlockBaseAddress(imageBuffer,0);
  }
```

We obtain a reference to the image buffer that stores our frame data. Then we lock it to prevent modifications by new frames. Now we have exclusive access to the frame data. With help of the CoreVideo API, we get the image dimensions, stride (number of pixels per row), and the pointer to the beginning of the image data.

> I draw your attention to the `CVPixelBufferLockBaseAddress`/ `CVPixelBufferUnlockBaseAddress` function call in the callback code. Until we hold a lock on the pixel buffer, it guarantees consistency and correctness of its data. Reading of pixels is available only after you have obtained a lock. When you're done, don't forget to unlock it to allow the OS to fill it with new data.

Marker detection

A marker is usually designed as a rectangle image holding black and white areas inside it. Due to known limitations, the marker detection procedure is a simple one. First of all we need to find closed contours on the input image and unwarp the image inside it to a rectangle and then check this against our marker model.

In this sample the 5 x 5 marker will be used. Here is what it looks like:

In the sample project that you will find in this book, the marker detection routine is encapsulated in the `MarkerDetector` class:

```cpp
/**
 * A top-level class that encapsulate marker detector algorithm
 */
class MarkerDetector
{
public:

  /**
   * Initialize a new instance of marker detector object
   * @calibration[in] - Camera calibration necessary for pose
estimation.
   */
  MarkerDetector(CameraCalibration calibration);

  void processFrame(const BGRAVideoFrame& frame);

  const std::vector<Transformation>& getTransformations() const;

  protected:
  bool findMarkers(const BGRAVideoFrame& frame, std::vector<Marker>&
  detectedMarkers);

  void prepareImage(const cv::Mat& bgraMat,
                    cv::Mat& grayscale);

  void performThreshold(const cv::Mat& grayscale,
                        cv::Mat& thresholdImg);

  void findContours(const cv::Mat& thresholdImg,
                    std::vector<std::vector<cv::Point> >& contours,
                    int minContourPointsAllowed);

  void findMarkerCandidates(const std::vector<std::vector<cv::Point>
>&
  contours, std::vector<Marker>& detectedMarkers);

  void detectMarkers(const cv::Mat& grayscale,
                     std::vector<Marker>& detectedMarkers);

  void estimatePosition(std::vector<Marker>& detectedMarkers);

private:
};
```

To help you better understand the marker detection routine, a step-by-step processing on one frame from a video will be shown. A source image taken from an iPad camera will be used as an example:

Marker identification

Here is the workflow of the marker detection routine:

1. Convert the input image to grayscale.

2. Perform binary threshold operation.

3. Detect contours.

4. Search for possible markers.

5. Detect and decode markers.

6. Estimate marker 3D pose.

Grayscale conversion

The conversion to grayscale is necessary because markers usually contain only black and white blocks and it's much easier to operate with them on grayscale images. Fortunately, OpenCV color conversion is simple enough.

Please take a look at the following code listing in C++:

```
void MarkerDetector::prepareImage(const cv::Mat& bgraMat, cv::Mat&
grayscale)
{
  // Convert to grayscale
  cv::cvtColor(bgraMat, grayscale, CV_BGRA2GRAY);
}
```

This function will convert the input BGRA image to grayscale (it will allocate image buffers if necessary) and place the result into the second argument. All further steps will be performed with the grayscale image.

Image binarization

The binarization operation will transform each pixel of our image to black (zero intensity) or white (full intensity). This step is required to find contours. There are several threshold methods; each has strong and weak sides. The easiest and fastest method is absolute threshold. In this method the resulting value depends on current pixel intensity and some threshold value. If pixel intensity is greater than the threshold value, the result will be white (255); otherwise it will be black (0).

This method has a huge disadvantage—it depends on lighting conditions and soft intensity changes. The more preferable method is the adaptive threshold. The major difference of this method is the use of all pixels in given radius around the examined pixel. Using average intensity gives good results and secures more robust corner detection.

The following code snippet shows the `MarkerDetector` function:

```
void MarkerDetector::performThreshold(const cv::Mat& grayscale,
cv::Mat& thresholdImg)
{
  cv::adaptiveThreshold(grayscale,    // Input image
                        thresholdImg,// Result binary image
                        255,          //
                        cv::ADAPTIVE_THRESH_GAUSSIAN_C, //
                        cv::THRESH_BINARY_INV, //
                        7, //
                        7 //
                        );
}
```

After applying adaptive threshold to the input image, the resulting image looks similar to the following one:

Each marker usually looks like a square figure with black and white areas inside it. So the best way to locate a marker is to find closed contours and approximate them with polygons of 4 vertices.

Contours detection

The `cv::findCountours` function will detect contours on the input binary image:

```
void MarkerDetector::findContours(const cv::Mat& thresholdImg,
                                  std::vector<std::vector<cv::Point>
>& contours,
int minContourPointsAllowed)
{
    std::vector< std::vector<cv::Point> > allContours;
    cv::findContours(thresholdImg, allContours, CV_RETR_LIST, CV_
CHAIN_APPROX_NONE);

    contours.clear();
    for (size_t i=0; i<allContours.size(); i++)
    {
        int contourSize = allContours[i].size();
        if (contourSize > minContourPointsAllowed)
        {
            contours.push_back(allContours[i]);
        }
    }
}
```

The return value of this function is a list of polygons where each polygon represents a single contour. The function skips contours that have their perimeter in pixels value set to be less than the value of the `minContourPointsAllowed` variable. This is because we are not interested in small contours. (They will probably contain no marker, or the contour won't be able to be detected due to a small marker size.)

The following figure shows the visualization of detected contours:

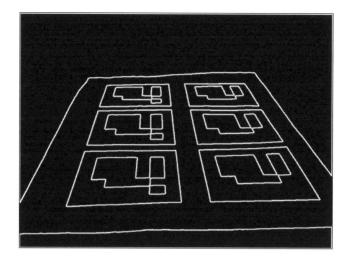

Candidates search

After finding contours, the polygon approximation stage is performed. This is done to decrease the number of points that describe the contour shape. It's a good quality check to filter out areas without markers because they can always be represented with a polygon that contains four vertices. If the approximated polygon has more than or fewer than 4 vertices, it's definitely not what we are looking for. The following code implements this idea:

```
void MarkerDetector::findCandidates
(
    const ContoursVector& contours,
    std::vector<Marker>& detectedMarkers
)
{
    std::vector<cv::Point>  approxCurve;
    std::vector<Marker>     possibleMarkers;

    // For each contour, analyze if it is a parallelepiped likely to
be the
    marker
    for (size_t i=0; i<contours.size(); i++)
    {
        // Approximate to a polygon
        double eps = contours[i].size() * 0.05;
```

```
cv::approxPolyDP(contours[i], approxCurve, eps, true);

// We interested only in polygons that contains only four
points
if (approxCurve.size() != 4)
    continue;

// And they have to be convex
if (!cv::isContourConvex(approxCurve))
    continue;

// Ensure that the distance between consecutive points is
large enough
float minDist = std::numeric_limits<float>::max();

for (int i = 0; i < 4; i++)
{
    cv::Point side = approxCurve[i] - approxCurve[(i+1)%4];
    float squaredSideLength = side.dot(side);
    minDist = std::min(minDist, squaredSideLength);
}

// Check that distance is not very small
if (minDist < m_minContourLengthAllowed)
    continue;

// All tests are passed. Save marker candidate:
Marker m;

for (int i = 0; i<4; i++)
    m.points.push_back( cv::Point2f(approxCurve[i].x,approxCu
rve[i].y) );

// Sort the points in anti-clockwise order
// Trace a line between the first and second point.
// If the third point is at the right side, then the points
are anti-
clockwise
cv::Point v1 = m.points[1] - m.points[0];
cv::Point v2 = m.points[2] - m.points[0];

double o = (v1.x * v2.y) - (v1.y * v2.x);

if (o < 0.0)            //if the third point is in the left side,
then
```

```
            sort in anti-clockwise order
                std::swap(m.points[1], m.points[3]);

            possibleMarkers.push_back(m);
    }


    // Remove these elements which corners are too close to each
other.
    // First detect candidates for removal:
    std::vector< std::pair<int,int> > tooNearCandidates;
    for (size_t i=0;i<possibleMarkers.size();i++)
    {
        const Marker& m1 = possibleMarkers[i];

        //calculate the average distance of each corner to the nearest
corner
        of the other marker candidate
        for (size_t j=i+1;j<possibleMarkers.size();j++)
        {
            const Marker& m2 = possibleMarkers[j];

            float distSquared = 0;

            for (int c = 0; c < 4; c++)
            {
                cv::Point v = m1.points[c] - m2.points[c];
                distSquared += v.dot(v);
            }

            distSquared /= 4;

            if (distSquared < 100)
            {
                tooNearCandidates.push_back(std::pair<int,int>(i,j));
            }
        }
    }

    // Mark for removal the element of the pair with smaller perimeter
    std::vector<bool> removalMask (possibleMarkers.size(), false);

    for (size_t i=0; i<tooNearCandidates.size(); i++)
    {
```

```
            float p1 = perimeter(possibleMarkers[tooNearCandidates[i].
first
            ].points);
            float p2 =
            perimeter(possibleMarkers[tooNearCandidates[i].second].
points);

            size_t removalIndex;
            if (p1 > p2)
                removalIndex = tooNearCandidates[i].second;
            else
                removalIndex = tooNearCandidates[i].first;

            removalMask[removalIndex] = true;
        }

        // Return candidates
        detectedMarkers.clear();
        for (size_t i=0;i<possibleMarkers.size();i++)
        {
            if (!removalMask[i])
                detectedMarkers.push_back(possibleMarkers[i]);
        }
    }
```

Now we have obtained a list of parallelepipeds that are likely to be the markers. To verify whether they are markers or not, we need to perform three steps:

1. First, we should remove the perspective projection so as to obtain a frontal view of the rectangle area.

2. Then we perform thresholding of the image using the Otsu algorithm. This algorithm assumes a bimodal distribution and finds the threshold value that maximizes the extra-class variance while keeping a low intra-class variance.

3. Finally we perform identification of the marker code. If it is a marker, it has an internal code. The marker is divided into a 7 x 7 grid, of which the internal 5 x 5 cells contain ID information. The rest correspond to the external black border. Here, we first check whether the external black border is present. Then we read the internal 5 x 5 cells and check if they provide a valid code. (It might be required to rotate the code to get the valid one.)

To get the rectangle marker image, we have to unwarp the input image using perspective transformation. This matrix can be calculated with the help of the `cv::getPerspectiveTransform` function. It finds the perspective transformation from four pairs of corresponding points. The first argument is the marker coordinates in image space and the second point corresponds to the coordinates of the square marker image. Estimated transformation will transform the marker to square form and let us analyze it:

```
cv::Mat canonicalMarker;
Marker& marker = detectedMarkers[i];

// Find the perspective transfomation that brings current marker to
rectangular form
cv::Mat M = cv::getPerspectiveTransform(marker.points, m_
markerCorners2d);

// Transform image to get a canonical marker image
cv::warpPerspective(grayscale, canonicalMarker,  M, markerSize);
```

Image warping transforms our image to a rectangle form using perspective transformation:

Now we can test the image to verify if it is a valid marker image. Then we try to extract the bit mask with the marker code. As we expect our marker to contain only black and white colors, we can perform Otsu thresholding to remove gray pixels and leave only black and white pixels:

```
//threshold image
cv::threshold(markerImage, markerImage, 125, 255, cv::THRESH_BINARY |
cv::THRESH_OTSU);
```

Marker code recognition

Each marker has an internal code given by 5 words of 5 bits each. The codification employed is a slight modification of the hamming code. In total, each word has only 2 bits of information out of the 5 bits employed. The other 3 are employed for error detection. As a consequence, we can have up to 1024 different IDs.

The main difference with the hamming code is that the first bit (parity of bits 3 and 5) is inverted. So, ID 0 (which in hamming code is 00000) becomes 10000 in our code. The idea is to prevent a completely black rectangle from being a valid marker ID, with the goal of reducing the likelihood of false positives with objects of the environment.

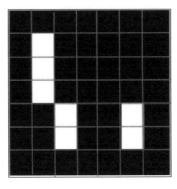

Counting the number of black and white pixels for each cell gives us a 5 x 5-bit mask with marker code. To count the number of non-zero pixels on a certain image, the cv::countNonZero function is used. This function counts non-zero array elements from a given 1D or 2D array. The cv::Mat type can return a subimage view—a new instance of cv::Mat that contains a portion of the original image. For example, if you have a cv::Mat of size 400 x 400, the following piece of code will create a submatrix for the 50 x 50 image block starting from (10, 10):

```
cv::Mat src(400,400,CV_8UC1);
cv::Rect r(10,10,50,50);
cv::Mat subView = src(r);
```

Reading marker code

Using this technique, we can easily find black and white cells on the marker board:

```
cv::Mat bitMatrix = cv::Mat::zeros(5,5,CV_8UC1);

//get information(for each inner square, determine if it is  black
or white)
```

```
for (int y=0;y<5;y++)
{
  for (int x=0;x<5;x++)
  {
    int cellX = (x+1)*cellSize;
    int cellY = (y+1)*cellSize;
    cv::Mat cell = grey(cv::Rect(cellX,cellY,cellSize,cellSize));

    int nZ = cv::countNonZero(cell);
    if (nZ> (cellSize*cellSize) /2)
      bitMatrix.at<uchar>(y,x) = 1;
  }
}
```

Take a look at the following figure. The same marker can have four possible representations depending on the camera's point of view:

As there are four possible orientations of the marker picture, we have to find the correct marker position. Remember, we introduced three parity bits for each two bits of information. With their help we can find the hamming distance for each possible marker orientation. The correct marker position will have zero hamming distance error, while the other rotations won't.

Here is a code snippet that rotates the bit matrix four times and finds the correct marker orientation:

```
//check all possible rotations
cv::Mat rotations[4];
int distances[4];

rotations[0] = bitMatrix;
distances[0] = hammDistMarker(rotations[0]);

std::pair<int,int> minDist(distances[0],0);

for (int i=1; i<4; i++)
```

```
{
  //get the hamming distance to the nearest possible word
  rotations[i] = rotate(rotations[i-1]);
  distances[i] = hammDistMarker(rotations[i]);

  if (distances[i] < minDist.first)
  {
    minDist.first  = distances[i];
    minDist.second = i;
  }
}
```

This code finds the orientation of the bit matrix in such a way that it gives minimal error for the hamming distance metric. This error should be zero for correct marker ID; if it's not, it means that we encountered a wrong marker pattern (corrupted image or false-positive marker detection).

Marker location refinement

After finding the right marker orientation, we rotate the marker's corners respectively to conform to their order:

```
//sort the points so that they are always in the same order
// no matter the camera orientation
std::rotate(marker.points.begin(), marker.points.begin() + 4 -
nRotations,
marker.points.end());
```

After detecting a marker and decoding its ID, we will refine its corners. This operation will help us in the next step when we will estimate the marker position in 3D. To find the corner location with subpixel accuracy, the `cv::cornerSubPix` function is used:

```
std::vector<cv::Point2f> preciseCorners(4 * goodMarkers.size());

for (size_t i=0; i<goodMarkers.size(); i++)
{
  Marker& marker = goodMarkers[i];

  for (int c=0;c<4;c++)
  {
    preciseCorners[i*4+c] = marker.points[c];
  }
}
```

```
cv::cornerSubPix(grayscale, preciseCorners, cvSize(5,5),
cvSize(-1,-1), cvTermCriteria(CV_TERMCRIT_ITER,30,0.1));

//copy back
for (size_t i=0;i<goodMarkers.size();i++)
{
  Marker&marker = goodMarkers[i];

  for (int c=0;c<4;c++)
  {
    marker.points[c] = preciseCorners[i*4+c];
  }
}
```

The first step is to prepare the input data for this function. We copy the list of vertices to the input array. Then we call `cv::cornerSubPix`, passing the actual image, list of points, and set of parameters that affect quality and performance of location refinement. When done, we copy the refined locations back to marker corners as shown in the following image.

We do not use `cornerSubPix` in the earlier stages of marker detection due to its complexity. It's very expensive to call this function for large numbers of points (in terms of computation time). Therefore we do this only for valid markers.

Placing a marker in 3D

Augmented Reality tries to fuse the real-world object with virtual content. To place a 3D model in a scene, we need to know its pose with regard to a camera that we use to obtain the video frames. We will use a Euclidian transformation in the Cartesian coordinate system to represent such a pose.

The position of the marker in 3D and its corresponding projection in 2D is restricted by the following equation:

P = A * [R | T] * M;

Where:

- *M* denotes a point in a 3D space
- *[R | T]* denotes a [3 | 4] matrix representing a Euclidian transformation
- *A* denotes a camera matrix or a matrix of intrinsic parameters
- *P* denotes projection of *M* in screen space

After performing the marker detection step we now know the position of the four marker corners in 2D (projections in screen space). In the next section you will learn how to obtain the *A* matrix and *M* vector parameters and calculate the [R | T] transformation.

Camera calibration

Each camera lens has unique parameters, such as focal length, principal point, and lens distortion model. The process of finding intrinsic camera parameters is called camera calibration. The camera calibration process is important for Augmented Reality applications because it describes the perspective transformation and lens distortion on an output image. To achieve the best user experience with Augmented Reality, visualization of an augmented object should be done using the same perspective projection.

To calibrate the camera, we need a special pattern image (chessboard plate or black circles on white background). The camera that is being calibrated takes 10-15 shots of this pattern from different points of view. A calibration algorithm then finds the optimal camera intrinsic parameters and the distortion vector:

To represent camera calibration in our program, we use the `CameraCalibration` class:

```
/**
 * A camera calibration class that stores intrinsic matrix and
distorsion coefficients.
 */
class CameraCalibration
{
  public:
  CameraCalibration();
  CameraCalibration(float fx, float fy, float cx, float cy);
  CameraCalibration(float fx, float fy, float cx, float cy, float
  distorsionCoeff[4]);

  void getMatrix34(float cparam[3][4]) const;

  const Matrix33& getIntrinsic() const;
  const Vector4&  getDistorsion() const;

  private:
  Matrix33 m_intrinsic;
  Vector4  m_distorsion;
};
```

Detailed explanation of the calibration procedure is beyond the scope of this chapter. Please refer to *OpenCV camera_calibration sample* or *OpenCV: Estimating Projective Relations in Images* at `http://www.packtpub.com/article/opencv-estimating-projective-relations-images` for additional information and source code.

For this sample we provide internal parameters for all modern iOS devices (iPad 2, iPad 3, and iPhone 4).

Marker pose estimation

With the precise location of marker corners, we can estimate a transformation between our camera and a marker in 3D space. This operation is known as pose estimation from 2D-3D correspondences. The pose estimation process finds a Euclidean transformation (that consists only of rotation and translation components) between the camera and the object.

Let's take a look at the following figure:

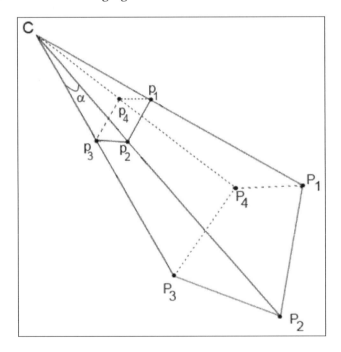

The **C** is used to denote the camera center. The **P1-P4** points are 3D points in the world coordinate system and the **p1-p4** points are their projections on the camera's image plane. Our goal is to find relative transformation between a known marker position in the 3D world (**p1-p4**) and the camera **C** using an intrinsic matrix and known point projections on image plane (**P1-P4**). But where do we get the coordinates of marker position in 3D space? We imagine them. As our marker always has a square form and all vertices lie in one plane, we can define their corners as follows:

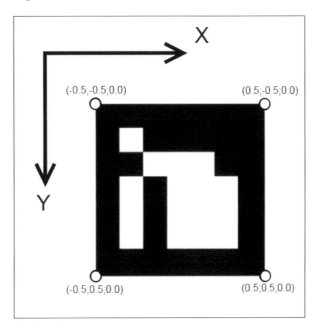

We put our marker in the XY plane (Z component is zero) and the marker center corresponds to the (0.0, 0.0, 0.0) point. It's a great hint, because in this case the beginning of our coordinate system will be in the center of the marker (Z axis is perpendicular to the marker plane).

To find the camera location with the known 2D-3D correspondences, the `cv::solvePnP` function can be used:

```
void solvePnP(const Mat& objectPoints, const Mat& imagePoints, const Mat&
cameraMatrix, const Mat& distCoeffs, Mat& rvec, Mat& tvec, bool
useExtrinsicGuess=false);
```

The `objectPoints` array is an input array of object points in the object coordinate space. `std::vector<cv::Point3f>` can be passed here. The OpenCV matrix 3 x *N* or *N* x 3, where *N* is the number of points, can also be passed as an input argument. Here we pass the list of marker coordinates in 3D space (a vector of four points).

The `imagePoints` array is an array of corresponding image points (or projections). This argument can also be `std::vector<cv::Point2f>` or `cv::Mat` of 2 x N or N x 2, where N is the number of points. Here we pass the list of found marker corners.

- `cameraMatrix`: This is the 3 x 3 camera intrinsic matrix.
- `distCoeffs`: This is the input 4 x 1, 1 x 4, 5 x 1, or 1 x 5 vector of distortion coefficients (k1, k2, p1, p2, [k3]). If it is NULL, all of the distortion coefficients are set to 0.
- `rvec`: This is the output rotation vector that (together with `tvec`) brings points from the model coordinate system to the camera coordinate system.
- `tvec`: This is the output translation vector.
- `useExtrinsicGuess`: If true, the function will use the provided `rvec` and `tvec` vectors as the initial approximations of the rotation and translation vectors, respectively, and will further optimize them.

The function calculates the camera transformation in such a way that it minimizes reprojection error, that is, the sum of squared distances between the observed projection's `imagePoints` and the projected `objectPoints`.

The estimated transformation is defined by rotation (`rvec`) and translation components (`tvec`). This is also known as Euclidean transformation or rigid transformation.

A rigid transformation is formally defined as a transformation that, when acting on any vector *v*, produces a transformed vector *T(v)* of the form:

$T(v) = R\,v + t$

where RT = R-1 (that is, R is an orthogonal transformation), and *t* is a vector giving the translation of the origin. A proper rigid transformation has, in addition,

$\det(R) = 1$

This means that R does not produce a reflection, and hence it represents a rotation (an orientation-preserving orthogonal transformation).

To obtain a 3 x 3 rotation matrix from the rotation vector, the function `cv::Rodrigues` is used. This function converts a rotation represented by a rotation vector and returns its equivalent rotation matrix.

Because `cv::solvePnP` finds the camera position with regards to marker pose in 3D space, we have to invert the found transformation. The resulting transformation will describe a marker transformation in the camera coordinate system, which is much friendlier for the rendering process.

Here is a listing of the `estimatePosition` function, which finds the position of the detected markers:

```
void MarkerDetector::estimatePosition(std::vector<Marker>&
detectedMarkers)
{
  for (size_t i=0; i<detectedMarkers.size(); i++)
  {
    Marker& m = detectedMarkers[i];

    cv::Mat Rvec;
    cv::Mat_<float> Tvec;
    cv::Mat raux,taux;
    cv::solvePnP(m_markerCorners3d, m.points, camMatrix,
distCoeff,raux,taux);
    raux.convertTo(Rvec,CV_32F);
    taux.convertTo(Tvec ,CV_32F);

    cv::Mat_<float> rotMat(3,3);
    cv::Rodrigues(Rvec, rotMat);

    // Copy to transformation matrix
    m.transformation = Transformation();

    for (int col=0; col<3; col++)
    {
      for (int row=0; row<3; row++)
      {
        m.transformation.r().mat[row][col] = rotMat(row,col); // Copy
rotation
        component
      }
      m.transformation.t().data[col] = Tvec(col); // Copy translation
      component
    }

    // Since solvePnP finds camera location, w.r.t to marker pose, to
get
    marker pose w.r.t to the camera we invert it.
    m.transformation = m.transformation.getInverted();
  }
```

Rendering the 3D virtual object

So, by now you already know how to find the markers on the image to calculate their exact position in space, relative to the camera. It's time to draw something. As already mentioned, to render the scene we will use OpenGL functions. 3D visualization is a core part of Augmented Reality. OpenGL provides all the basic features for creating high-quality rendering.

> There are a large number of commercial and open source 3D-engines (Unity, Unreal Engine, Ogre, and so on). But all these engines use either OpenGL or DirectX to pass commands to the video card. DirectX is a proprietary API and it's supported only on the Windows platform. For this reason, OpenGL is the first and last candidate for building cross-platform rendering systems.

Understanding the principles of the rendering system will give you the necessary experience and knowledge to use these engines in the future or to write your own.

Creating the OpenGL rendering layer

In order to use OpenGL functions in your application you should obtain an iOS graphics context surface, which will present the rendered scene to the user. This context is usually bound to **View**, which the user sees. The following screenshot shows the hierarchy of the application interface in XCode's **Interface Builder**:

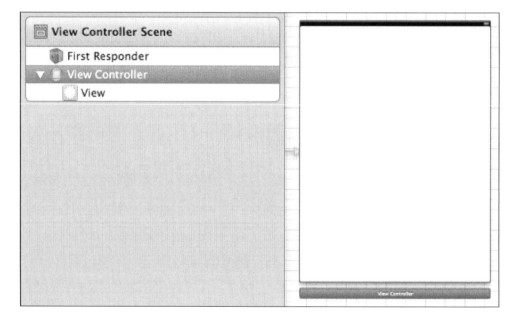

To encapsulate the OpenGL context initialization logic, we introduce the
EAGLView class:

```
@class EAGLContext;

// This class wraps the CAEAGLLayer from CoreAnimation into a
convenient UIView subclass.
// The view content is basically an EAGL surface you render your
OpenGL scene into.
// Note that setting the view non-opaque will only work if the EAGL
surface has an alpha channel.
@interface EAGLView : UIView
{
@private
    // The OpenGL ES names for the framebuffer and renderbuffer used
to render
    to this view.
    GLuint defaultFramebuffer, colorRenderbuffer;
}

@property (nonatomic, retain) EAGLContext *context;
// The pixel dimensions of the CAEAGLLayer.
@property (readonly) GLint framebufferWidth;
@property (readonly) GLint framebufferHeight;

- (void)setFramebuffer;
- (BOOL)presentFramebuffer;
- (void)initContext;
@end
```

This class is connected to our View in our interface definition file, so when the NIB
file is loaded, the runtime will instantiate a new instance of our EAGLView. When
created, it will receive events from iOS and initialize the OpenGL rendering context.

The following is a code listing showing the initWithCoder function:

```
//The EAGL view is stored in the nib file. When it's unarchived it's
sent -initWithCoder:.
- (id)initWithCoder:(NSCoder*)coder
{
  self = [super initWithCoder:coder];
  if (self) {
    CAEAGLLayer *eaglLayer = (CAEAGLLayer *)self.layer;

    eaglLayer.opaque = TRUE;
```

```
    eaglLayer.drawableProperties = [NSDictionary
dictionaryWithObjectsAndKeys:
                                   [NSNumber numberWithBool:FALSE],

kEAGLDrawablePropertyRetainedBacking,
                                   kEAGLColorFormatRGBA8,
                                   kEAGLDrawablePropertyColorFormat,
                                   nil];

    [self initContext];
  }

  return self;
}

- (void)createFramebuffer
{
  if (context && !defaultFramebuffer) {
    [EAGLContext setCurrentContext:context];

    // Create default framebuffer object.
    glGenFramebuffers(1, &defaultFramebuffer);
    glBindFramebuffer(GL_FRAMEBUFFER, defaultFramebuffer);

    // Create color render buffer and allocate backing store.
    glGenRenderbuffers(1, &colorRenderbuffer);
    glBindRenderbuffer(GL_RENDERBUFFER, colorRenderbuffer);
    [context renderbufferStorage:GL_RENDERBUFFER
fromDrawable:(CAEAGLLayer *)self.layer];
    glGetRenderbufferParameteriv(GL_RENDERBUFFER, GL_RENDERBUFFER_
WIDTH, &framebufferWidth);
    glGetRenderbufferParameteriv(GL_RENDERBUFFER, GL_RENDERBUFFER_
HEIGHT, &framebufferHeight);

    glFramebufferRenderbuffer(GL_FRAMEBUFFER, GL_COLOR_ATTACHMENT0,
    GL_RENDERBUFFER, colorRenderbuffer);

    if (glCheckFramebufferStatus(GL_FRAMEBUFFER) != GL_FRAMEBUFFER_
COMPLETE)
    NSLog(@"Failed to make complete framebuffer object %x",
```

```
    glCheckFramebufferStatus(GL_FRAMEBUFFER));

    //glClearColor(0, 0, 0, 0);
    NSLog(@"Framebuffer created");
  }
}
```

Rendering an AR scene

As you can see, the EAGLView class does not contain methods for the visualization of 3D objects and video. This is done on purpose. The task of EAGLView is to provide rendering context. The separation of responsibilities allows us to change the logic of the visualization later.

For visualization of Augmented Reality, we will create a separate class called as VisualizationController:

```
@interface SimpleVisualizationController : NSObject<VisualizationCont
roller>
{
  EAGLView * m_glview;
  GLuint m_backgroundTextureId;
  std::vector<Transformation> m_transformations;
  CameraCalibration m_calibration;
  CGSize m_frameSize;
}

-(id) initWithGLView:(EAGLView*)view calibration:(CameraCalibration)
calibration frameSize:(CGSize) size;

-(void) drawFrame;
-(void) updateBackground:(BGRAVideoFrame) frame;
-(void) setTransformationList:(const std::vector<Transformation>&)
transformations;
```

The drawFrame function performs rendering of the AR onto the given EAGLView target view. It performs the following steps:

1. Clears the scene.
2. Sets up orthographic projection for drawing the background.
3. Draws the latest received image from the camera on a viewport.
4. Sets up perspective projection with regards to a camera's intrinsic parameters.

5. For each detected marker, it moves the coordinate system to marker position in 3D. (It puts 4 x 4-transformation matrix to the OpenGl model-view matrix.)

6. Renders an arbitrary 3D object.

7. Shows the frame buffer.

The `drawFrame` function is called when the frame is ready to be drawn. It happens when a new camera frame has been uploaded to video memory and the marker detection stage has been completed.

The following code shows the `drawFrame` function:

```
- (void)drawFrame
{
  // Set the active framebuffer
  [m_glview setFramebuffer];

  // Draw a video on the background
  [self drawBackground];

  // Draw 3D objects on the position of the detected markers
  [self drawAR];

  // Present framebuffer
  bool ok = [m_glview presentFramebuffer];

  int glErCode = glGetError();
  if (!ok || glErCode != GL_NO_ERROR)
  {
    std::cerr << "GL error detected. Error code:" << glErCode <<
std::endl;
  }
}
```

Drawing a background is easy enough; we set the orthographic projection and draw a fullscreen texture with image from the current frame. Here is a code listing that uses the GLES 1 API to do this:

```
- (void) drawBackground
{
  GLfloat w = m_glview.bounds.size.width;
  GLfloat h = m_glview.bounds.size.height;
  const GLfloat squareVertices[] =
  {
    0, 0,
    w, 0,
```

```
    0, h,
    w, h
};

static const GLfloat textureVertices[] =
{
  1, 0,
  1, 1,
  0, 0,
  0, 1
};

static const GLfloat proj[] =
{
  0, -2.f/w, 0, 0,
  -2.f/h, 0, 0, 0,
  0, 0, 1, 0,
  1, 1, 0, 1
};

glMatrixMode(GL_PROJECTION);
glLoadMatrixf(proj);

glMatrixMode(GL_MODELVIEW);
glLoadIdentity();

glDisable(GL_COLOR_MATERIAL);

glEnable(GL_TEXTURE_2D);
glBindTexture(GL_TEXTURE_2D, m_backgroundTextureId);

// Update attribute values.
glVertexPointer(2, GL_FLOAT, 0, squareVertices);
glEnableClientState(GL_VERTEX_ARRAY);
glTexCoordPointer(2, GL_FLOAT, 0, textureVertices);
glEnableClientState(GL_TEXTURE_COORD_ARRAY);

glColor4f(1,1,1,1);
glDrawArrays(GL_TRIANGLE_STRIP, 0, 4);

glDisableClientState(GL_VERTEX_ARRAY);
glDisableClientState(GL_TEXTURE_COORD_ARRAY);
glDisable(GL_TEXTURE_2D);
}
```

Rendering of artificial objects in a scene is somewhat tricky. First of all we have to adjust the OpenGL projection matrix with regards to the camera intrinsic (calibration) matrix. Without this step we will have the wrong perspective projection. Wrong perspective makes artificial objects look unnatural, as if they are "flying in the air" and not a part of the real world. Correct perspective is a must-have for any Augmented Reality application.

Here is a code snippet that creates an OpenGL projection matrix from camera intrinsics:

```
- (void)buildProjectionMatrix:(Matrix33)cameraMatrix: (int)screen_
width: (int)screen_height: (Matrix44&) projectionMatrix
{
  float near = 0.01;  // Near clipping distance
  float far = 100;  // Far clipping distance

  // Camera parameters
  float f_x = cameraMatrix.data[0]; // Focal length in x axis
  float f_y = cameraMatrix.data[4]; // Focal length in y axis (usually
the
  same?)
  float c_x = cameraMatrix.data[2]; // Camera primary point x
  float c_y = cameraMatrix.data[5]; // Camera primary point y

  projectionMatrix.data[0] =  - 2.0 * f_x / screen_width;
  projectionMatrix.data[1] = 0.0;
  projectionMatrix.data[2] = 0.0;
  projectionMatrix.data[3] = 0.0;

  projectionMatrix.data[4] = 0.0;
  projectionMatrix.data[5] = 2.0 * f_y / screen_height;
  projectionMatrix.data[6] = 0.0;
  projectionMatrix.data[7] = 0.0;

  projectionMatrix.data[8] = 2.0 * c_x / screen_width - 1.0;
  projectionMatrix.data[9] = 2.0 * c_y / screen_height - 1.0;
  projectionMatrix.data[10] = -( far+near ) / ( far - near );
  projectionMatrix.data[11] = -1.0;

  projectionMatrix.data[12] = 0.0;
  projectionMatrix.data[13] = 0.0;
  projectionMatrix.data[14] = -2.0 * far * near / ( far - near );
  projectionMatrix.data[15] = 0.0;
}
```

After we load this matrix to the OpenGL pipeline, it's time to draw some objects. Each transformation can be presented as a 4 x 4 matrix and loaded to the OpenGL model view matrix. This will move the coordinate system to the marker position in the world coordinate system.

For example, let's draw a coordinate axis on the top of each marker that will show its orientation in space, and a rectangle with gradient fill that overlays the whole marker. This visualization will give us visual feedback that our code is working as expected.

The following is a code snippet showing the `drawAR` function:

```
- (void) drawAR
{
  Matrix44 projectionMatrix;
  [self buildProjectionMatrix:m_calibration.getIntrinsic():m_
frameSize.width
   :m_frameSize.height :projectionMatrix];

  glMatrixMode(GL_PROJECTION);
  glLoadMatrixf(projectionMatrix.data);

  glMatrixMode(GL_MODELVIEW);
  glLoadIdentity();

  glEnableClientState(GL_VERTEX_ARRAY);
  glEnableClientState(GL_NORMAL_ARRAY);

  glPushMatrix();
  glLineWidth(3.0f);

  float lineX[] = {0,0,0,1,0,0};
  float lineY[] = {0,0,0,0,1,0};
  float lineZ[] = {0,0,0,0,0,1};

  const GLfloat squareVertices[] = {
    -0.5f, -0.5f,
     0.5f, -0.5f,
    -0.5f,  0.5f,
     0.5f,  0.5f,
  };
  const GLubyte squareColors[] = {
    255, 255,   0, 255,
    0,   255, 255, 255,
    0,     0,   0,   0,
```

```
    255,    0, 255, 255,
  };

  for (size_t transformationIndex=0;
  transformationIndex<m_transformations.size(); transformationIndex++)
  {
    const Transformation& transformation =
    m_transformations[transformationIndex];

    Matrix44 glMatrix = transformation.getInverted().getMat44();

    glLoadMatrixf(reinterpret_cast<const GLfloat*>(&glMatrix.
data[0]));

    // draw data
    glVertexPointer(2, GL_FLOAT, 0, squareVertices);
    glEnableClientState(GL_VERTEX_ARRAY);
    glColorPointer(4, GL_UNSIGNED_BYTE, 0, squareColors);
    glEnableClientState(GL_COLOR_ARRAY);

    glDrawArrays(GL_TRIANGLE_STRIP, 0, 4);
    glDisableClientState(GL_COLOR_ARRAY);

    float scale = 0.5;
    glScalef(scale, scale, scale);

    glColor4f(1.0f, 0.0f, 0.0f, 1.0f);
    glVertexPointer(3, GL_FLOAT, 0, lineX);
    glDrawArrays(GL_LINES, 0, 2);

    glColor4f(0.0f, 1.0f, 0.0f, 1.0f);
    glVertexPointer(3, GL_FLOAT, 0, lineY);
    glDrawArrays(GL_LINES, 0, 2);

    glColor4f(0.0f, 0.0f, 1.0f, 1.0f);
    glVertexPointer(3, GL_FLOAT, 0, lineZ);
    glDrawArrays(GL_LINES, 0, 2);
  }

  glPopMatrix();
  glDisableClientState(GL_VERTEX_ARRAY);
}
```

If you run the application, you will get the following figure:

Despite the fact that we do not use a special 3D rendering engine for visualization of our scene, we have all the necessary data to do this by ourselves. Let's summarize the data we obtain:

- A frame from the camera device in BGRA format
- A correct projection matrix that gives us the right perspective projection for AR scene rendering
- A list of found marker poses

You can easily put this data to any 3D engine and create your own finished marker-based AR application

As you can see, the quads with gradient fill and pivots are placed exactly on the markers. This is the key feature of Augmented Reality—seamless fusion of real pictures and artificial objects.

Summary

In this chapter we learned how to create a mobile Augmented Reality application for iPhone/iPad devices. You gained knowledge on how to use the OpenCV library within the XCode projects to create stunning state-of-the-art applications. Usage of OpenCV enables your application to perform complex image processing computations on mobile devices with real-time performance.

From this chapter you also learned how to perform the initial image processing (translation in shades of gray and binarization), how to find closed contours in the image and approximate them with polygons, how to find markers in the image and decode them, how to compute the marker position in space, and the visualization of 3D objects in Augmented Reality.

References

- *ArUco: a minimal library for Augmented Reality applications based on OpenCV* (http://www.uco.es/investiga/grupos/ava/node/26)

- *OpenCV Camera Calibration and 3D Reconstruction* (http://opencv.itseez.com/modules/calib3d/doc/camera_calibration_and_3d_reconstruction.html)

- *OpenCV: Estimating Projective Relations in Images* (http://www.packtpub.com/article/opencv-estimating-projective-relations-images)

- *Multiple View Geometry in Computer Vision* (*second edition*), *R.I. Hartley and A. Zisserman, Cambridge University Press, ISBN 0-521-54051-8*

3
Marker-less Augmented Reality

In this chapter readers will learn how to create a standard real-time project using OpenCV (for desktop), and how to perform a new method of marker-less augmented reality, using the actual environment as the input instead of printed square markers. This chapter will cover some of the theory of marker-less AR and show how to apply it in useful projects.

The following is a list of topics that will be covered in this chapter:

- Marker-based versus marker-less AR
- Using feature descriptors to find an arbitrary image on video
- Pattern pose estimation
- Application infrastructure
- Enabling support for OpenGL visualization in OpenCV
- Rendering the augmented reality
- Demonstration

Before we start, let me give you a brief list of the knowledge required for this chapter and the software you will need:

- Basic knowledge of CMake. CMake is a cross-platform, open-source build system designed to build, test, and package software. Like the OpenCV library, the demonstration project for this chapter also uses the CMake build system. CMake can be downloaded from `http://www.cmake.org/`.

- A basic knowledge of C++ programming language is also necessary. However, all complex parts of the application source code will be explained in detail.

Marker-based versus marker-less AR

From the previous chapter you've learned how to use special images called markers to augment a real scene. The strong aspects of the markers are as follows:

- Cheap detection algorithm
- Robust against lighting changes

Markers also have several weaknesses. They are as follows:

- Doesn't work if partially overlapped
- Marker image has to be black and white
- Has square form in most cases (because it's easy to detect)
- Non-esthetic visual look of the marker
- Has nothing in common with real-world objects

So, markers are a good point to start working with augmented reality; but if you want more, it's time to move on from marker-based to marker-less AR. Marker-less AR is a technique that is based on recognition of objects that exist in the real world. A few examples of a target for marker-less AR are: magazine covers, company logos, toys, and so on. In general, any object that has enough descriptive and discriminative information regarding the rest of the scene can be a target for marker-less AR.

The strong sides of the marker-less AR approach are:

- Can be used to detect real-world objects
- Works even if the target object is partially overlapped
- Can have arbitrary form and texture (except solid or smooth gradient textures)

Marker-less AR systems can use real images and objects to position the camera in 3D space and present eye-catching effects on top of the real picture. The heart of the marker-less AR are image recognition and object detection algorithms. Unlike markers, whose shape and internal structure is fixed and known, real objects cannot be defined in such a way. Also, objects can have a complex shape and require modified pose estimation algorithms to find their correct 3D transformations.

 To give you an idea of marker-less AR, we will use a planar image as a target. Objects with complex shapes will not be considered here in detail. We will discuss the use of complex shapes for AR later in this chapter.

Marker-less AR performs heavy CPU calculations, so a mobile device often is not capable to secure smooth FPS. In this chapter, we will be targeting desktop platforms such as PC or Mac. For this purpose, we need a cross-platform build system. In this chapter we use the CMake build system.

Using feature descriptors to find an arbitrary image on video

Image recognition is a computer vision technique that searches the input image for a particular bitmap pattern. Our image recognition algorithm should be able to detect the pattern even if it is scaled, rotated, or has different brightness than of the original image.

How do we compare the pattern image against other images? As the pattern can be affected by perspective transformation, it's obvious that we can't directly compare pixels of the pattern and test image. The feature points and feature descriptors are helpful in this case. There is no universal or exact definition of what the feature is. The exact definition often depends on the problem or the type of application. Usually a feature is defined as an "interesting" part of an image, and features are used as a starting point for many computer vision algorithms. In this chapter we will use a **feature point** term, which is a part of the image defined by a center point, radius, and orientation. Each feature-detection algorithm tries to detect the same feature points regardless of the perspective transformation applied.

Feature extraction

Feature detection is the method of finding areas of interest from the input image. There are a lot of feature-detection algorithms, which search for edges, corners, or blobs. In our case we are interested in corner detection. The corner detection is based on an analysis of the edges in the image. A corner-based edge detection algorithm searches for rapid changes in the image gradient. Usually it's done by looking for extremums of the first derivative of the image gradients in the X and Y directions.

Feature-point orientation is usually computed as a direction of dominant image gradient in a particular area. When the image is rotated or scaled, the orientation of dominant gradient is recomputed by the feature-detection algorithm. This means that regardless of image rotation, the orientation of feature points will not change. Such features are called **rotation invariant**.

Also, I have to mention a few points about the size feature point. Some of the feature-detection algorithms use fixed-size features, while others calculate the optimal size for each keypoint separately. Knowing the feature size allows us to find the same feature points on scaled images. This makes features scale invariant.

OpenCV has several feature-detection algorithms. All of them are derived from the base class `cv::FeatureDetector`. Creation of the feature-detection algorithm can be done in two ways:

- Via an explicit call of the concrete feature detector class constructor:

```
cv::Ptr<cv::FeatureDetector> detector =
cv::Ptr<cv::FeatureDetector>(new cv::SurfFeatureDetector());
```

- Or by creating a feature detector by algorithm name:

```
cv::Ptr<cv::FeatureDetector> detector =
cv::FeatureDetector::create("SURF");
```

Both methods have their advantages, so choose the one you most prefer. The explicit class creation allows you to pass additional arguments to the feature detector constructor, while the creation by algorithm name makes it easier to switch the algorithm during runtime.

To detect feature points, you should call the `detect` method:

```
std::vector<cv::KeyPoint> keypoints;
detector->detect(image, keypoints);
```

The detected feature points are placed in the `keypoints` container. Each keypoint contains its center, radius, angle, and score, and has some correlation with the "quality" or "strength" of the feature point. Each feature-detection algorithm has its own score computation algorithm, so it's valid to compare scores of the keypoints detected by a particular detection algorithm.

> Corner-based feature detectors use a grayscale image to find feature points. Descriptor-extraction algorithms also work with grayscale images. Of course, both of them can do color conversion implicitly. But in this case the color conversion will be done twice. We can improve performance by doing an explicit color conversion of the input image to grayscale and use that for feature detection and descriptor extraction.

The best results in pattern detection are achieved if the detector computes keypoint orientation and size. This makes keypoints invariant to rotation and scale. The most famous and robust keypoint detection algorithms are well known, they are used in SIFT and SURF feature detection/description extraction. Unfortunately, they are patented; so they are not free for commercial use. However, their implementation is present in OpenCV, so you can evaluate them freely. But there are good and free replacements available. You can use the ORB or FREAK algorithm instead. The ORB detection is a modified FAST feature detector. The original FAST detector is amazingly fast but does not calculate the orientation or the size of the keypoint. Fortunately, the ORB algorithm does estimate keypoint orientation, but the feature size is still fixed. From the following paragraphs you will learn nice and cheap tricks of dealing with this. But first, let me explain why the feature point matters so much in image recognition.

If we deal with images, which usually have a color depth of 24 bits per pixel, for a resolution of 640 x 480, we have 912 KB of data. How do we find our pattern image in the real world? Pixel-to-pixel matching takes too long and we will have to deal with rotation and scaling too. It's definitely not an option. Using feature points can solve this problem. By detecting keypoints, we can be sure that returned features describe parts of the image that contains lot of information (that's because corner-based detectors return edges, corners, and other sharp figures). So to find correspondences between two frames, we only have to match keypoints.

From the patch defined by the keypoint, we extract a vector called descriptor. It's a form of representation of the feature point. There are many methods of extraction of the descriptor from the feature point. All of them have their strengths and weaknesses. For example, SIFT and SURF descriptor-extraction algorithms are CPU-intensive but provide robust descriptors with good distinctiveness. In our sample project we use the ORB descriptor-extraction algorithm because we choose it as a feature detector too.

 It's always a good idea to use both feature detector and descriptor extractor from the same algorithm, as they will then fit each other perfectly.

Feature descriptor is represented as a vector of fixed size (16 or more elements). Let's say our image has a resolution of 640 x 480 pixels and it has 1,500 feature points. Then, it will require `1500 * 16 * sizeof(float) = 96 KB` (for SURF). It's ten times smaller than the original image data. Also, it's much easier to operate with descriptors rather than with raster bitmaps. For two feature descriptors we can introduce a similarity score—a metric that defines the level of similarity between two vectors. Usually its L2 norm or hamming distance (based upon the kind of feature descriptor used).

The feature descriptor-extraction algorithms are derived from the `cv::DescriptorExtractor` base class. Likewise, as feature-detection algorithms they can be created by either specifying their name or with explicit constructor calls.

Definition of a pattern object

To describe a pattern object we introduce a class called `Pattern`, which holds a train image, list of features and extracted descriptors, and 2D and 3D correspondences for initial pattern position:

```
/**
 * Store the image data and computed descriptors of target pattern
 */
struct Pattern
{
  cv::Size                  size;
  cv::Mat                   data;
  std::vector<cv::KeyPoint> keypoints;
  cv::Mat                   descriptors;

  std::vector<cv::Point2f>  points2d;
  std::vector<cv::Point3f>  points3d;
};
```

Matching of feature points

The process of finding frame-to-frame correspondences can be formulated as the search of the nearest neighbor from one set of descriptors for every element of another set. It's called the "matching" procedure. There are two main algorithms for descriptor matching in OpenCV:

- Brute-force matcher (`cv::BFMatcher`)
- Flann-based matcher (`cv::FlannBasedMatcher`)

The brute-force matcher looks for each descriptor in the first set and the closest descriptor in the second set by trying each one (exhaustive search). `cv::FlannBasedMatcher` uses the fast approximate nearest neighbor search algorithm to find correspondences (it uses fast third-party library for approximate nearest neighbors library for this).

The result of descriptor matching is a list of correspondences between two sets of descriptors. The first set of descriptors is usually called the train set because it corresponds to our pattern image. The second set is called the query set as it belongs to the image where we will be looking for the pattern. The more correct matches found (more patterns to image correspondences exist) the more chances are that the pattern is present on the image.

To increase the matching speed, you can train a matcher before by calling the `match` function. The training stage can be used to optimize the performance of `cv::FlannBasedMatcher`. For this, the `train` class will build index trees for train descriptors. And this will increase the matching speed for large data sets (for example, if you want to find a match from hundreds of images). For `cv::BFMatcher` the `train` class does nothing as there is nothing to preprocess; it simply stores the train descriptors in the internal fields.

PatternDetector.cpp

The following code block trains the descriptor matcher using the pattern image:

```cpp
void PatternDetector::train(const Pattern& pattern)
{
    // Store the pattern object
    m_pattern = pattern;

    // API of cv::DescriptorMatcher is somewhat tricky
    // First we clear old train data:
    m_matcher->clear();

    // That we add vector of descriptors
    // (each descriptors matrix describe one image).
    // This allows us to perform search across multiple images:
    std::vector<cv::Mat> descriptors(1);
    descriptors[0] = pattern.descriptors.clone();
    m_matcher->add(descriptors);

    // After adding train data perform actual train:
    m_matcher->train();
}
```

To match query descriptors, we can use one of the following methods of
`cv::DescriptorMatcher:`

- To find the simple list of best matches:

```
void match(const Mat& queryDescriptors,
           vector<DMatch>& matches,
           const vector<Mat>& masks=vector<Mat>() );
```

- To find *K* nearest matches for each descriptor:

```
void knnMatch(const Mat& queryDescriptors,
vector<vector<DMatch> >& matches, int k,
const vector<Mat>& masks=vector<Mat>(),
bool compactResult=false );
```

- To find correspondences whose distances are not farther than the specified distance:

```
void radiusMatch(const Mat& queryDescriptors,
vector<vector<DMatch> >& matches, maxDistance,
const vector<Mat>& masks=vector<Mat>(),
bool compactResult=false );
```

Outlier removal

Mismatches during the matching stage can happen. It's normal. There are two kinds of errors in matching:

- **False-positive matches**: When the feature-point correspondence is wrong
- **False-negative matches**: The absence of a match when the feature points are visible on both images

False-negative matches are obviously bad. But we can't deal with them because the matching algorithm has rejected them. Our goal is therefore to minimize the number of false-positive matches. To reject wrong correspondences, we can use a cross-match technique. The idea is to match train descriptors with the query set and vice versa. Only common matches for these two matches are returned. Such techniques usually produce best results with minimal number of outliers when there are enough matches.

Cross-match filter

Cross-match is available in the `cv::BFMatcher` class. To enable a cross-check test, create `cv::BFMatcher` with the second argument set to `true`:

```
cv::Ptr<cv::DescriptorMatcher>
matcher(new cv::BFMatcher(cv::NORM_HAMMING, true));
```

The result of matching using cross-checks can be seen in the following screenshot:

Ratio test

The second well-known outlier-removal technique is the ratio test. We perform KNN-matching first with K=2. Two nearest descriptors are returned for each match. The match is returned only if the distance ratio between the first and second matches is big enough (the ratio threshold is usually near two).

PatternDetector.cpp

The following code performs robust descriptor matching using a ratio test:

```
void PatternDetector::getMatches(const cv::Mat& queryDescriptors,
std::vector<cv::DMatch>& matches)
{
    matches.clear();

    if (enableRatioTest)
    {
        // To avoid NaNs when best match has
        // zero distance we will use inverse ratio.
```

```
const float minRatio = 1.f / 1.5f;

// KNN match will return 2 nearest
// matches for each query descriptor
m_matcher->knnMatch(queryDescriptors, m_knnMatches, 2);

for (size_t i=0; i<m_knnMatches.size(); i++)
{
    const cv::DMatch& bestMatch   = m_knnMatches[i][0];
    const cv::DMatch& betterMatch = m_knnMatches[i][1];

    float distanceRatio = bestMatch.distance /
        betterMatch.distance;

    // Pass only matches where distance ratio between
    // nearest matches is greater than 1.5
    // (distinct criteria)
    if (distanceRatio < minRatio)
    {
        matches.push_back(bestMatch);
    }
}
}
else
{
    // Perform regular match
    m_matcher->match(queryDescriptors, matches);
}
}
```

The ratio test can remove almost all outliers. But in some cases, false-positive matches can pass through this test. In the next section, we will show you how to remove the rest of outliers and leave only correct matches.

Homography estimation

To improve our matching even more, we can perform outlier filtration using the random sample consensus (RANSAC) method. As we're working with an image (a planar object) and we expect it to be rigid, it's ok to find the homography transformation between feature points on the pattern image and feature points on the query image. Homography transformations will bring points from a pattern to the query image coordinate system. To find this transformation, we use the cv::findHomography function. It uses RANSAC to find the best homography matrix by probing subsets of input points. As a side effect, this function marks each correspondence as either inlier or outlier, depending on the reprojection error for the calculated homography matrix.

PatternDetector.cpp

The following code uses a homography matrix estimation using a RANSAC algorithm to filter out geometrically incorrect matches:

```
bool PatternDetector::refineMatchesWithHomography
    (
        const std::vector<cv::KeyPoint>& queryKeypoints,
        const std::vector<cv::KeyPoint>& trainKeypoints,
        float reprojectionThreshold,
        std::vector<cv::DMatch>& matches,
        cv::Mat& homography
    )
{
    const int minNumberMatchesAllowed = 8;

    if (matches.size() < minNumberMatchesAllowed)
        return false;

    // Prepare data for cv::findHomography
    std::vector<cv::Point2f> srcPoints(matches.size());
    std::vector<cv::Point2f> dstPoints(matches.size());

    for (size_t i = 0; i < matches.size(); i++)
    {
        srcPoints[i] = trainKeypoints[matches[i].trainIdx].pt;
        dstPoints[i] = queryKeypoints[matches[i].queryIdx].pt;
    }

    // Find homography matrix and get inliers mask
    std::vector<unsigned char> inliersMask(srcPoints.size());
    homography = cv::findHomography(srcPoints,
                                    dstPoints,
                                    CV_FM_RANSAC,
                                    reprojectionThreshold,
                                    inliersMask);

    std::vector<cv::DMatch> inliers;
    for (size_t i=0; i<inliersMask.size(); i++)
    {
        if (inliersMask[i])
            inliers.push_back(matches[i]);
    }

    matches.swap(inliers);
    return matches.size() > minNumberMatchesAllowed;
}
```

Here is a visualization of matches that were refined using this technique:

The homography search step is important because the obtained transformation is a key to find the pattern location in the query image.

Homography refinement

When we look for homography transformations, we already have all the necessary data to find their locations in 3D. However, we can improve its position even more by finding more accurate pattern corners. For this we warp the input image using estimated homography to obtain a pattern that has been found. The result should be very close to the source train image. Homography refinement can help to find more accurate homography transformations.

Then we obtain another homography and another set of inlier features. The resultant precise homography will be the matrix product of the first (H1) and second (H2) homography.

PatternDetector.cpp

The following code block contains the final version of the pattern detection routine:

```
bool PatternDetector::findPattern(const cv::Mat& image,
PatternTrackingInfo& info)
{
    // Convert input image to gray
    getGray(image, m_grayImg);

    // Extract feature points from input gray image
    extractFeatures(m_grayImg, m_queryKeypoints,
        m_queryDescriptors);

    // Get matches with current pattern
    getMatches(m_queryDescriptors, m_matches);

    // Find homography transformation and detect good matches
    bool homographyFound = refineMatchesWithHomography(
        m_queryKeypoints,
        m_pattern.keypoints,
        homographyReprojectionThreshold,
        m_matches,
        m_roughHomography);

    if (homographyFound)
    {
        // If homography refinement enabled
        // improve found transformation
        if (enableHomographyRefinement)
        {
            // Warp image using found homography
            cv::warpPerspective(m_grayImg, m_warpedImg,
                m_roughHomography, m_pattern.size,
                cv::WARP_INVERSE_MAP | cv::INTER_CUBIC);

            // Get refined matches:
            std::vector<cv::KeyPoint> warpedKeypoints;
            std::vector<cv::DMatch> refinedMatches;

            // Detect features on warped image
```

```
        extractFeatures(m_warpedImg, warpedKeypoints,
            m_queryDescriptors);

        // Match with pattern
        getMatches(m_queryDescriptors, refinedMatches);

        // Estimate new refinement homography
        homographyFound = refineMatchesWithHomography(
            warpedKeypoints,
            m_pattern.keypoints,
            homographyReprojectionThreshold,
            refinedMatches,
            m_refinedHomography);

        // Get a result homography as result of matrix product
        // of refined and rough homographies:
        info.homography = m_roughHomography *
            m_refinedHomography;

        // Transform contour with precise homography
        cv::perspectiveTransform(m_pattern.points2d,
            info.points2d, info.homography);
    }
    else
    {
        info.homography = m_roughHomography;

        // Transform contour with rough homography
        cv::perspectiveTransform(m_pattern.points2d,
            info.points2d, m_roughHomography);
    }
}

return homographyFound;
}
```

If, after all the outlier removal stages, the number of matches is still reasonably large (at least 25 percent of features from the pattern image have correspondences with the input one), you can be sure the pattern image is located correctly. If so, we proceed to the next stage—estimation of the 3D position of the pattern pose with regards to the camera.

Putting it all together

To hold instances of the feature detector, descriptor extractor, and matcher algorithms, we create a class `PatternMatcher`, which will encapsulate all this data. It takes ownership on the feature detection and descriptor-extraction algorithm, feature matching logic, and settings that control the detection process.

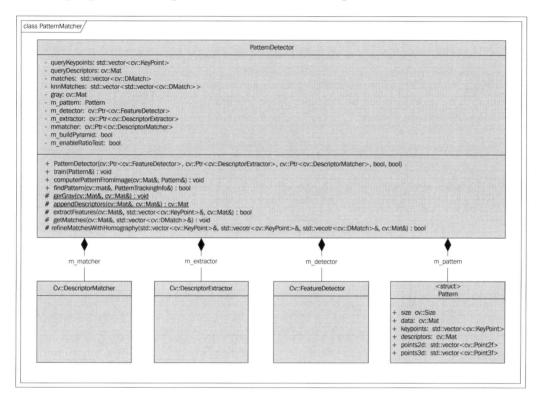

The class provides a method to compute all the necessary data to build a pattern structure from a given image:

```
void PatternDetector::computePatternFromImage(const cv::Mat&
image, Pattern& pattern);
```

This method finds feature points on the input image and extracts descriptors using the specified detector and extractor algorithms, and fills the pattern structure with this data for later use.

When `Pattern` is computed, we can train a detector with it by calling the `train` method:

```
void PatternDetector::train(const Pattern& pattern)
```

This function sets the argument as the current target pattern that we are going to find. Also, it trains a descriptor matcher with a pattern's descriptor set. After calling this method we are ready to find our train image. The pattern detection is done in the last public function `findPattern`. This method encapsulates the whole routine as described previously, including feature detection, descriptors extraction, and matching with outlier filtration.

Let's conclude again with a brief list of the steps we performed:

1. Converted input image to grayscale.
2. Detected features on the query image using our feature-detection algorithm.
3. Extracted descriptors from the input image for the detected feature points.
4. Matched descriptors against pattern descriptors.
5. Used cross-checks or ratio tests to remove outliers.
6. Found the homography transformation using inlier matches.
7. Refined the homography by warping the query image with homography from the previous step.
8. Found the precise homography as a result of the multiplication of rough and refined homography.
9. Transformed the pattern corners to an image coordinate system to get pattern locations on the input image.

Pattern pose estimation

The pose estimation is done in a similar manner to marker pose estimation from the previous chapter. As usual we need 2D-3D correspondences to estimate the camera-extrinsic parameters. We assign four 3D points to coordinate with the corners of the unit rectangle that lies in the XY plane (the Z axis is up), and 2D points correspond to the corners of the image bitmap.

PatternDetector.cpp

The `buildPatternFromImage` class creates a `Pattern` object from the input image as follows:

```
void PatternDetector::buildPatternFromImage(const cv::Mat& image,
    Pattern& pattern) const
{
    int numImages = 4;
```

```
float step = sqrtf(2.0f);

// Store original image in pattern structure
pattern.size = cv::Size(image.cols, image.rows);
pattern.frame = image.clone();
getGray(image, pattern.grayImg);

// Build 2d and 3d contours (3d contour lie in XY plane since
// it's planar)
pattern.points2d.resize(4);
pattern.points3d.resize(4);

// Image dimensions
const float w = image.cols;
const float h = image.rows;

// Normalized dimensions:
const float maxSize = std::max(w,h);
const float unitW = w / maxSize;
const float unitH = h / maxSize;

pattern.points2d[0] = cv::Point2f(0,0);
pattern.points2d[1] = cv::Point2f(w,0);
pattern.points2d[2] = cv::Point2f(w,h);
pattern.points2d[3] = cv::Point2f(0,h);

pattern.points3d[0] = cv::Point3f(-unitW, -unitH, 0);
pattern.points3d[1] = cv::Point3f( unitW, -unitH, 0);
pattern.points3d[2] = cv::Point3f( unitW,  unitH, 0);
pattern.points3d[3] = cv::Point3f(-unitW,  unitH, 0);

extractFeatures(pattern.grayImg, pattern.keypoints,
    pattern.descriptors);
}
```

This configuration of corners is useful as this pattern coordinate system will be placed directly in the center of the pattern location lying in the XY plane, with the Z axis looking in the direction of the camera.

Obtaining the camera-intrinsic matrix

The camera-intrinsic parameters can be calculated using a sample program from the OpenCV distribution package called `camera_cailbration.exe`. This program will find the internal lens parameters such as focal length, principal point, and distortion coefficients using a series of pattern images. Let's say we have a set of eight calibration pattern images from various points of view, as follows:

Then the command-line syntax to perform calibration will be as follows:

```
imagelist_creator imagelist.yaml *.png
```

```
calibration -w 9 -h 6 -o camera_intrinsic.yaml imagelist.yaml
```

The first command will create an image list of YAML format that the calibration tool expects as input from all PNG files in the current directory. You can use the exact file names, such as `img1.png`, `img2.png`, and `img3.png`. The generated file `imagelist.yaml` is then passed to the calibration application. Also, the calibration tool can take images from a regular web camera.

We specify the dimensions of the calibration pattern and input and output files where the calibration data will be written.

After calibration is done, you'll get the following result in a YAML file:

```
%YAML:1.0
calibration_time: "06/12/12 11:17:56"
image_width: 640
image_height: 480
board_width: 9
```

```
board_height: 6
square_size: 1.
flags: 0
camera_matrix: !!opencv-matrix
    rows: 3
    cols: 3
    dt: d
    data: [ 5.2658037684199849e+002, 0., 3.1841744018680112e+002, 0.,
        5.2465577209994706e+002, 2.0296659047014398e+002, 0., 0., 1. ]
distortion_coefficients: !!opencv-matrix
    rows: 5
    cols: 1
    dt: d
    data: [ 7.3253671786835686e-002, -8.6143199924308911e-002,
        -2.0800255026966759e-002, -6.8004894417795971e-004,
        -1.7750733073535208e-001 ]
avg_reprojection_error: 3.6539552933501085e-001
```

We are mainly interested in `camera_matrix`, which is the 3 x 3 camera-calibration matrix. It has the following notation:

$$\begin{bmatrix} f_x & 0 & c_y \\ 0 & f_y & c_y \\ 0 & 0 & 1 \end{bmatrix}$$

We're mainly interested in four components: f_x, f_y, c_x, and c_y. With this data we can create an instance of the camera-calibration object using the following code for calibration:

```
CameraCalibration calibration(526.58037684199849e,
524.65577209994706e, 318.41744018680112, 202.96659047014398)
```

Without correct camera calibration it's impossible to create a natural-looking augmented reality. The estimated perspective transformation will differ from the transformation that the camera has. This will cause the augmented objects to look like they are too close or too far. The following is an example screenshot where the camera calibration was changed intentionally:

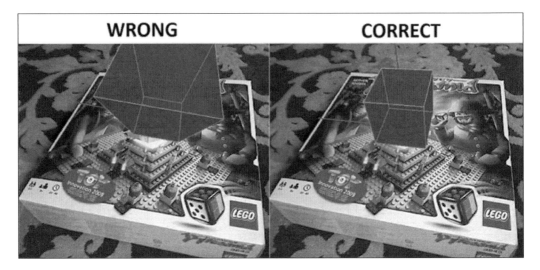

As you can see, the perspective look of the box differs from the overall scene.

To estimate the pattern position, we solve the PnP problem using the OpenCV function `cv::solvePnP`. You are probably familiar with this function because we used it in the marker-based AR too. We need the coordinates of the pattern corners on the current image, and its reference 3D coordinates we defined previously.

> The `cv::solvePnP` function can work with more than four points. Also, it's a key function if you want to create an AR with complex shape patterns. The idea remains the same—you just have to define a 3D structure of your pattern and the 2D find point correspondences. Of course, the homography estimation is not applicable here.

We take the reference 3D points from the trained pattern object and their corresponding projections in 2D from the `PatternTrackingInfo` structure; the camera calibration is stored in a `PatternDetector` private field.

Pattern.cpp

The pattern location in 3D space is estimated by the computePose function as follows:

```
void PatternTrackingInfo::computePose(const Pattern& pattern, const
CameraCalibration& calibration)
{
  cv::Mat camMatrix, distCoeff;
  cv::Mat(3,3, CV_32F,
    const_cast<float*>(&calibration.getIntrinsic().data[0]))
    .copyTo(camMatrix);
  cv::Mat(4,1, CV_32F,
    const_cast<float*>(&calibration.getDistorsion().data[0])).
    copyTo(distCoeff);

  cv::Mat Rvec;
  cv::Mat_<float> Tvec;
  cv::Mat raux,taux;
  cv::solvePnP(pattern.points3d, points2d, camMatrix,
    distCoeff,raux,taux);
  raux.convertTo(Rvec,CV_32F);
  taux.convertTo(Tvec ,CV_32F);

  cv::Mat_<float> rotMat(3,3);
  cv::Rodrigues(Rvec, rotMat);

  // Copy to transformation matrix
  pose3d = Transformation();

  for (int col=0; col<3; col++)
  {
    for (int row=0; row<3; row++)
    {
     pose3d.r().mat[row][col] = rotMat(row,col);
     // Copy rotation component
    }
    pose3d.t().data[col] = Tvec(col);
    // Copy translation component
  }

  // Since solvePnP finds camera location, w.r.t to marker pose,
  // to get marker pose w.r.t to the camera we invert it.
  pose3d = pose3d.getInverted();
}
```

Application infrastructure

So far, we've learned how to detect a pattern and estimate its 3D position with regards to the camera. Now it's time to show how to put these algorithms into a real application. So our goal for this section is to show how to use OpenCV to capture a video from a web camera and create the visualization context for 3D rendering.

As our goal is to show how to use key features of marker-less AR, we will create a simple command-line application that will be capable of detecting arbitrary pattern images either in a video sequence or in still images.

To hold all image-processing logic and intermediate data, we introduce the `ARPipeline` class. It's a root object that holds all subcomponents necessary for augmented reality and performs all processing routines on the input frames. The following is a UML diagram of `ARPipeline` and its subcomponents:

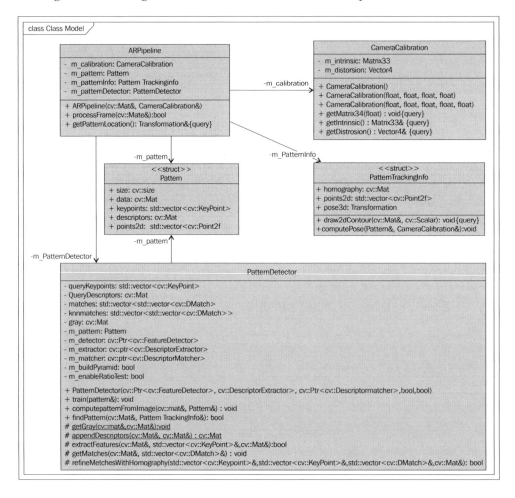

It consists of:

- The camera-calibration object
- An Instance of the pattern-detector object
- A trained pattern object
- Intermediate data of pattern tracking

ARPipeline.hpp

The following code contains a declaration of the ARPipeline class:

```
class ARPipeline
{
public:
  ARPipeline(const cv::Mat& patternImage,
    const CameraCalibration& calibration);

  bool processFrame(const cv::Mat& inputFrame);

  const Transformation& getPatternLocation() const;

private:
  CameraCalibration    m_calibration;
  Pattern              m_pattern;
  PatternTrackingInfo  m_patternInfo;
  PatternDetector      m_patternDetector;
};
```

In the ARPipeline constructor, a pattern object is initialized and the calibration data is saved to the private field. The processFrame function implements pattern detection and the person's pose-estimation routine. The return value indicates the success of pattern detection. You can get the calculated pattern pose by calling the getPatternLocation function.

ARPipeline.cpp

The following code contains the implementation of the ARPipeline class:

```
ARPipeline::ARPipeline(const cv::Mat& patternImage,
  const CameraCalibration& calibration)
  : m_calibration(calibration)
{
```

```
    m_patternDetector.buildPatternFromImage (patternImage,
      m_pattern);
    m_patternDetector.train(m_pattern);
}

bool ARPipeline::processFrame(const cv::Mat& inputFrame)
{
  bool patternFound = m_patternDetector.findPattern(inputFrame,
    m_patternInfo);

  if (patternFound)
  {
    m_patternInfo.computePose(m_pattern, m_calibration);
  }

  return patternFound;
}

const Transformation& ARPipeline::getPatternLocation() const
{
  return m_patternInfo.pose3d;
}
```

Enabling support for 3D visualization in OpenCV

As in the previous chapter, we will use OpenGL to render our 3D working. But unlike the iOS environment, where we had to follow the iOS application architecture requirements, we now have much more freedom. On Windows and Mac you can choose from many 3D engines. In this chapter, we will learn how to create cross-platform 3D visualization using OpenCV. Starting from version 2.4.2, OpenCV has OpenGL's support in visualization windows. This means you can now easily render any 3D content in OpenCV.

To set up an OpenGL window in OpenCV, the first thing you need to do is to build OpenCV with OpenGL support. Otherwise, an exception will be thrown when you attempt to use the OpenGL-related functions of OpenCV. To enable OpenGL support, you should build the OpenCV library with the ENABLE_OPENGL=YES flag.

As of the current version (OpenCV 2.4.2), OpenGL support is turned off by default. We cannot guarantee it, but OpenGL may be enabled by default in future releases. If so, there will be no need to build OpenCV manually.

To set up an OpenGL window in OpenCV, perform the following:

- Clone the OpenCV repository from GitHub (`https://github.com/Itseez/opencv`). You will need either command-line git tools or the GitHub Application installed on your computer to perform this step.

- Configure OpenCV and generate a workspace for your IDE. You will need a CMake application to complete this step. CMake can be freely downloaded from `http://www.cmake.org/cmake/resources/software.html`.

To configure OpenCV, you can either use the command-line CMake command as follows (run from the directory where you want the generated project to be placed):

```
cmake -D ENABLE_OPENGL=YES <path to the OpenCV source directory>
```

Or, if you prefer GUI-style, use CMake-GUI for a more user-friendly project configuration:

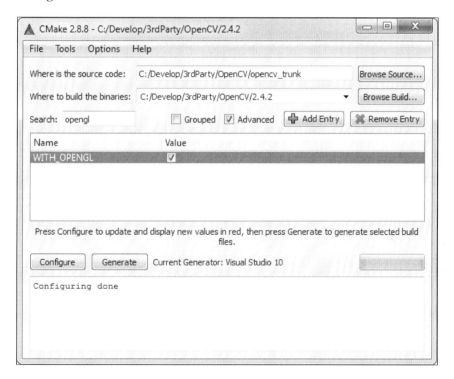

After the generation of the OpenCV workspace for the selected IDE, open the project and execute the install target to build the library and install it. When this process is done, you can configure the sample project using the new OpenCV library you've just built.

Creating OpenGL windows using OpenCV

Now that we have OpenCV binaries with OpenGL support, it's time to create our first OpenGL window. The initialization of the OpenGL window starts with creating the named window with an OpenGL flag:

```
cv::namedWindow(ARWindowName, cv::WINDOW_OPENGL);
```

`ARWindowName` is a string constant for the name of our window. We will use `Markerless AR` here. This call will create a window with the specified name. The `cv::WINDOW_OPENGL` flag indicates we're going to use OpenGL in this window. Then we set the desired window size:

```
cv::resizeWindow(ARWindowName, 640, 480);
```

We then set up the drawing context for this window:

```
cv::setOpenGlContext(ARWindowName);
```

Now our window is ready for use. To draw something on it, we should register a callback function using the following method:

```
cv::setOpenGlDrawCallback(ARWindowName, drawAR, NULL);
```

This callback will be called on the repaint window. The first argument sets the window name, the second is a callback function, and the third optional argument will be passed to the callback function.

The `drawAR` function should have following signature:

```
void drawAR(void* param)
{
  // Draw something using OpenGL here
}
```

To notify the system that you want to redraw your window, use the `cv::updateWindow` function:

```
cv::updateWindow(ARWindowName);
```

Video capture using OpenCV

OpenCV allows you to easily retrieve frames from almost every web camera and video file as well. To capture video from either a webcam or a video file, we can use the `cv::VideoCapture` class, as shown in the *Accessing the webcam* section from *Chapter 1, Cartoonifier and Skin Changer for Android*.

Rendering augmented reality

We introduce the ARDrawingContext structure to hold all the necessary data that visualization may need:

- The most recent image taken from the camera
- The camera-calibration matrix
- The pattern pose in 3D (if present)
- The internal data related to OpenGL (texture ID and so on)

ARDrawingContext.hpp

The following code contains a declaration of the ARDrawingContext class:

```
class ARDrawingContext
{
public:
  ARDrawingContext(const CameraCalibration& c);

  bool              patternPresent;
  Transformation    patternPose;

  //! Request the redraw of the OpenGl window
  void draw();

  //! Set the new frame for the background
  void updateBackground(const cv::Mat& frame);

private:
  //! Draws the background with video
  void drawCameraFrame ();

  //! Draws the AR
  void drawAugmentedScene();

  //! Builds the right projection matrix
  //! from the camera calibration for AR
  void buildProjectionMatrix(const Matrix33& calibration,
    int w, int h, Matrix44& result);

  //! Draws the coordinate axis
  void drawCoordinateAxis();

  //! Draw the cube model
```

```
      void drawCubeModel();


   private:
     bool                 m_textureInitialized;
     unsigned int         m_backgroundTextureId;
     CameraCalibration    m_calibration;
     cv::Mat              m_backgroundImage;
   };
```

ARDrawingContext.cpp

Initialization of the OpenGL window is done in the constructor of the `ARDrawingContext` class as follows:

```
ARDrawingContext::ARDrawingContext(std::string windowName, cv::Size
frameSize, const CameraCalibration& c)
  : m_isTextureInitialized(false)
  , m_calibration(c)
  , m_windowName(windowName)
{
  // Create window with OpenGL support
  cv::namedWindow(windowName, cv::WINDOW_OPENGL);

  // Resize it exactly to video size
  cv::resizeWindow(windowName, frameSize.width, frameSize.height);

  // Initialize OpenGL draw callback:
  cv::setOpenGlContext(windowName);
  cv::setOpenGlDrawCallback(windowName,
    ARDrawingContextDrawCallback, this);
}
```

As we now have a separate class for storing the visualization state, we modify the `cv::setOpenGlDrawCallback` call and pass an instance of `ARDrawingContext` as the parameter.

The modified callback function is as follows:

```
void ARDrawingContextDrawCallback(void* param)
{
  ARDrawingContext * ctx = static_cast<ARDrawingContext*>(param);
  if (ctx)
  {
    ctx->draw();
  }
}
```

`ARDrawingContext` takes all the responsibility of rendering the augmented reality. The frame rendering starts by drawing a background with an orthography projection. Then we render a 3D model with the correct perspective projection and model transformation. The following code contains the final version of the `draw` function:

```
void ARDrawingContext::draw()
{
  // Clear entire screen
  glClear(GL_DEPTH_BUFFER_BIT | GL_COLOR_BUFFER_BIT);
  // Render background
  drawCameraFrame();
  // Draw AR
  drawAugmentedScene();
}
```

After clearing the screen and depth buffer, we check if a texture for presenting a video is initialized. If so, we proceed to drawing a background, otherwise we create a new 2D texture by calling `glGenTextures`.

To draw a background, we set up an orthographic projection and draw a solid rectangle that covers all the screen viewports. This rectangle is bound with a texture unit. This texture is filled with the content of an `m_backgroundImage` object. Its content is uploaded to the OpenGL memory beforehand. This function is identical to the function from the previous chapter, so we will omit its code here.

After drawing the picture from a camera, we switch to drawing an AR. It's necessary to set the correct perspective projection that matches our camera calibration.

The following code shows how to build the correct OpenGL projection matrix from the camera calibration and render the scene:

```
void ARDrawingContext::drawAugmentedScene()
{
  // Init augmentation projection
  Matrix44 projectionMatrix;
  int w = m_backgroundImage.cols;
  int h = m_backgroundImage.rows;
  buildProjectionMatrix(m_calibration, w, h, projectionMatrix);

  glMatrixMode(GL_PROJECTION);
  glLoadMatrixf(projectionMatrix.data);

  glMatrixMode(GL_MODELVIEW);
  glLoadIdentity();
```

```
  if (isPatternPresent)
  {
    // Set the pattern transformation
    Matrix44 glMatrix = patternPose.getMat44();
    glLoadMatrixf(reinterpret_cast<const
      GLfloat*>(&glMatrix.data[0]));

    // Render model
    drawCoordinateAxis();
    drawCubeModel();
  }
}
```

The `buildProjectionMatrix` function was taken from the previous chapter, so it's the same. After applying perspective projection, we set the `GL_MODELVIEW` matrix to pattern transformation. To prove that our pose estimation works correctly, we draw a unit coordinate system in the pattern position.

Almost all things are done. We create a pattern-detection algorithm and then we estimate the pose of the found pattern in 3D space, a visualization system to render the AR. Let's take a look at the following UML sequence diagram that demonstrates the frame-processing routine in our app:

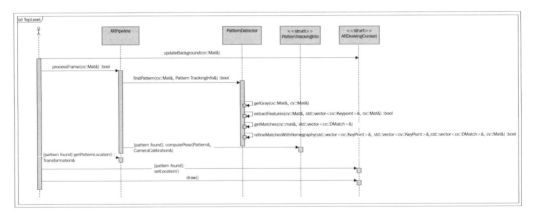

Demonstration

Our demonstration project supports the processing of still images, recorded videos, and live views from a web camera. We create two functions that help us with this.

main.cpp

The function `processVideo` handles the processing of the video and the function `processSingleImage` is used to process a single image, as follows:

```
void processVideo(const cv::Mat& patternImage,
  CameraCalibration& calibration, cv::VideoCapture& capture);

void processSingleImage(const cv::Mat& patternImage,
  CameraCalibration& calibration, const cv::Mat& image);
```

From the function names it's clear that the first function processed the video source, and the second one works with a single image (this function is useful for debugging purposes). Both of them have a very common routine of image processing, pattern detection, scene rendering, and user interaction.

The `processFrame` function wraps these steps as follows:

```
/**
 * Performs full detection routine on camera frame
.* and draws the scene using drawing context.
 * In addition, this function draw overlay with debug information
.* on top of the AR window. Returns true
.* if processing loop should be stopped; otherwise - false.
 */
bool processFrame(const cv::Mat& cameraFrame, ARPipeline&
  pipeline, ARDrawingContext& drawingCtx)
{
    // Clone image used for background (we will
    // draw overlay on it)
    cv::Mat img = cameraFrame.clone();

    // Draw information:
    if (pipeline.m_patternDetector.enableHomographyRefinement)
        cv::putText(img, "Pose refinement: On    ('h' to switch
            off)", cv::Point(10,15), CV_FONT_HERSHEY_PLAIN, 1,
            CV_RGB(0,200,0));
    else
        cv::putText(img, "Pose refinement: Off   ('h' to switch
            on)",   cv::Point(10,15), CV_FONT_HERSHEY_PLAIN, 1,
            CV_RGB(0,200,0));

    cv::putText(img, "RANSAC threshold: " +
        ToString(pipeline.m_patternDetector.
        homographyReprojectionThreshold) + "( Use'-'/'+' to
        adjust)", cv::Point(10, 30), CV_FONT_HERSHEY_PLAIN, 1,
        CV_RGB(0,200,0));
```

```cpp
    // Set a new camera frame:
    drawingCtx.updateBackground(img);

    // Find a pattern and update its detection status:
    drawingCtx.isPatternPresent =
      pipeline.processFrame(cameraFrame);

    // Update a pattern pose:
    drawingCtx.patternPose = pipeline.getPatternLocation();

    // Request redraw of the window:
    drawingCtx.updateWindow();


    // Read the keyboard input:
    int keyCode = cv::waitKey(5);

    bool shouldQuit = false;
    if (keyCode == '+' || keyCode == '=')
    {
        pipeline.m_patternDetector.homographyReprojectionThreshold
            += 0.2f;
        pipeline.m_patternDetector.homographyReprojectionThreshold
            = std::min(10.0f, pipeline.m_patternDetector.
            homographyReprojectionThreshold);
    }
    else if (keyCode == '-')
    {
        pipeline.m_patternDetector.
            homographyReprojectionThreshold -= 0.2f;
        pipeline.m_patternDetector.homographyReprojectionThreshold
            = std::max(0.0f, pipeline.m_patternDetector.
            homographyReprojectionThreshold);
    }
    else if (keyCode == 'h')
    {
        pipeline.m_patternDetector.enableHomographyRefinement =
            !pipeline.m_patternDetector.enableHomographyRefinement;
    }
    else if (keyCode == 27 || keyCode == 'q')
    {
        shouldQuit = true;
    }

    return shouldQuit;
}
```

The initialization of `ARPipeline` and `ARDrawingContext` is done either in the `processSingleImage` or `processVideo` function as follows:

```
void processSingleImage(const cv::Mat& patternImage,
CameraCalibration& calibration, const cv::Mat& image)
{
    cv::Size frameSize(image.cols, image.rows);
    ARPipeline pipeline(patternImage, calibration);
    ARDrawingContext drawingCtx("Markerless AR", frameSize,
      calibration);

    bool shouldQuit = false;
    do
    {
        shouldQuit = processFrame(image, pipeline, drawingCtx);
    } while (!shouldQuit);
}
```

We create `ARPipeline` from the pattern image and calibration arguments. Then we initialize `ARDrawingContext` using calibration again. After these steps, the OpenGL window is created. Then we upload the query image into a drawing context and call `ARPipeline.processFrame` to find a pattern. If the pose pattern has been found, we copy its location to the drawing context for further frame rendering. If the pattern has not been detected, we render only the camera frame without any AR.

You can run the demo application in one of the following ways:

- To run on a single image call:

  markerless_ar_demo pattern.png test_image.png

- To run on a recorded video call:

  markerless_ar_demo pattern.png test_video.avi

- To run using live feed from a web camera, call:

  markerless_ar_demo pattern.png

The result of augmenting a single image is shown in the following screenshot:

Summary

In this chapter you have learned about feature descriptors and how to use them to define a scale and a rotation invariant pattern description. This description can be used to find similar entries in other images. The strengths and weaknesses of most popular feature descriptors were also explained. In the second half of the chapter, we learned how to use OpenGL and OpenCV together for rendering augmented reality.

References

- *Distinctive Image Features from Scale-Invariant Keypoints* (`http://www.cs.ubc.ca/~lowe/papers/ijcv04.pdf`)

- *SURF: Speeded Up Robust Features* (`http://www.vision.ee.ethz.ch/~surf/eccv06.pdf`)

- *Model-Based Object Pose in 25 Lines of Code, Dementhon and L.S Davis, International Journal of Computer Vision, edition 15, pp. 123-141, 1995*

- *Linear N-Point Camera Pose Determination, L.Quan, IEEE Trans. on Pattern Analysis and Machine Intelligence, vol. 21, edition. 7, July 1999*

- *Random Sample Consensus: A Paradigm for Model Fitting with Applications to Image Analysis and Automated Cartography, M. Fischer and R. Bolles, Graphics and Image Processing, vol. 24, edition. 6, pp. 381-395, June 1981*

- *Multiple View Geometry in Computer Vision, R. Hartley and A.Zisserman, Cambridge University Press* (`http://www.umiacs.umd.edu/~ramani/cmsc828d/lecture9.pdf`)

- *Camera Pose Revisited – New Linear Algorithms, M. Ameller, B.Triggs, L.Quan* (`http://hal.inria.fr/docs/00/54/83/06/PDF/Ameller-eccv00.pdf`)

- *Closed-form solution of absolute orientation using unit quaternions, Berthold K. P. Horn, Journal of the Optical Society A, vol. 4, 629–642*

4

Exploring Structure from Motion Using OpenCV

In this chapter we will discuss the notion of **Structure from Motion (SfM)**, or better put as extracting geometric structures from images taken through a camera's motion, using functions within OpenCV's API to help us. First, let us constrain the otherwise lengthy footpath of our approach to using a single camera, usually called a **monocular** approach, and a discrete and sparse set of frames rather than a continuous video stream. These two constrains will greatly simplify the system we will sketch in the coming pages, and help us understand the fundamentals of any SfM method. To implement our method we will follow in the footsteps of Hartley and Zisserman (hereafter referred to as H and Z), as documented in chapters 9 through 12 of their seminal book *Multiple View Geometry in Computer Vision*.

In this chapter we cover the following:

- Structure from Motion concepts
- Estimating the camera motion from a pair of images
- Reconstructing the scene
- Reconstruction from many views
- Refinement of the reconstruction
- Visualizing 3D point clouds

Throughout the chapter we assume the use of a calibrated camera—one that was calibrated beforehand. **Calibration** is a ubiquitous operation in computer vision, fully supported in OpenCV using command-line tools and was discussed in previous chapters. We therefore assume the existence of the camera's intrinsic parameters embodied in the K matrix, one of the outputs from the calibration process.

To make things clear in terms of language, from this point on we will refer to a camera as a single view of the scene rather than to the optics and hardware taking the image. A camera has a position in space, and a direction of view. Between two cameras, there is a translation element (movement through space) and a rotation of the direction of view.

We will also unify the terms for the point in the scene, world, real, or 3D to be the same thing, a point that exists in our real world. The same goes for points in the image or 2D, which are points in the image coordinates, of some real 3D point that was projected on the camera sensor at that location and time.

In the chapter's code sections you will notice references to *Multiple View Geometry in Computer Vision*, for example // HZ 9.12. This refers to equation number 12 of chapter 9 of the book. Also, the text will include excerpts of code only, while the complete runnable code is included in the material accompanied with the book.

Structure from Motion concepts

The first discrimination we should make is the difference between stereo (or indeed any multiview), 3D reconstruction using calibrated rigs, and SfM. While a rig of two or more cameras assume we already know what the motion between the cameras is, in SfM we don't actually know this motion and we wish to find it. Calibrated rigs, from a simplistic point of view, allow a much more accurate reconstruction of 3D geometry because there is no error in estimating the distance and rotation between the cameras—it is already known. The first step in implementing an SfM system is finding the motion between the cameras. OpenCV may help us in a number of ways to obtain this motion, specifically using the findFundamentalMat function.

Let us think for one moment of the goal behind choosing an SfM algorithm. In most cases we wish to obtain the geometry of the scene, for example, where objects are in relation to the camera and what their form is. Assuming we already know the motion between the cameras picturing the same scene, from a reasonably similar point of view, we would now like to reconstruct the geometry. In computer vision jargon this is known as **triangulation**, and there are plenty of ways to go about it. It may be done by way of ray intersection, where we construct two rays: one from each camera's center of projection and a point on each of the image planes. The intersection of these rays in space will, ideally, intersect at one 3D point in the real world that was imaged in each camera, as shown in the following diagram:

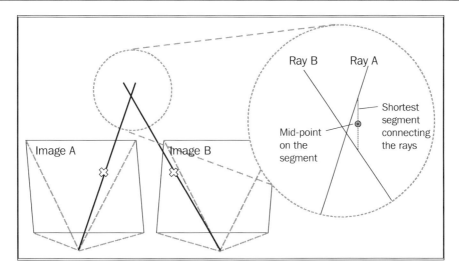

In reality, ray intersection is highly unreliable; H and Z recommend against it. This is because the rays usually do not intersect, making us fall back to using the middle point on the shortest segment connecting the two rays. Instead, H and Z suggest a number of ways to triangulate 3D points, of which we will discuss a couple of them in the *Reconstructing the scene* section. The current version of OpenCV does not contain a simple API for triangulation, so this part we will code on our own.

After we have learned how to recover 3D geometry from two views, we will see how we can incorporate more views of the same scene to get an even richer reconstruction. At that point, most SfM methods try to optimize the bundle of estimated positions of our cameras and 3D points by means of Bundle Adjustment, in the *Refinement of the reconstruction* section. OpenCV contains means for Bundle Adjustment in its new Image Stitching Toolbox. However, the beauty of working with OpenCV and C++ is the abundance of external tools that can be easily integrated into the pipeline. We will therefore see how to integrate an external bundle adjuster, the neat SSBA library.

Now that we have sketched an outline of our approach to SfM using OpenCV, we will see how each element can be implemented.

Estimating the camera motion from a pair of images

Before we set out to actually find the motion between two cameras, let us examine the inputs and the tools we have at hand to perform this operation. First, we have two images of the same scene from (hopefully not extremely) different positions in space. This is a powerful asset, and we will make sure to use it. Now as far as tools go, we should take a look at mathematical objects that impose constraints over our images, cameras, and the scene.

Two very useful mathematical objects are the fundamental matrix (denoted by F) and the essential matrix (denoted by E). They are mostly similar, except that the essential matrix is assuming usage of calibrated cameras; this is the case for us, so we will choose it. OpenCV only allows us to find the fundamental matrix via the `findFundamentalMat` function; however, it is extremely simple to get the essential matrix from it using the calibration matrix K as follows:

```
Mat_<double> E = K.t() * F * K; //according to HZ (9.12)
```

The essential matrix, a 3 x 3 sized matrix, imposes a constraint between a point in one image and a point in the other image with x'Ex=0, where x is a point in image one and x' is the corresponding point in image two. This is extremely useful, as we are about to see. Another important fact we use is that the essential matrix is all we need in order to recover both cameras for our images, although only up to scale; but we will get to that later. So, if we obtain the essential matrix, we know where each camera is positioned in space, and where it is looking. We can easily calculate the matrix if we have enough of those constraint equations, simply because each equation can be used to solve for a small part of the matrix. In fact, OpenCV allows us to calculate it using just seven point-pairs, but hopefully we will have many more pairs and get a more robust solution.

Point matching using rich feature descriptors

Now we will make use of our constraint equations to calculate the essential matrix. To get our constraints, remember that for each point in image A we must find a corresponding point in image B. How can we achieve such a matching? Simply by using OpenCV's extensive feature-matching framework, which has greatly matured in the past few years.

Feature extraction and descriptor matching is an essential process in computer vision, and is used in many methods to perform all sorts of operations. For example, detecting the position and orientation of an object in the image or searching a big database of images for similar images through a given query. In essence, **extraction** means selecting points in the image that would make the features good, and computing a descriptor for them. A **descriptor** is a vector of numbers that describes the surrounding environment around a feature point in an image. Different methods have different length and data type for their descriptor vectors. **Matching** is the process of finding a corresponding feature from one set in another using its descriptor. OpenCV provides very easy and powerful methods to support feature extraction and matching. More information about feature matching may be found in *Chapter 3, Marker-less Augmented Reality*.

Let us examine a very simple feature extraction and matching scheme:

```
// detectingkeypoints
SurfFeatureDetectordetector();
vector<KeyPoint> keypoints1, keypoints2;
detector.detect(img1, keypoints1);
detector.detect(img2, keypoints2);

// computing descriptors
SurfDescriptorExtractor extractor;
Mat descriptors1, descriptors2;
extractor.compute(img1, keypoints1, descriptors1);
extractor.compute(img2, keypoints2, descriptors2);

// matching descriptors
BruteForceMatcher<L2<float>> matcher;
vector<DMatch> matches;
matcher.match(descriptors1, descriptors2, matches);
```

You may have already seen similar OpenCV code, but let us review it quickly. Our goal is to obtain three elements: Feature points for two images, descriptors for them, and a matching between the two sets of features. OpenCV provides a range of feature detectors, descriptor extractors, and matchers. In this simple example we use the `SurfFeatureDetector` function to get the 2D location of the **Speeded-Up Robust Features (SURF)** features, and the `SurfDescriptorExtractor` function to get the SURF descriptors. We use a brute-force matcher to get the matching, which is the most straightforward way to match two feature sets implemented by comparing each feature in the first set to each feature in the second set (hence the phrasing brute-force) and getting the best match.

In the next image we will see a matching of feature points on two images from the Fountain-P11 sequence found at `http://cvlab.epfl.ch/~strecha/multiview/ denseMVS.html`.

Practically, raw matching like we just performed is good only up to a certain level, and many matches are probably erroneous. For that reason, most SfM methods perform some form of filtering on the matches to ensure correctness and reduce errors. One form of filtering, which is the built-in OpenCV's brute-force matcher, is cross-check filtering. That is, a match is considered true if a feature of the first image matched a feature of the second image, and the reverse check also matched the feature of the second image with the feature of the first image. Another common filtering mechanism, used in the provided code, is to filter based on the fact that the two images are of the same scene and have a certain stereo-view relationship between them. In practice, the filter tries to robustly calculate the fundamental matrix, of which we will learn in the *Finding camera matrices* section, and retain those feature pairs that correspond with this calculation with small errors.

Point matching using optical flow

An alternative to using rich features, such as SURF, is using **optical flow (OF)**. The following information box provides a short overview of optical flow. OpenCV recently extended its API for getting the flow field from two images and now it is faster and more powerful. We will try to use it as an alternative to matching features.

Optical flow is the process of matching selected points from one image to another, assuming both images are part of a sequence and relatively close to one another. Most optical flow methods compare a small region, known as the search window or patch, around each point from image A to the same area in image B. Following a very common rule in computer vision, called the brightness constancy constraint (and other names), the small patches of the image will not change drastically from one image to the other, and therefore the magnitude of their subtraction should be close to zero. In addition to matching patches, newer methods of optical flow use a number of additional methods to get better results. One is using image pyramids, which are smaller and smaller resized versions of the image, which allow for working "from-coarse-to-fine" — a very well-used trick in computer vision. Another method is to define global constraints on the flow field, assuming that the points close to each other "move together" in the same direction. A more in-depth review of optical flow methods in OpenCV can be found in *Chapter Developing Fluid Wall Using the Microsoft Kinect* which is available on the Packt website..

Using optical flow in OpenCV is fairly easy by invoking the `calcOpticalFlowPyrLK` function. However, we would like to keep the result matching from OF similar to that using rich features, as in the future we would like the two approaches to be interchangeable. To that end, we must install a special matching method — one that is interchangeable with the previous feature-based method, which we are about to see in the code section that follows:

```
Vector<KeyPoint>left_keypoints,right_keypoints;

// Detect keypoints in the left and right images
FastFeatureDetectorffd;
ffd.detect(img1, left_keypoints);
ffd.detect(img2, right_keypoints);

vector<Point2f>left_points;
KeyPointsToPoints(left_keypoints,left_points);

vector<Point2f>right_points(left_points.size());

// making sure images are grayscale
Mat prevgray,gray;
if (img1.channels() == 3) {
    cvtColor(img1,prevgray,CV_RGB2GRAY);
    cvtColor(img2,gray,CV_RGB2GRAY);
} else {
        prevgray = img1;
```

```
        gray = img2;
}

// Calculate the optical flow field:
//  how each left_point moved across the 2 images
vector<uchar>vstatus; vector<float>verror;
calcOpticalFlowPyrLK(prevgray, gray, left_points, right_points,
vstatus, verror);

// First, filter out the points with high error
vector<Point2f>right_points_to_find;
vector<int>right_points_to_find_back_index;
for (unsigned inti=0; i<vstatus.size(); i++) {
    if (vstatus[i] &&verror[i] < 12.0) {
    // Keep the original index of the point in the
    // optical flow array, for future use
    right_points_to_find_back_index.push_back(i);
    // Keep the feature point itself
right_points_to_find.push_back(j_pts[i]);
} else {
        vstatus[i] = 0; // a bad flow
}
}

// for each right_point see which detected feature it belongs to
Mat right_points_to_find_flat = Mat(right_points_to_find).
reshape(1,to_find.size()); //flatten array

vector<Point2f>right_features; // detected features
KeyPointsToPoints(right_keypoints,right_features);

Mat right_features_flat = Mat(right_features).reshape(1,right_
features.size());

// Look around each OF point in the right image
//  for any features that were detected in its area
//  and make a match.
BFMatchermatcher(CV_L2);
vector<vector<DMatch>>nearest_neighbors;
matcher.radiusMatch(
right_points_to_find_flat,
right_features_flat,
nearest_neighbors,
```

```
2.0f);

// Check that the found neighbors are unique (throw away neighbors
//  that are too close together, as they may be confusing)
std::set<int>found_in_right_points; // for duplicate prevention
for(inti=0;i<nearest_neighbors.size();i++) {
DMatch _m;
if(nearest_neighbors[i].size()==1) {
    _m = nearest_neighbors[i][0]; // only one neighbor
} else if(nearest_neighbors[i].size()>1) {
        // 2 neighbors - check how close they are
        double ratio = nearest_neighbors[i][0].distance /
        nearest_neighbors[i][1].distance;
if(ratio < 0.7) { // not too close
    // take the closest (first) one
    _m = nearest_neighbors[i][0];
} else { // too close - we cannot tell which is better
        continue; // did not pass ratio test - throw away
}
} else {
        continue; // no neighbors... :(
}

// prevent duplicates
if (found_in_right_points.find(_m.trainIdx) == found_in_right_points.
end()) {
    // The found neighbor was not yet used:
    // We should match it with the original indexing
    // ofthe left point
    _m.queryIdx = right_points_to_find_back_index[_m.queryIdx];
    matches->push_back(_m); // add this match
    found_in_right_points.insert(_m.trainIdx);
    }
}
cout<<"pruned "<< matches->size() <<" / "<<nearest_neighbors.size()
<<" matches"<<endl;
```

The functions `KeyPointsToPoints` and `PointsToKeyPoints` are simply convenience functions for conversion between the `cv::Point2f` and the `cv::KeyPoint` structs.

In the previous segment of code we can see a number of interesting things. The first thing to note is that when we use optical flow, our result shows a feature moved from a position in the image on the left-hand side to another position in the image on the right-hand side. But we have a new set of features detected in the image to the right-hand side, not necessarily aligning with the features that flowed from the image to the left-hand side in optical flow. We must align them. To find those lost features we use a **k-nearest neighbor (kNN)** radius search, which gives us up to two features that fall within a 2-pixel radius to the points of interest.

One more thing that we can see is an implementation of the ratio test for kNN, which is a common practice in SfM to reduce errors. In essence, it is a filter that removes confusing matches when we have a match between one feature in the left-hand side image and two features in the right-hand side image. If the two features in the right-hand side image are too close together, or the ratio between them is too big (close to 1.0), we consider them confusing and do not use them. We also install a duplicate prevention filter to further prune the matches.

The following image shows the flow field from one image to another. Pink arrows in the left-hand side image show the movement of patches from the left-hand side image to the right-hand side image. In the second image to the left, we see a small area of the flow field zoomed in. The pink arrows again show the motion of patches, and we can see it makes sense by looking at the two original image segments on the right-hand side. Visual features in the left-hand side image are moving leftwards across the image, in the directions of the pink arrows as shown in the following image:

The advantage of using optical flow in place of rich features is that the process is usually faster and can accommodate the matching many more points, making the reconstruction denser. In many optical flow methods there is also a monolithic model of the overall movement of patches, where matching rich features are usually not taken into account. The caveat in working with optical flow is that it works best for consecutive images taken by the same hardware, whereas rich features are mostly agnostic to that. The differences result from the fact that optical flow methods usually use very rudimentary features, like image patches around a keypoint, whereas higher-order richer features (for example, SURF) take into account higher-level information for each keypoint. Using optical flow or rich features is a decision the designer of the application should make depending on the input.

Finding camera matrices

Now that we have obtained matches between keypoints, we can calculate the fundamental matrix and from that obtain the essential matrix. However, we must first align our matching points into two arrays, where an index in one array corresponds to the same index in the other. This is required by the `findFundamentalMat` function. We would also need to convert the `KeyPoint` structure to a `Point2f` structure. We must pay special attention to the `queryIdx` and `trainIdx` member variables of `DMatch`, the OpenCV struct that holds a match between two keypoints, as they must align with the way we used the `matcher.match()` function. The following code section shows how to align a matching into two corresponding sets of 2D points, and how these can be used to find the fundamental matrix:

```
vector<Point2f>imgpts1,imgpts2;
for( unsigned inti = 0; i<matches.size(); i++ )
{
// queryIdx is the "left" image
imgpts1.push_back(keypoints1[matches[i].queryIdx].pt);
// trainIdx is the "right" image
imgpts2.push_back(keypoints2[matches[i].trainIdx].pt);
}

Mat F = findFundamentalMat(imgpts1, imgpts2, FM_RANSAC, 0.1, 0.99,
status);
Mat_<double> E = K.t() * F * K; //according to HZ (9.12)
```

We may later use the `status` binary vector to prune those points that align with the recovered fundamental matrix. See the following image for an illustration of point matching after pruning with the fundamental matrix. The red arrows mark feature matches that were removed in the process of finding the F matrix, and the green arrows are feature matches that were kept.

Now we are ready to find the camera matrices. This process is described at length in chapter 9 of H and Z's book; however, we are going to use a very straightforward and simplistic implementation of it, and OpenCV makes things very easy for us. But first, we will briefly examine the structure of the camera matrix we are going to use.

$$P = [R|t] = \begin{bmatrix} r_1 & r_2 & r_3 & t_1 \\ r_4 & r_5 & r_6 & t_2 \\ r_7 & r_8 & r_9 & t_3 \end{bmatrix}$$

This is the model for our camera, it consists of two elements, rotation (denoted as **R**) and translation (denoted as **t**). The interesting thing about it is that it holds a very essential equation: x=PX, where x is a 2D point on the image and X is a 3D point in space. There is more to it, but this matrix gives us a very important relationship between the image points and the scene points. So, now that we have a motivation for finding the camera matrices, we will see how it can be done. The following code section shows how to decompose the essential matrix into the rotation and translation elements:

```
SVD svd(E);
Matx33d W(0,-1,0,//HZ 9.13
```

```
    1,0,0,
    0,0,1);
Mat_<double> R = svd.u * Mat(W) * svd.vt; //HZ 9.19
Mat_<double> t = svd.u.col(2); //u3
Matx34d P1( R(0,0),R(0,1), R(0,2), t(0),
R(1,0),R(1,1), R(1,2), t(1),
R(2,0),R(2,1), R(2,2), t(2));
```

Very simple. All we had to do is take the **Singular Value Decomposition (SVD)** of the essential matrix we obtained from before, and multiply it by a special matrix W. Without going too deeply into the mathematical interpretation of what we did, we can say the SVD operation decomposed our matrix E into two parts, a rotation element and a translation element. In fact, the essential matrix was originally composed by the multiplication of these two elements. Strictly for satisfying our curiosity we can look at the following equation for the essential matrix, which appears in the literature: E=[t]$_x$R. We see it is composed of (some form of) a translation element and a rotational element R.

We notice that what we just did only gives us one camera matrix, so where is the other camera matrix? Well, we perform this operation under the assumption that one camera matrix is fixed and canonical (no rotation and no translation). The next camera matrix is also canonical:

$$P_0 = \begin{bmatrix} 1 & 0 & 0 & 0 \\ 0 & 1 & 0 & 0 \\ 0 & 0 & 1 & 0 \end{bmatrix}$$

The other camera that we recovered from the essential matrix has moved and rotated in relation to the fixed one. This also means that any of the 3D points that we recover from these two camera matrices will have the first camera at the world origin point (0, 0, 0).

This, however, is not the complete solution. H and Z show in their book how and why this decomposition has in fact four possible camera matrices, but only one of them is the true one. The correct matrix is the one that will produce reconstructed points with a positive Z value (points that are in front of the camera). But we can only understand that after learning about triangulation and 3D reconstruction, which will be discussed in the next section.

One more thing we can think of adding to our method is error checking. Many a times the calculation of the fundamental matrix from the point matching is erroneous, and this affects the camera matrices. Continuing triangulation with faulty camera matrices is pointless. We can install a check to see if the rotation element is a valid rotation matrix. Keeping in mind that rotation matrices must have a determinant of 1 (or -1), we can simply do the following:

```
bool CheckCoherentRotation(cv::Mat_<double>& R) {
if(fabsf(determinant(R))-1.0 > 1e-07) {
    cerr<<"det(R) != +-1.0, this is not a rotation matrix"<<endl;
    return false;
    }
return true;
}
```

We can now see how all these elements combine into a function that recovers the P matrices, as follows:

```
void FindCameraMatrices(const Mat& K,
const Mat& Kinv,
const vector<KeyPoint>& imgpts1,
const vector<KeyPoint>& imgpts2,
Matx34d& P,
Matx34d& P1,
vector<DMatch>& matches,
vector<CloudPoint>& outCloud
)
{
//Find camera matrices

//Get Fundamental Matrix
Mat F = GetFundamentalMat(imgpts1,imgpts2,matches);

//Essential matrix: compute then extract cameras [R|t]
Mat_<double> E = K.t() * F * K; //according to HZ (9.12)

//decompose E to P' , HZ (9.19)
SVD svd(E,SVD::MODIFY_A);
Mat svd_u = svd.u;
Mat svd_vt = svd.vt;
Mat svd_w = svd.w;

Matx33d W(0,-1,0,//HZ 9.13
1,0,0,
0,0,1);
```

```
Mat_<double> R = svd_u * Mat(W) * svd_vt; //HZ 9.19
Mat_<double> t = svd_u.col(2); //u3

if (!CheckCoherentRotation(R)) {
    cout<<"resulting rotation is not coherent\n";
    P1 = 0;
    return;
}

P1 = Matx34d(R(0,0),R(0,1),R(0,2),t(0),
R(1,0),R(1,1),R(1,2),t(1),
R(2,0),R(2,1),R(2,2),t(2));
}
```

At this point we have the two cameras that we need in order to reconstruct the scene. The canonical first camera, in the P variable, and the second camera we calculated, form the fundamental matrix in the P1 variable. The next section will reveal how we use these cameras to obtain a 3D structure of the scene.

Reconstructing the scene

Next we look into the matter of recovering the 3D structure of the scene from the information we have acquired so far. As we had done before, we should look at the tools and information we have at hand to achieve this. In the preceding section we obtained two camera matrices from the essential and fundamental matrices; we already discussed how these tools will be useful for obtaining the 3D position of a point in space. Then, we can go back to our matched point pairs to fill in our equations with numerical data. The point pairs will also be useful in calculating the error we get from all our approximate calculations.

This is the time to see how we can perform triangulation using OpenCV. This time we will follow the steps Hartley and Sturm take in their article *Triangulation*, where they implement and compare a few triangulation methods. We will implement one of their linear methods, as it is very simple to code with OpenCV.

Remember we had two key equations arising from the 2D point matching and P matrices: x=PX and x'= P'X, where x and x' are matching 2D points and X is a real world 3D point imaged by the two cameras. If we rewrite the equations, we can formulate a system of linear equations that can be solved for the value of X, which is what we desire to find. Assuming X = (x, y, z, 1)t (a reasonable assumption for points that are not too close or too far from the camera center) creates an inhomogeneous linear equation system of the form AX = B. We can code and solve this equation system as follows:

```
Mat_<double> LinearLSTriangulation(
Point3d u,//homogenous image point (u,v,1)
Matx34d P,//camera 1 matrix
Point3d u1,//homogenous image point in 2nd camera
Matx34d P1//camera 2 matrix
)
{
//build A matrix
 Matx43d A(u.x*P(2,0)-P(0,0),u.x*P(2,1)-P(0,1),u.x*P(2,2)-P(0,2),
u.y*P(2,0)-P(1,0),u.y*P(2,1)-P(1,1),u.y*P(2,2)-P(1,2),
u1.x*P1(2,0)-P1(0,0), u1.x*P1(2,1)-P1(0,1),u1.x*P1(2,2)-P1(0,2),
u1.y*P1(2,0)-P1(1,0), u1.y*P1(2,1)-P1(1,1),u1.y*P1(2,2)-P1(1,2)
  );
//build B vector
Matx41d B(-(u.x*P(2,3)-P(0,3)),
 -(u.y*P(2,3)-P(1,3)),
 -(u1.x*P1(2,3)-P1(0,3)),
 -(u1.y*P1(2,3)-P1(1,3)));

//solve for X
Mat_<double> X;
solve(A,B,X,DECOMP_SVD);

return X;
}
```

This will give us an approximation for the 3D points arising from the two 2D points. One more thing to note is that the 2D points are represented in homogenous coordinates, meaning the x and y values are appended with a 1. We should make sure these points are in normalized coordinates, meaning that they were multiplied by the calibration matrix K beforehand. We may notice that instead of multiplying each point by the matrix K we can simply make use of the KP matrix (the K matrix multiplied by the P matrix), as H and Z do throughout chapter 9. We can now write a loop over the point matches to get a complete triangulation as follows:

```
double TriangulatePoints(
const vector<KeyPoint>& pt_set1,
const vector<KeyPoint>& pt_set2,
const Mat&Kinv,
const Matx34d& P,
const Matx34d& P1,
vector<Point3d>& pointcloud)
{
vector<double> reproj_error;
for (unsigned int i=0; i<pts_size; i++) {
    //convert to normalized homogeneous coordinates
    Point2f kp = pt_set1[i].pt;
    Point3d u(kp.x,kp.y,1.0);
    Mat_<double> um = Kinv * Mat_<double>(u);
    u = um.at<Point3d>(0);
    Point2f kp1 = pt_set2[i].pt;
    Point3d u1(kp1.x,kp1.y,1.0);
    Mat_<double> um1 = Kinv * Mat_<double>(u1);
    u1 = um1.at<Point3d>(0);

    //triangulate
    Mat_<double> X = LinearLSTriangulation(u,P,u1,P1);

    //calculate reprojection error
    Mat_<double> xPt_img = K * Mat(P1) * X;
    Point2f xPt_img_(xPt_img(0)/xPt_img(2),xPt_img(1)/xPt_img(2));
    reproj_error.push_back(norm(xPt_img_-kp1));

    //store 3D point
    pointcloud.push_back(Point3d(X(0),X(1),X(2)));
}

//return mean reprojection error
Scalar me = mean(reproj_error);
return me[0];
}
```

In the following image we will see a triangulation result of two images out of the Fountain P-11 sequence at `http://cvlab.epfl.ch/~strecha/multiview/denseMVS.html`. The two images at the top are the original two views of the scene, and the bottom pair is the view of the reconstructed point cloud from the two views, including the estimated cameras looking at the fountain. We can see how the right-hand side section of the red brick wall was reconstructed, and also the fountain that protrudes from the wall.

However, as we discussed earlier, we have an issue with the reconstruction being only up-to-scale. We should take a moment to understand what up-to-scale means. The motion we obtained between our two cameras is going to have an arbitrary unit of measurement, that is, it is not in centimeters or inches but simply a given unit of scale. Our reconstructed cameras we will be one unit of scale distance apart. This has big implications should we decide to recover more cameras later, as each pair of cameras will have their own units of scale, rather than a common one.

We will now discuss how the error measure that we set up may help us in finding a more robust reconstruction. First we should note that reprojection means we simply take the triangulated 3D point and reimage it on a camera to get a reprojected 2D point, we then compare the distance between the original 2D point and the reprojected 2D point. If this distance is large this means we may have an error in triangulation, so we may not want to include this point in the final result. Our global measure is the average reprojection distance and may give us a hint to how our triangulation performed overall. High average reprojection rates may point to a problem with the P matrices, and therefore a possible problem with the calculation of the essential matrix or the matched feature points.

We should briefly go back to our discussion of camera matrices in the previous section. We mentioned that composing the camera matrix P1 can be performed in four different ways, but only one composition is correct. Now that we know how to triangulate a point, we can add a check to see which one of the four camera matrices is valid. We shall skip the implementation details at this point, as they are featured in the sample code attached to the book.

Next we are going to take a look at recovering more cameras looking at the same scene, and combining the 3D reconstruction results.

Reconstruction from many views

Now that we know how to recover the motion and scene geometry from two cameras, it would seem trivial to get the parameters of additional cameras and more scene points simply by applying the same process. This matter is in fact not so simple as we can only get a reconstruction that is up-to-scale, and each pair of pictures gives us a different scale.

There are a number of ways to correctly reconstruct the 3D scene data from multiple views. One way is of resection or camera pose estimation, also known as **Perspective N-Point(PNP)**, where we try to solve for the position of a new camera using the scene points we have already found. Another way is to triangulate more points and see how they fit into our existing scene geometry; this will tell us the position of the new camera by means of the **Iterative Closest Point(ICP)** procedure. In this chapter we will discuss using OpenCV's solvePnP functions to achieve the first method.

The first step we choose in this kind of reconstruction—incremental 3D reconstruction with camera resection—is to get a baseline scene structure. As we are going to look for the position of any new camera based on a known structure of the scene, we need to find an initial structure and a baseline to work with. We can use the method we previously discussed—for example, between the first and second frames—to get a baseline by finding the camera matrices (using the `FindCameraMatrices` function) and triangulate the geometry (using the `TriangulatePoints` function).

Having found an initial structure, we may continue; however, our method requires quite a bit of bookkeeping. First we should note that the `solvePnP` function needs two aligned vectors of 3D and 2D points. Aligned vectors mean that the ith position in one vector aligns with the ith position in the other. To obtain these vectors we need to find those points among the 3D points that we recovered earlier, which align with the 2D points in our new frame. A simple way to do this is to attach, for each 3D point in the cloud, a vector denoting the 2D points it came from. We can then use feature matching to get a matching pair.

Let us introduce a new structure for a 3D point as follows:

```
struct CloudPoint {
cv::Point3d pt;
std::vector<int>index_of_2d_origin;
};
```

It holds, on top of the 3D point, an index to the 2D point inside the vector of 2D points that each frame has, which had contributed to this 3D point. The information for `index_of_2d_origin` must be initialized when triangulating a new 3D point, recording which cameras were involved in the triangulation. We can then use it to trace back from our 3D point cloud to the 2D point in each frame, as follows:

```
std::vector<CloudPoint> pcloud; //our global 3D point cloud

//check for matches between i'th frame and 0'th frame (and thus the
current cloud)
std::vector<cv::Point3f> ppcloud;
std::vector<cv::Point2f> imgPoints;
vector<int> pcloud_status(pcloud.size(),0);

//scan the views we already used (good_views)
for (set<int>::iterator done_view = good_views.begin(); done_view !=
good_views.end(); ++done_view)
{
    int old_view = *done_view; //a view we already used for
reconstrcution
```

```
//check for matches_from_old_to_working between
<working_view>'th frame and <old_view>'th frame (and thus
the current cloud)
std::vector<cv::DMatch> matches_from_old_to_working =
matches_matrix[std::make_pair(old_view,working_view)];
//scan the 2D-2D matched-points
for (unsigned int match_from_old_view=0;
match_from_old_view<matches_from_old_to_working.size();
match_from_old_view++) {
// the index of the matching 2D point in <old_view>
int idx_in_old_view =
matches_from_old_to_working[match_from_old_view].queryIdx;

//scan the existing cloud to see if this point from <old_view>
exists for (unsigned int pcldp=0; pcldp<pcloud.size(); pcldp++) {
// see if this 2D point from <old_view> contributed to this 3D
point in the cloud
if (idx_in_old_view == pcloud[pcldp].index_of_2d_origin[old_view]
   && pcloud_status[pcldp] == 0) //prevent duplicates
   {
     //3d point in cloud
     ppcloud.push_back(pcloud[pcldp].pt);
     //2d point in image <working_view>
     Point2d pt_ = imgpts[working_view][matches_from_old_to_
     working[match_from_old_view].trainIdx].pt;
     imgPoints.push_back(pt_);

     pcloud_status[pcldp] = 1;
     break;
     }
   }
 }
}
cout<<"found "<<ppcloud.size() <<" 3d-2d point correspondences"<<endl;
```

Now we have an aligned pairing of 3D points in the scene to the 2D points in a new frame, and we can use them to recover the camera position as follows:

```
cv::Mat_<double> t,rvec,R;
cv::solvePnPRansac(ppcloud, imgPoints, K, distcoeff, rvec, t, false);

//get rotation in 3x3 matrix form
Rodrigues(rvec, R);

P1 = cv::Matx34d(R(0,0),R(0,1),R(0,2),t(0),
R(1,0),R(1,1),R(1,2),t(1),
R(2,0),R(2,1),R(2,2),t(2));
```

Note that we are using the `solvePnPRansac` function rather than the `solvePnP` function as it is more robust to outliers. Now that we have a new `P1` matrix, we can simply use the `TriangulatePoints` function we defined earlier again and populate our point cloud with more 3D points.

In the following image we see an incremental reconstruction of the Fountain-P11 scene at `http://cvlab.epfl.ch/~strecha/multiview/denseMVS.html`, starting from the 4th image. The top-left image is the reconstruction after four images were used; the participating cameras are shown as red pyramids with a white line showing the direction. The other images show how more cameras add more points to the cloud.

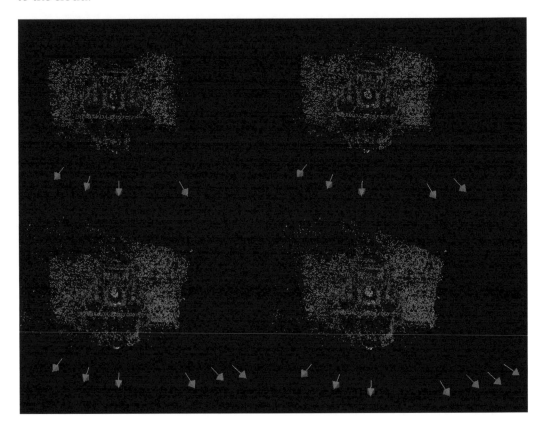

Refinement of the reconstruction

One of the most important parts of an SfM method is refining and optimizing the reconstructed scene, also known as the process of **Bundle Adjustment (BA)**. This is an optimizing step where all the data we gathered is fitted to a monolithic model. Both the position of the 3D points and the positions of cameras are optimized, so reprojection errors are minimized (that is, approximated 3D points are projected on the image close to the position of originating 2D points). This process usually entails the solving of very big linear equations of the order of tens of thousands of parameters. The process may be slightly laborious, but the steps we took earlier will allow for an easy integration with the bundle adjuster. Some things that seemed strange earlier may become clear; for example, the reason we retain the origin 2D points for each 3D point in the cloud.

One implementation of a bundle adjustment algorithm is the **Simple Sparse Bundle Adjustment (SSBA)** library; we will choose it as our BA optimizer as it has a simple API. It requires only a few input arguments that we can create rather easily from our data structures. The key object we will use from SSBA is the `CommonInternalsMetricBundleOptimizer` function, which performs the optimization. It needs the camera parameters, the 3D point cloud, the 2D image points that corresponds to each point in the point cloud, and cameras looking at the scene. By now it should be straightforward to come up with these parameters. We should note that this method of BA assumes all images were taken by the same hardware, hence the common internals, other modes of operation may not assume this. We can perform Bundle Adjustment as follows:

```
voidBundleAdjuster::adjustBundle(
vector<CloudPoint>&pointcloud,
const Mat&cam_intrinsics,
conststd::vector<std::vector<cv::KeyPoint>>&imgpts,
std::map<int ,cv::Matx34d>&Pmats
)
{
int N = Pmats.size(), M = pointcloud.size(), K = -1;

cout<<"N (cams) = "<< N <<" M (points) = "<< M <<" K (measurements) =
"<< K <<endl;

StdDistortionFunction distortion;

// intrinsic parameters matrix
Matrix3x3d KMat;
makeIdentityMatrix(KMat);
KMat[0][0] = cam_intrinsics.at<double>(0,0);
```

```cpp
KMat[0][1] = cam_intrinsics.at<double>(0,1);
KMat[0][2] = cam_intrinsics.at<double>(0,2);
KMat[1][1] = cam_intrinsics.at<double>(1,1);
KMat[1][2] = cam_intrinsics.at<double>(1,2);

...

// 3D point cloud
vector<Vector3d >Xs(M);
for (int j = 0; j < M; ++j)
{
Xs[j][0] = pointcloud[j].pt.x;
Xs[j][1] = pointcloud[j].pt.y;
Xs[j][2] = pointcloud[j].pt.z;
}
cout<<"Read the 3D points."<<endl;

// convert cameras to BA datastructs
vector<CameraMatrix> cams(N);
for (inti = 0; i< N; ++i)
{
intcamId = i;
Matrix3x3d R;
Vector3d T;

Matx34d& P = Pmats[i];

R[0][0] = P(0,0); R[0][1] = P(0,1); R[0][2] = P(0,2); T[0] = P(0,3);
R[1][0] = P(1,0); R[1][1] = P(1,1); R[1][2] = P(1,2); T[1] = P(1,3);
R[2][0] = P(2,0); R[2][1] = P(2,1); R[2][2] = P(2,2); T[2] = P(2,3);

cams[i].setIntrinsic(Knorm);
cams[i].setRotation(R);
cams[i].setTranslation(T);
}
cout<<"Read the cameras."<<endl;

vector<Vector2d > measurements;
vector<int> correspondingView;
vector<int> correspondingPoint;

// 2D corresponding points
for (unsigned int k = 0; k <pointcloud.size(); ++k)
{
```

```
for (unsigned int i=0; i<pointcloud[k].imgpt_for_img.size(); i++) {
if (pointcloud[k].imgpt_for_img[i] >= 0) {
int view = i, point = k;
Vector3d p, np;

Point cvp = imgpts[i][pointcloud[k].imgpt_for_img[i]].pt;
p[0] = cvp.x;
p[1] = cvp.y;
p[2] = 1.0;

// Normalize the measurements to match the unit focal length.
scaleVectorIP(1.0/f0, p);
measurements.push_back(Vector2d(p[0], p[1]));
correspondingView.push_back(view);
correspondingPoint.push_back(point);
}
}
} // end for (k)

K = measurements.size();

cout<<"Read "<< K <<" valid 2D measurements."<<endl;

...

// perform the bundle adjustment
{
CommonInternalsMetricBundleOptimizeropt(V3D::FULL_BUNDLE_FOCAL_
LENGTH_PP, inlierThreshold, K0, distortion, cams, Xs, measurements,
correspondingView, correspondingPoint);

opt.tau = 1e-3;
opt.maxIterations = 50;
opt.minimize();

cout<<"optimizer status = "<<opt.status<<endl;
}

...

//extract 3D points
for (unsigned int j = 0; j <Xs.size(); ++j)
{
pointcloud[j].pt.x = Xs[j][0];
```

```
pointcloud[j].pt.y = Xs[j][1];
pointcloud[j].pt.z = Xs[j][2];
}
//extract adjusted cameras
for (int i = 0; i< N; ++i)
{
Matrix3x3d R = cams[i].getRotation();
Vector3d T = cams[i].getTranslation();
Matx34d P;
P(0,0) = R[0][0]; P(0,1) = R[0][1]; P(0,2) = R[0][2]; P(0,3) = T[0];
P(1,0) = R[1][0]; P(1,1) = R[1][1]; P(1,2) = R[1][2]; P(1,3) = T[1];
P(2,0) = R[2][0]; P(2,1) = R[2][1]; P(2,2) = R[2][2]; P(2,3) = T[2];
Pmats[i] = P;
}
}
```

This code, albeit long, is primarily about converting our internal data structures to and from SSBA's data structures, and invoking the optimization process.

The following image shows the effects of BA. The two images on the left are the points of the point cloud before adjustment, from two perspectives, and the images on the right show the optimized cloud. The change is quite dramatic, and many misalignments between points triangulated from different views are now mostly consolidated. We can also notice how the adjustment created a far better reconstruction of flat surfaces.

Visualizing 3D point clouds with PCL

While working with 3D data, it is hard to quickly understand if a result is correct simply by looking at reprojection error measures or raw point information. On the other hand, if we look at the point cloud itself we can immediately verify whether it makes sense or there was an error. For visualization we will use an up-and-coming sister project for OpenCV, called the **Point Cloud Library (PCL)**. It comes with many tools for visualizing and also analyzing point clouds, such as finding flat surfaces, matching point clouds, segmenting objects, and eliminating outliers. These tools are highly useful if our goal is not a point cloud but rather some higher-order information such as a 3D model.

First, we should represent our cloud (essentially a list of 3D points) in PCL's data structures. This can be done as follows:

```
pcl::PointCloud<pcl::PointXYZRGB>::Ptr cloud;

void PopulatePCLPointCloud(const vector<Point3d>& pointcloud,
const std::vector<cv::Vec3b>& pointcloud_RGB
)
//Populate point cloud
{
cout<<"Creating point cloud...";
cloud.reset(new pcl::PointCloud<pcl::PointXYZRGB>);

for (unsigned int i=0; i<pointcloud.size(); i++) {
// get the RGB color value for the point
Vec3b rgbv(255,255,255);
if (pointcloud_RGB.size() >= i) {
rgbv = pointcloud_RGB[i];
}

// check for erroneous coordinates (NaN, Inf, etc.)
if (pointcloud[i].x != pointcloud[i].x || isnan(pointcloud[i].x) ||
pointcloud[i].y != pointcloud[i].y || isnan(pointcloud[i].y) ||
pointcloud[i].z != pointcloud[i].z || isnan(pointcloud[i].z) ||
fabsf(pointcloud[i].x) > 10.0 ||
fabsf(pointcloud[i].y) > 10.0 ||
fabsf(pointcloud[i].z) > 10.0) {
continue;
}

pcl::PointXYZRGB pclp;

// 3D coordinates
```

```
pclp.x = pointcloud[i].x;
pclp.y = pointcloud[i].y;
pclp.z = pointcloud[i].z;

// RGB color, needs to be represented as an integer
uint32_t rgb = ((uint32_t)rgbv[2] << 16 | (uint32_t)rgbv[1] << 8 |
(uint32_t)rgbv[0]);
pclp.rgb = *reinterpret_cast<float*>(&rgb);

cloud->push_back(pclp);
}

cloud->width = (uint32_t) cloud->points.size(); // number of points
cloud->height = 1; // a list of points, one row of data
}
```

To have a nice effect for the purpose of visualization, we can also supply color data as RGB values taken from the images. We can also apply a filter to the raw cloud that will eliminate points that are likely to be outliers, using the **statistical outlier removal (SOR)** tool as follows:

```
Void SORFilter() {

pcl::PointCloud<pcl::PointXYZRGB>::Ptr cloud_filtered (new pcl::PointC
loud<pcl::PointXYZRGB>);

std::cerr<<"Cloud before SOR filtering: "<< cloud->width * cloud-
>height <<" data points"<<std::endl;


// Create the filtering object
pcl::StatisticalOutlierRemoval<pcl::PointXYZRGB>sor;
sor.setInputCloud (cloud);
sor.setMeanK (50);
sor.setStddevMulThresh (1.0);
sor.filter (*cloud_filtered);

std::cerr<<"Cloud after SOR filtering: "<<cloud_filtered->width *
cloud_filtered->height <<" data points "<<std::endl;

copyPointCloud(*cloud_filtered,*cloud);
}
```

Then we can use PCL's API for running a simple point cloud visualizer as follows:

```
Void RunVisualization(const vector<cv::Point3d>& pointcloud,
const std::vector<cv::Vec3b>& pointcloud_RGB) {
PopulatePCLPointCloud(pointcloud,pointcloud_RGB);
SORFilter();
copyPointCloud(*cloud,*orig_cloud);

pcl::visualization::CloudViewer viewer("Cloud Viewer");

// run the cloud viewer
viewer.showCloud(orig_cloud,"orig");

while (!viewer.wasStopped ())
    {
// NOP
}
}
```

The following image shows the output after the statistical outlier removal tool has been used. The image on the left-hand side is the original resultant cloud of the SfM, with the cameras location and a zoomed-in view of a particular part of the cloud. The image on the right-hand side shows the filtered cloud after the SOR operation. We can notice some stray points were removed, leaving a cleaner point cloud:

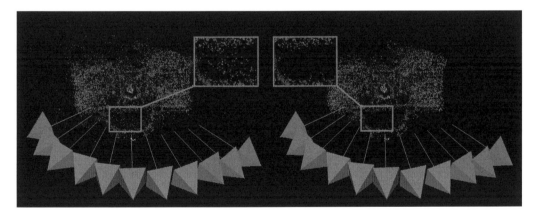

Using the example code

We can find the example code for SfM with the supporting material of this book. We will now see how we can build, run, and make use of it. The code makes use of CMake, a cross-platform build environment similar to Maven or SCons. We should also make sure we have all the following prerequisites to build the application:

- OpenCV v2.3 or higher
- PCL v1.6 or higher
- SSBA v3.0 or higher

First we must set up the build environment. To that end, we may create a folder named `build` in which all build-related files will go; we will now assume all command-line operations are within the `build/`folder, although the process is similar (up to the locations of the files) even if not using the `build` folder.

We should make sure CMake can find SSBA and PCL. If PCL was installed properly, there should not be a problem; however, we must set the correct location to find SSBA's prebuilt binaries via the **-DSSBA_LIBRARY_DIR=...** build parameter. If we are using Windows as the operating system, we can use Microsoft Visual Studio to build; therefore, we should run the following command:

```
cmake –G "Visual Studio 10" -DSSBA_LIBRARY_DIR=../3rdparty/SSBA-3.0/
build/ ..
```

If we are using Linux, Mac OS, or another Unix-like operating system, we execute the following command:

```
cmake –G "Unix Makefiles" -DSSBA_LIBRARY_DIR=../3rdparty/SSBA-3.0/build/
..
```

If we prefer to use XCode on Mac OS, execute the following command:

```
cmake –G Xcode -DSSBA_LIBRARY_DIR=../3rdparty/SSBA-3.0/build/ ..
```

CMake also has the ability to build macros for Eclipse, Codeblocks, and more. After CMake is done creating the environment, we are ready to build. If we are using a Unix-like system we can simply execute the make utility, else we should use our development environment's building process.

After the build has finished, we should be left with an executable named ExploringSfMExec, which runs the SfM process. Running it with no arguments will result in the following: **USAGE: ./ExploringSfMExec <path_to_images>**

To execute the process over a set of images, we should supply a location on the drive to find image files. If a valid location is supplied, the process should start and we should see the progress and debug information on the screen. The process will end with a display of the point cloud that arises from the images. Pressing the *1* and *2* keys will switch between the adjusted and non-adjusted point cloud.

Summary

In this chapter we have seen how OpenCV can help us approach Structure from Motion in a manner that is both simple to code and to understand. OpenCV's API contains a number of useful functions and data structures that make our lives easier and also assist in a cleaner implementation.

However, the state-of-the-art SfM methods are far more complex. There are many issues we choose to disregard in favor of simplicity, and plenty more error examinations that are usually in place. Our chosen methods for the different elements of SfM can also be revisited. For one, H and Z propose a highly accurate triangulation method that minimizes the reprojection error in the image domain. Some methods even use the N-view triangulation once they understand the relationship between the features in multiple images.

If we would like to extend and deepen our familiarity with SfM, we will certainly benefit from looking at other open-source SfM libraries. One particularly interesting project is libMV, which implements a vast array of SfM elements that may be interchanged to get the best results. There is a great body of work from University of Washington that provides tools for many flavors of SfM (Bundler and VisualSfM). This work inspired an online product from Microsoft called PhotoSynth. There are many more implementations of SfM readily available online, and one must only search to find quite a lot of them.

Another important relationship we have not discussed in depth is that of SfM and Visual Localization and Mapping, better known in as **Simultaneous Localization and Mapping (SLAM)** methods. In this chapter we have dealt with a given dataset of images and a video sequence, and using SfM is practical in those cases; however, some applications have no prerecorded dataset and must bootstrap the reconstruction on the fly. This process is better known as **Mapping**, and it is done while we are creating a 3D map of the world, using feature matching and tracking in 2D, and after triangulation.

In the next chapter we will see how OpenCV can be used for extracting license plate numbers from images, using various techniques in machine learning.

References

- *Multiple View Geometry in Computer Vision, Richard Hartley and Andrew Zisserman, Cambridge University Press*

- *Triangulation, Richard I. Hartley and Peter Sturm, Computer vision and image understanding, Vol. 68, pp. 146-157*

- http://cvlab.epfl.ch/~strecha/multiview/denseMVS.html

- *On Benchmarking Camera Calibration and Multi-View Stereo for High Resolution Imagery,C. Strecha, W. von Hansen, L. Van Gool, P. Fua, and U. Thoennessen, CVPR*

- http://www.inf.ethz.ch/personal/chzach/opensource.html

- http://www.ics.forth.gr/~lourakis/sba/

- http://code.google.com/p/libmv/

- http://www.cs.washington.edu/homes/ccwu/vsfm/

- http://phototour.cs.washington.edu/bundler/

- http://photosynth.net/

- http://en.wikipedia.org/wiki/Simultaneous_localization_and_mapping

- http://pointclouds.org

- http://www.cmake.org

5
Number Plate Recognition Using SVM and Neural Networks

This chapter introduces us to the steps needed to create an application for **Automatic Number Plate Recognition (ANPR)**. There are different approaches and techniques based on different situations, for example, IR cameras, fixed car positions, light conditions, and so on. We can proceed to construct an ANPR application to detect automobile license plates in a photograph taken between 2-3 meters from a car, in ambiguous light condition, and with non-parallel ground with minor perspective distortions of the automobile's plate.

The main purpose of this chapter is to introduce us to image segmentation and feature extraction, pattern recognition basics, and two important pattern recognition algorithms **Support Vector Machines** and **Artificial Neural Networks**. In this chapter, we will cover:

- ANPR
- Plate detection
- Plate recognition

Introduction to ANPR

Automatic Number Plate Recognition (ANPR), also known as **Automatic License-Plate Recognition (ALPR)**, **Automatic Vehicle Identification (AVI)**, or **Car Plate Recognition (CPR)**, is a surveillance method that uses **Optical Character Recognition (OCR)** and other methods such as segmentations and detection to read vehicle registration plates.

The best results in an ANPR system can be obtained with an **infrared (IR)** camera, because the segmentation steps for detection and OCR segmentation are easy, clean, and minimize errors. This is due to the laws of light, the basic one being that the angle of incidence equals the angle of reflection; we can see this basic reflection when we see a smooth surface such as a plane mirror. Reflection off of rough surfaces such as paper leads to a type of reflection known as diffuse or scatter reflection. The majority of number plates have a special characteristic named retro-reflection — the surface of the plate is made with a material that is covered with thousands of tiny hemispheres that cause light to be reflected back to the source as we can see in the following figure:

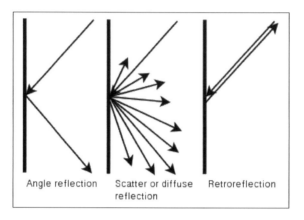

Angle reflection   Scatter or diffuse   Retroreflection
                          reflection

If we use a camera with a filter coupled with a structured infrared light projector, we can retrieve just the infrared light and then we have a very high-quality image to segment and subsequently detect, and recognize the plate number that is independent of any light environment as shown in the following figure:

We do not use IR photographs in this chapter; we use regular photographs. We do this so that we do not obtain the best results and get a higher level of detection errors and higher false recognition rate as opposed to the results we would expect if we used an IR camera; however, the steps for both are the same.

Each country has different license plate sizes and specifications; it is useful to know these specifications in order to get the best results and reduce errors. The algorithms used in this chapter are intended to explain the basics of ANPR and the specifications for license plates from Spain, but we can extend them to any country or specification.

In this chapter, we will work with license plates from Spain. In Spain, there are three different sizes and shapes of license plates; we will only use the most common (large) license plate which is 520 x 110 mm. Two groups of characters are separated by a 41 mm space and then a 14 mm width separates each individual character. The first group of characters has four numeric digits, and the second group has three letters without the vowels A, E, I, O, U, nor the letters Ñ or Q; all characters have dimensions of 45 x 77 mm.

This data is important for character segmentation since we can check both the character and blank spaces to verify that we get a character and no other image segment. The following is a figure of one such license plate:

ANPR algorithm

Before explaining the ANPR code, we need to define the main steps and tasks in the ANPR algorithm. ANPR is divided in two main steps: plate detection and plate recognition. Plate detection has the purpose of detecting the location of the plate in the whole camera frame. When a plate is detected in an image, the plate segment is passed to the second step — plate recognition — which uses an OCR algorithm to determine the alphanumeric characters on the plate.

In the next figure we can see the two main algorithm steps, plate detection and plate recognition. After these steps the program draws over the camera frame the plate's characters that have been detected. The algorithms can return bad results or even no result:

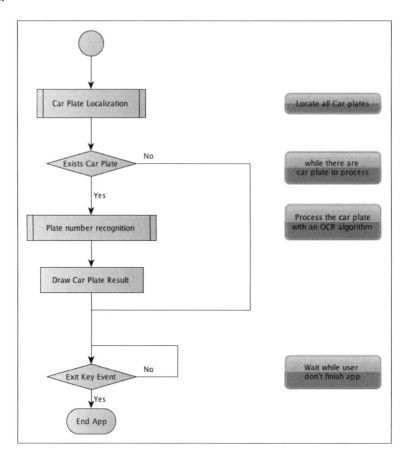

In each step shown in the previous figure, we will define three additional steps that are commonly used in pattern recognition algorithms:

1. **Segmentation**: This step detects and removes each patch/region of interest in the image.

2. **Feature extraction**: This step extracts from each patch a set of characteristics.

3. **Classification**: This step extracts each character from the plate recognition step or classifies each image patch into "plate" or "no plate" in the plate-detection step.

The following figure shows us the pattern recognition steps in the whole algorithm application:

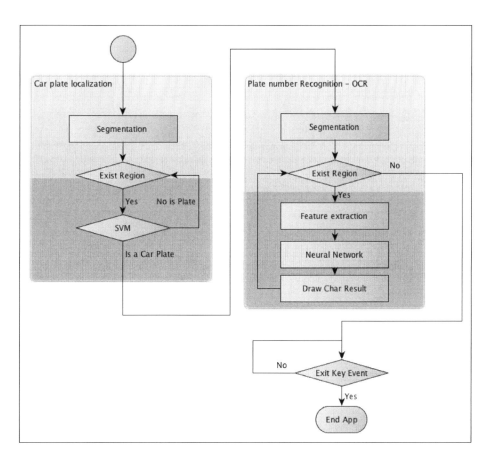

Aside from the main application, whose purpose is to detect and recognize a car's license plate number, we will briefly explain two more tasks that are usually not explained:

- How to train a pattern recognition system
- How to evaluate such a system

These tasks, however, can be more important than the main application itself, because if we do not train the pattern recognition system correctly, our system can fail and not work correctly; different patterns need different types of training and evaluation. We need to evaluate our system in different environments, conditions, and with different features to get the best results. These two tasks are sometimes used together since different features can produce different results that we can see in the evaluation section.

Plate detection

In this step we have to detect all the plates in the current camera frame. To do this task, we divide it in two main steps: segmentation and segment classification. The feature step is not explained because we use the image patch as a vector feature.

In the first step (segmentation), we apply different filters, morphological operations, contour algorithms, and validations to retrieve those parts of the image that could have a plate.

In the second step (classification), we apply a **Support Vector Machine (SVM)** classifier to each image patch—our feature. Before creating our main application we train with two different classes—plate and non-plate. We work with parallel frontal-view color images that are 800 pixels wide and taken 2–4 meters from a car. These requirements are important to ensure correct segmentations. We can perform detection if we create a multi-scale image algorithm.

In the next image we have shown all the processes involved in plate detection:

- Sobel filter
- Threshold operation
- Close morphologic operation
- Mask of one filled area
- Possible detected plates marked in red (features images)
- Detected plates after the SVM classifier

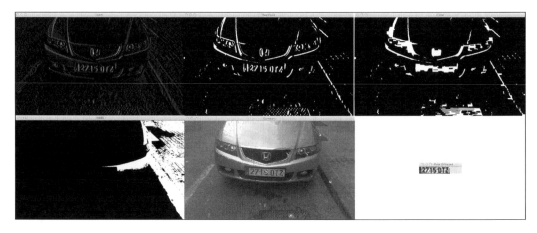

Segmentation

Segmentation is the process of dividing an image into multiple segments. This process is to simplify the image for analysis and make feature extraction easier.

One important feature of plate segmentation is the high number of vertical edges in a license plate assuming that the image was taken frontally, and the plate is not rotated and is without perspective distortion. This feature can be exploited during the first segmentation step to eliminate regions that don't have any vertical edges.

Before finding vertical edges, we need to convert the color image to a grayscale image, (because color can't help us in this task), and remove possible noise generated by the camera or other ambient noise. We will apply a Gaussian blur of 5 x 5 and remove noise. If we don't apply a noise-removal method, we can get a lot of vertical edges that produce a falied detection.

```
//convert image to gray
Mat img_gray;
cvtColor(input, img_gray, CV_BGR2GRAY);
blur(img_gray, img_gray, Size(5,5));
```

To find the vertical edges, we will use a Sobel filter and find the first horizontal derivative. The derivative is a mathematical function that allows us to find the vertical edges on an image. The definition of a Sobel function in OpenCV is:

```
void Sobel(InputArray src, OutputArray dst, int ddepth, int xorder,
int yorder, int ksize=3, double scale=1, double delta=0, int
borderType=BORDER_DEFAULT )
```

Here, `ddepth` is the destination image depth, `xorder` is the order of the derivative by x, `yorder` is the order of derivative by y, `ksize` is the kernel size of either 1, 3, 5, or 7, `scale` is an optional factor for computed derivative values, `delta` is an optional value added to the result, and `borderType` is the pixel interpolation method.

For our case we can use a `xorder=1`, `yorder=0`, and a `ksize=3`:

```
//Find vertical lines. Car plates have high density of vertical lines
Mat img_sobel;
Sobel(img_gray, img_sobel, CV_8U, 1, 0, 3, 1, 0);
```

After a Sobel filter, we apply a threshold filter to obtain a binary image with a threshold value obtained through Otsu's method. Otsu's algorithm needs an 8-bit input image and Otsu's method automatically determines the optimal threshold value:

```
//threshold image
Mat img_threshold;
threshold(img_sobel, img_threshold, 0, 255, CV_THRESH_OTSU+CV_THRESH_
BINARY);
```

To define Otsu's method in the `threshold` function, if we combine the type parameter with the `CV_THRESH_OTSU` value, then the threshold value parameter is ignored.

> When the value of `CV_THRESH_OTSU` is defined, the threshold function returns the optimal threshold value obtained by the Otsu's algorithm.

By applying a close morphological operation, we can remove blank spaces between each vertical edge line, and connect all regions that have a high number of edges. In this step we have the possible regions that can contain plates.

First we define our structural element to use in our morphological operation. We will use the `getStructuringElement` function to define a structural rectangular element with a 17 x 3 dimension size in our case; this may be different in other image sizes:

```
Mat element = getStructuringElement(MORPH_RECT, Size(17, 3));
```

And use this structural element in a close morphological operation using the `morphologyEx` function:

```
morphologyEx(img_threshold, img_threshold, CV_MOP_CLOSE, element);
```

After applying these functions, we have regions in the image that could contain a plate; however, most of the regions will not contain license plates. These regions can be split with a connected-component analysis or by using the `findContours` function. This last function retrieves the contours of a binary image with different methods and results. We only need to get the external contours with any hierarchical relationship and any polygonal approximation results:

```
//Find contours of possibles plates
vector< vector< Point> > contours;
findContours(img_threshold,
            contours,              // a vector of contours
            CV_RETR_EXTERNAL,   // retrieve the external contours
            CV_CHAIN_APPROX_NONE); // all pixels of each contour
```

For each contour detected, extract the bounding rectangle of minimal area. OpenCV brings up the `minAreaRect` function for this task. This function returns a rotated rectangle class called `RotatedRect`. Then using a vector iterator over each contour, we can get the rotated rectangle and make some preliminary validations before we classify each region:

```
//Start to iterate to each contour found
vector<vector<Point> >::iterator itc= contours.begin();
vector<RotatedRect> rects;

//Remove patch that has  no inside limits of aspect ratio and area.
while (itc!=contours.end()) {
//Create bounding rect of object
  RotatedRect mr= minAreaRect(Mat(*itc));
  if( !verifySizes(mr)){
    itc= contours.erase(itc);
  }else{
  ++itc;
  rects.push_back(mr);
  }
}
```

We make basic validations about the regions detected based on its area and aspect ratio. We only consider that a region can be a plate if the aspect ratio is approximately 520/110 = 4.727272 (plate width divided by plate height) with an error margin of 40 percent and an area based on a minimum of 15 pixels and maximum of 125 pixels for the height of the plate. These values are calculated depending on the image sizes and camera position:

```
bool DetectRegions::verifySizes(RotatedRect candidate ){

  float error=0.4;
//Spain car plate size: 52x11 aspect 4,7272
  const float aspect=4.7272;
//Set a min and max area. All other patches are discarded
  int min= 15*aspect*15; // minimum area
  int max= 125*aspect*125; // maximum area
//Get only patches that match to a respect ratio.
  float rmin= aspect-aspect*error;
  float rmax= aspect+aspect*error;

  int area= candidate.size.height * candidate.size.width;
  float r= (float)candidate.size.width / (float)candidate.size.height;
  if(r<1)
```

```
    r= 1/r;

    if(( area < min || area > max ) || ( r < rmin || r > rmax )){
      return false;
    }else{
    return true;
    }
  }
```

We can make more improvements using the license plate's white background property. All plates have the same background color and we can use a flood fill algorithm to retrieve the rotated rectangle for precise cropping.

The first step to crop the license plate is to get several seeds near the last rotated rectangle center. Then get the minimum size of plate between the width and height, and use it to generate random seeds near the patch center.

We want to select the white region and we need several seeds to touch at least one white pixel. Then for each seed, we use a floodFill function to draw a new mask image to store the new closest cropping region:

```
for(int i=0; i< rects.size(); i++){
//For better rect cropping for each possible box
//Make floodfill algorithm because the plate has white background
//And then we can retrieve more clearly the contour box
circle(result, rects[i].center, 3, Scalar(0,255,0), -1);
//get the min size between width and height
float minSize=(rects[i].size.width < rects[i].size.height)?rects[i].
size.width:rects[i].size.height;
minSize=minSize-minSize*0.5;
//initialize rand and get 5 points around center for floodfill
algorithm
srand ( time(NULL) );
//Initialize floodfill parameters and variables
Mat mask;
mask.create(input.rows + 2, input.cols + 2, CV_8UC1);
mask= Scalar::all(0);
int loDiff = 30;
int upDiff = 30;
int connectivity = 4;
```

```
int newMaskVal = 255;
int NumSeeds = 10;
Rect ccomp;
int flags = connectivity + (newMaskVal << 8 ) + CV_FLOODFILL_FIXED_
RANGE + CV_FLOODFILL_MASK_ONLY;
for(int j=0; j<NumSeeds; j++){
  Point seed;
  seed.x=rects[i].center.x+rand()%(int)minSize-(minSize/2);
  seed.y=rects[i].center.y+rand()%(int)minSize-(minSize/2);
  circle(result, seed, 1, Scalar(0,255,255), -1);
  int area = floodFill(input, mask, seed, Scalar(255,0,0), &ccomp,
Scalar(loDiff, loDiff, loDiff), Scalar(upDiff, upDiff, upDiff),
flags);
  }
```

The `floodFill` function fills a connected component with color into a mask image starting from a seed point, and sets maximal lower and upper brightness/color difference between the pixel to fill and the pixel neighbors or seed pixel:

```
int floodFill(InputOutputArray image, InputOutputArray mask, Point
seed, Scalar newVal, Rect* rect=0, Scalar loDiff=Scalar(), Scalar
upDiff=Scalar(), int flags=4 )
```

The `newVal` parameter is the new color we want to put into the image when filling. Parameters `loDiff` and `upDiff` are the maximal lower and maximal upper brightness/color difference between the pixel to fill and the pixel neighbors or seed pixel.

The `flag` parameter is a combination of:

- Lower bits: These bits contain connectivity value, 4 (by default), or 8, used within the function. Connectivity determines which neighbors of a pixel are considered.

- Upper bits: These can be 0 or a combination of the following values: CV_FLOODFILL_FIXED_RANGE and CV_FLOODFILL_MASK_ONLY.

CV_FLOODFILL_FIXED_RANGE sets the difference between the current pixel and the seed pixel. CV_FLOODFILL_MASK_ONLY will only fill the image mask and not change the image itself.

Once we have a crop mask, we get a minimal area rectangle from the image-mask points and check the valid size again. For each mask, a white pixel gets the position and uses the `minAreaRect` function for retrieving the closest crop region:

```
//Check new floodfill mask match for a correct patch.
//Get all points detected for minimal rotated Rect
vector<Point> pointsInterest;
Mat_<uchar>::iterator itMask= mask.begin<uchar>();
Mat_<uchar>::iterator end= mask.end<uchar>();
for( ; itMask!=end; ++itMask)
  if(*itMask==255)
  pointsInterest.push_back(itMask.pos());
  RotatedRect minRect = minAreaRect(pointsInterest);
  if(verifySizes(minRect)){
...
```

Now that the segmentation process is finished and we have valid regions, we can crop each detected region, remove any possible rotation, crop the image region, resize the image, and equalize the light of cropped image regions.

First, we need to generate the transform matrix with `getRotationMatrix2D` to remove possible rotations in the detected region. We need to pay attention to height, because the `RotatedRect` class can be returned and rotated at 90 degrees, so we have to check the rectangle aspect, and if it is less than 1 then rotate it by 90 degrees:

```
//Get rotation matrix
float r= (float)minRect.size.width / (float)minRect.size.height;
float angle=minRect.angle;
if(r<1)
  angle=90+angle;
  Mat rotmat= getRotationMatrix2D(minRect.center, angle,1);
```

With the transform matrix, we can now rotate the input image by an affine transformation (an affine transformation in geometry is a transformation that takes parallel lines to parallel lines) with the `warpAffine` function where we set the input and destination images, the transform matrix, the output size (same as the input in our case), and which interpolation method to use. We can define the border method and border value if needed:

```
//Create and rotate image
Mat img_rotated;
warpAffine(input, img_rotated, rotmat, input.size(), CV_INTER_CUBIC);
```

After we rotate the image, we crop the image with `getRectSubPix`, which crops and copies an image portion of given width and height centered in a point. If the image was rotated, we need to change the width and height sizes with the C++ `swap` function.

```
//Crop image
Size rect_size=minRect.size;
if(r < 1)
swap(rect_size.width, rect_size.height);
Mat img_crop;
getRectSubPix(img_rotated, rect_size, minRect.center, img_crop);
```

Cropped images are not good for use in training and classification since they do not have the same size. Also, each image contains different light conditions, increasing their relative differences. To resolve this, we resize all images to the same width and height and apply light histogram equalization:

```
Mat resultResized;
resultResized.create(33,144, CV_8UC3);
resize(img_crop, resultResized, resultResized.size(), 0, 0, INTER_
CUBIC);
//Equalize cropped image
Mat grayResult;
cvtColor(resultResized, grayResult, CV_BGR2GRAY);
blur(grayResult, grayResult, Size(3,3));
equalizeHist(grayResult, grayResult);
```

For each detected region, we store the cropped image and its position in a vector:

```
output.push_back(Plate(grayResult,minRect.boundingRect()));
```

Classification

After we preprocess and segment all possible parts of an image, we now need to decide if each segment is (or is not) a license plate. To do this, we will use a **Support Vector Machine (SVM)** algorithm.

A Support Vector Machine is a pattern recognition algorithm included in a family of supervised-learning algorithms originally created for binary classification. Supervised learning is machine-learning algorithm that learns through the use of labeled data. We need to train the algorithm with an amount of data that is labeled; each data set needs to have a class.

The SVM creates one or more hyperplanes that are used to discriminate each class of the data.

A classic example is a 2D point set that defines two classes; the SVM searches the optimal line that differentiates each class:

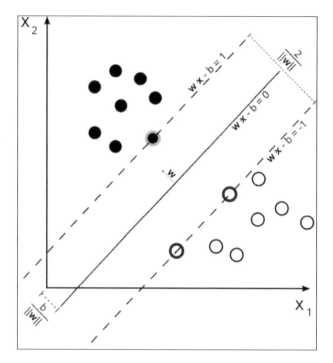

The first task before any classification is to train our classifier; this job is done prior to beginning the main application and it's named offline training. This is not an easy job because it requires a sufficient amount of data to train the system, but a bigger dataset does not always imply the best results. In our case, we do not have enough data due to the fact that there are no public license-plate databases. Because of this, we need to take hundreds of car photos and then preprocess and segment all the photos.

We trained our system with 75 license-plate images and 35 images without license plates of 144 x 33 pixels. We can see a sample of this data in the following image. This is not a large dataset, but it is sufficient enough to get decent results for our requirements. In a real application, we would need to train with more data:

To easily understand how machine learning works, we proceed to use image pixel features of the classifier algorithm (keep in mind, there are better methods and features to train an SVM, such as Principal Components Analysis, Fourier transform, texture analysis, and so on).

We need to create the images to train our system using the `DetectRegions` class and set the `savingRegions` variable to true in order to save the images. We can use the `segmentAllFiles.sh` bash script to repeat the process on all image files under a folder. This can be taken from the source code of this book.

To make this easier, we store all image training data that is processed and prepared, into an XML file for use directly with the SVM function. The `trainSVM.cpp` application creates this file using the folders and number of image files.

Training data for a machine-learning OpenCV algorithm is stored in an *N* x *M* matrix with *N* samples and *M* features. Each data set is saved as a row in the training matrix.

The classes are stored in another matrix with *N* x 1 size, where each class is identified by a float number.

OpenCV has an easy way to manage a data file in XML or JSON format with the `FileStorage` class, this class lets us store and read OpenCV variables and structures or our custom variables. With this function, we can read the training-data matrix and training classes and save it in `SVM_TrainingData` and `SVM_Classes`:

```
FileStorage fs;
fs.open("SVM.xml", FileStorage::READ);
Mat SVM_TrainingData;
Mat SVM_Classes;
fs["TrainingData"] >> SVM_TrainingData;
fs["classes"] >> SVM_Classes;
```

Now we need to set the SVM parameters that define the basic parameters to use in an SVM algorithm; we will use the CvSVMParams structure to define it. It is a mapping done to the training data to improve its resemblance to a linearly separable set of data. This mapping consists of increasing the dimensionality of the data and is done efficiently using a kernel function. We choose here the CvSVM::LINEAR types which means that no mapping is done:

```
//Set SVM params
CvSVMParams SVM_params;
SVM_params.kernel_type = CvSVM::LINEAR;
```

We then create and train our classifier. OpenCV defines the CvSVM class for the Support Vector Machine algorithm and we initialize it with the training data, classes, and parameter data:

```
CvSVM svmClassifier(SVM_TrainingData, SVM_Classes, Mat(), Mat(), SVM_
params);
```

Our classifier is ready to predict a possible cropped image using the predict function of our SVM class; this function returns the class identifier i. In our case, we label a plate class with 1 and no plate class with 0. Then for each detected region that can be a plate, we use SVM to classify it as a plate or no plate, and save only the correct responses. The following code is a part of main application, that is called online processing:

```
vector<Plate> plates;
for(int i=0; i< possible_regions.size(); i++)
{
  Mat img=possible_regions[i].plateImg;
  Mat p= img.reshape(1, 1);//convert img to 1 row m features
  p.convertTo(p, CV_32FC1);
  int response = (int)svmClassifier.predict( p );
  if(response==1)
    plates.push_back(possible_regions[i]);
}
```

Plate recognition

The second step in license plate recognition aims to retrieve the characters of the license plate with optical character recognition. For each detected plate, we proceed to segment the plate for each character, and use an **Artificial Neural Network (ANN)** machine-learning algorithm to recognize the character. Also in this section we will learn how to evaluate a classification algorithm.

OCR segmentation

First, we obtain a plate image patch as the input to the segmentation OCR function with an equalized histogram, we then need to apply a threshold filter and use this threshold image as the input of a **Find contours** algorithm; we can see this process in the next figure:

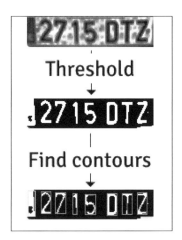

This segmentation process is coded as:

```
Mat img_threshold;
threshold(input, img_threshold, 60, 255, CV_THRESH_BINARY_INV);
if(DEBUG)
  imshow("Threshold plate", img_threshold);
Mat img_contours;
img_threshold.copyTo(img_contours);
//Find contours of possibles characters
vector< vector< Point> > contours;
findContours(img_contours,
            contours,              // a vector of contours
            CV_RETR_EXTERNAL,      // retrieve the external contours
            CV_CHAIN_APPROX_NONE); // all pixels of each contour
```

We use the `CV_THRESH_BINARY_INV` parameter to invert the threshold output by turning the white input values black and black input values white. This is needed to get the contours of each character, because the contours algorithm looks for white pixels.

For each detected contour, we can make a size verification and remove all regions where the size is smaller or the aspect is not correct. In our case, the characters have a 45/77 aspect, and we can accept a 35 percent error of aspect for rotated or distorted characters. If an area is higher than 80 percent, we consider that region to be a black block, and not a character. For counting the area, we can use the `countNonZero` function that counts the number of pixels with a value higher than 0:

```
bool OCR::verifySizes(Mat r)
{
  //Char sizes 45x77
  float aspect=45.0f/77.0f;
  float charAspect= (float)r.cols/(float)r.rows;
  float error=0.35;
  float minHeight=15;
  float maxHeight=28;
  //We have a different aspect ratio for number 1, and it can be
  //~0.2
  float minAspect=0.2;
  float maxAspect=aspect+aspect*error;
  //area of pixels
  float area=countNonZero(r);
  //bb area
  float bbArea=r.cols*r.rows;
  //% of pixel in area
  float percPixels=area/bbArea;
  if(percPixels < 0.8 && charAspect > minAspect && charAspect <
  maxAspect && r.rows >= minHeight && r.rows < maxHeight)
  return true;
  else
  return false;
}
```

If a segmented character is verified, we have to preprocess it to set the same size and position for all characters and save it in a vector with the auxiliary `CharSegment` class. This class saves the segmented character image and the position that we need to order the characters because the Find Contour algorithm does not return the contours in the required order.

Feature extraction

The next step for each segmented character is to extract the features for training and classifying the Artificial Neural Network algorithm.

Unlike the plate detection feature-extraction step that is used in SVM, we don't use all of the image pixels; we will apply more common features used in optical character recognition containing horizontal and vertical accumulation histograms and a low-resolution image sample. We can see this feature more graphically in the next image, where each image has a low-resolution 5 x 5 and the histogram accumulations:

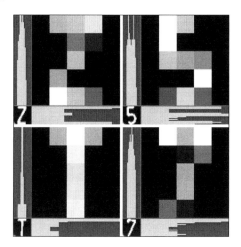

For each character, we count the number of pixels in a row or column with a non-zero value using the countNonZero function and store it in a new data matrix called mhist. We normalize it by looking for the maximum value in the data matrix using the minMaxLoc function and divide all elements of mhist by the maximum value with the convertTo function. We create the ProjectedHistogram function to create the accumulation histograms that have as input a binary image and the type of histogram we need—horizontal or vertical:

```
Mat OCR::ProjectedHistogram(Mat img, int t)
{
    int sz=(t)?img.rows:img.cols;
    Mat mhist=Mat::zeros(1,sz,CV_32F);

    for(int j=0; j<sz; j++){
        Mat data=(t)?img.row(j):img.col(j);
        mhist.at<float>(j)=countNonZero(data);
    }

//Normalize histogram
double min, max;
minMaxLoc(mhist, &min, &max);

if(max>0)
```

```
mhist.convertTo(mhist,-1 , 1.0f/max, 0);


    return mhist;
}
```

Other features use a low-resolution sample image. Instead of using the whole character image, we create a low-resolution character, for example 5 x 5. We train the system with 5 x 5, 10 x 10, 15 x 15, and 20 x 20 characters, and then evaluate which one returns the best result so that we can use it in our system. Once we have all the features, we create a matrix of *M* columns by one row where the columns are the features:

```
Mat OCR::features(Mat in, int sizeData)
{
//Histogram features
  Mat vhist=ProjectedHistogram(in,VERTICAL);
  Mat hhist=ProjectedHistogram(in,HORIZONTAL);
//Low data feature
  Mat lowData;
  resize(in, lowData, Size(sizeData, sizeData) );
  int numCols=vhist.cols + hhist.cols + lowData.cols *
  lowData.cols;
  Mat out=Mat::zeros(1,numCols,CV_32F);
  //Assign values to feature
  int j=0;
  for(int i=0; i<vhist.cols; i++)
  {
    out.at<float>(j)=vhist.at<float>(i);
    j++;
  }
  for(int i=0; i<hhist.cols; i++)
  {
  out.at<float>(j)=hhist.at<float>(i);
  j++;
  }
  for(int x=0; x<lowData.cols; x++)
  {
    for(int y=0; y<lowData.rows; y++)
    {
      out.at<float>(j)=(float)lowData.at<unsigned char>(x,y);
      j++;
    }
  }
  return out;
}
```

OCR classification

In the classification step, we use an Artificial Neural Network machine-learning algorithm. More specifically, a **Multi-Layer Perceptron (MLP)**, which is the most commonly used ANN algorithm.

MLP consists of a network of neurons with an input layer, output layer, and one or more hidden layers. Each layer has one or more neurons connected with the previous and next layer.

The following example represents a 3-layer perceptron (it is a binary classifier that maps a real-valued vector input to a single binary value output) with three inputs, two outputs, and the hidden layer including five neurons:

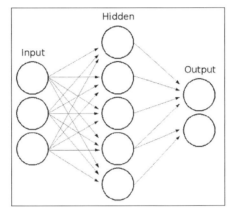

All neurons in an MLP are similar and each one has several inputs (the previous linked neurons) and several output links with the same value (the next linked neurons). Each neuron calculates the output value as a sum of the weighted inputs plus a bias term and is transformed by a selected activation function:

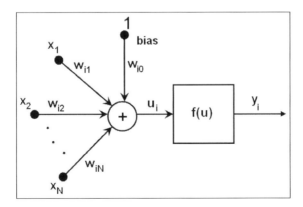

There are three widely used activation functions: Identity, Sigmoid, and Gaussian; the most common and default activation function is the Sigmoid function. It has an alpha and beta value set to 1:

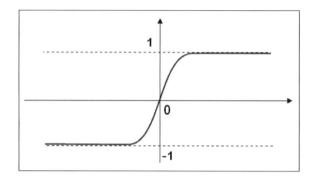

An ANN-trained network has a vector of input with features. It passes the values to the hidden layer and computes the results with the weights and activation function. It passes outputs further downstream until it gets the output layer that has the number of neuron classes.

The weight of each layer, synapses, and neuron is computed and learned by training the ANN algorithm. To train our classifier, we create two matrices of data as we did in the SVM training, but the training labels are a bit different. Instead of an $N \times 1$ matrix where N stands for training data rows and 1 is the column, we use the label number identifier. We have to create an $N \times M$ matrix where N is the training/samples data and M is the classes (10 digits + 20 letters in our case), and set 1 in a position (i, j) if the data row i is classified with class j.

$$
\begin{vmatrix}
1 & 0 & 0 & \cdots & 0 & 0 \\
1 & 0 & 0 & \cdots & 0 & 0 \\
0 & 1 & 0 & \cdots & 0 & 0 \\
0 & 1 & 0 & \cdots & 0 & 0 \\
0 & 1 & 0 & \cdots & 0 & 0 \\
\cdots & \cdots & \cdots & \cdots & \cdots & \cdots \\
0 & 0 & 0 & \cdots & 0 & 1 \\
0 & 0 & 0 & \cdots & 0 & 1 \\
0 & 0 & 0 & \cdots & 0 & 1
\end{vmatrix}
$$

We create an `OCR::train` function to create all the needed matrices and train our system, with the training data matrix, classes matrix, and the number of hidden neurons in the hidden layers. The training data is loaded from an XML file just as we did for the SVM training.

We have to define the number of neurons in each layer to initialize the ANN class. For our sample, we only use one hidden layer, then we define a matrix of 1 row and 3 columns. The first column position is the number of features, the second column position is the number of hidden neurons in the hidden layer, and the third column position is the number of classes.

OpenCV defines a `CvANN_MLP` class for ANN. With the `create` function, we can initiate the class by defining the number of layers and neurons, the activation function, and the `alpha` and `beta` parameters:

```
void OCR::train(Mat TrainData, Mat classes, int nlayers)
{
  Mat layerSizes(1,3,CV_32SC1);
  layerSizes.at<int>(0)= TrainData.cols;
  layerSizes.at<int>(1)= nlayers;
  layerSizes.at<int>(2)= numCharacters;
  ann.create(layerSizes, CvANN_MLP::SIGMOID_SYM, 1, 1); //ann is
  global class variable

  //Prepare trainClasses
  //Create a mat with n trained data by m classes
  Mat trainClasses;
  trainClasses.create( TrainData.rows, numCharacters, CV_32FC1 );
  for( int i = 0; i <  trainClasses.rows; i++ )
  {
    for( int k = 0; k < trainClasses.cols; k++ )
    {
    //If class of data i is same than a k class
    if( k == classes.at<int>(i) )
    trainClasses.at<float>(i,k) = 1;
    else
    trainClasses.at<float>(i,k) = 0;
    }
  }
  Mat weights( 1, TrainData.rows, CV_32FC1, Scalar::all(1) );

  //Learn classifier
  ann.train( TrainData, trainClasses, weights );
  trained=true;
}
```

After training, we can classify any segmented plate feature using the
`OCR::classify` function:

```
int OCR::classify(Mat f)
{
  int result=-1;
  Mat output(1, numCharacters, CV_32FC1);
  ann.predict(f, output);
  Point maxLoc;
  double maxVal;
  minMaxLoc(output, 0, &maxVal, 0, &maxLoc);
  //We need to know where in output is the max val, the x (cols) is
  //the class.

  return maxLoc.x;
}
```

The CvANN_MLP class uses the `predict` function for classifying a feature vector in a
class. Unlike the SVM `classify` function, the ANN's `predict` function returns a row
with the size equal to the number of classes with the probability of belonging to the
input feature of each class.

To get the best result, we can use the `minMaxLoc` function to get the maximum and
minimum response and the position in the matrix. The class of our character is
specified by the x position of a higher value:

To finish each plate detected, we order its characters and return a string using the
`str()` function of the `Plate` class and we can draw it on the original image:

```
string licensePlate=plate.str();
rectangle(input_image, plate.position, Scalar(0,0,200));
putText(input_image, licensePlate, Point(plate.position.x, plate.
position.y), CV_FONT_HERSHEY_SIMPLEX, 1, Scalar(0,0,200),2);
```

Evaluation

Our project is finished, but when we train a machine-learning algorithm like OCR for example, we need to know the best features and parameters to use and how to correct the classification, recognition, and detection errors in our system.

We need to evaluate our system with different situations and parameters, and evaluate the errors produced, and get the best parameters that minimize those errors.

In this chapter, we evaluated the OCR task with the following variables: the size of low-level resolution image features and the number of hidden neurons in the hidden layer.

We have created the `evalOCR.cpp` application where we use the XML training data file generated by the `trainOCR.cpp` application. The `OCR.xml` file contains the training data matrix for 5 x 5, 10 x10, 15 x 15, and 20 x 20 downsampled image features.

```
Mat classes;
Mat trainingData;
//Read file storage.
FileStorage fs;
fs.open("OCR.xml", FileStorage::READ);
fs[data] >> trainingData;
fs["classes"] >> classes;
```

The evaluation application gets each downsampled matrix feature and gets 100 random rows for training, as well as other rows for testing the ANN algorithm and checking the error.

Before training the system, we test each random sample and check if the response is correct. If the response is not correct, we increment the error-counter variable and then divide by the number of samples to evaluate. This indicates the error ratio between 0 and 1 for training with random data:

```
float test(Mat samples, Mat classes)
{
  float errors=0;
  for(int i=0; i<samples.rows; i++)
  {
    int result= ocr.classify(samples.row(i));
    if(result!= classes.at<int>(i))
    errors++;
  }
  return errors/samples.rows;
}
```

The application returns the output command-line error ratio for each sample size. For a good evaluation, we need to train the application with different random training rows; this produces different test error values, then we can add up all errors and make an average. To do this task, we create the following bash Unix script to automate it:

```bash
#!/bin/bash
echo "#ITS \t 5 \t 10 \t 15 \t 20" > data.txt
folder=$(pwd)

for numNeurons in 10 20 30 40 50 60 70 80 90 100 120 150 200 500
do
  s5=0;
  s10=0;
  s15=0;
  s20=0;
  for j  in {1..100}
  do
    echo $numNeurons $j
    a=$($folder/build/evalOCR $numNeurons TrainingDataF5)
    s5=$(echo "scale=4; $s5+$a" | bc -q 2>/dev/null)

    a=$($folder/build/evalOCR $numNeurons TrainingDataF10)
    s10=$(echo "scale=4; $s10+$a" | bc -q 2>/dev/null)

    a=$($folder/build/evalOCR $numNeurons TrainingDataF15)
    s15=$(echo "scale=4; $s15+$a" | bc -q 2>/dev/null)

    a=$($folder/build/evalOCR $numNeurons TrainingDataF20)
    s20=$(echo "scale=4; $s20+$a" | bc -q 2>/dev/null)
  done

  echo "$i \t $s5 \t $s10 \t $s15 \t $s20"
  echo "$i \t $s5 \t $s10 \t $s15 \t $s20" >> data.txt
done
```

This script saves a `data.txt` file that contains all results for each size and neuron-hidden layer number. This file can be used for plotting with gnuplot. We can see the result in the following figure:

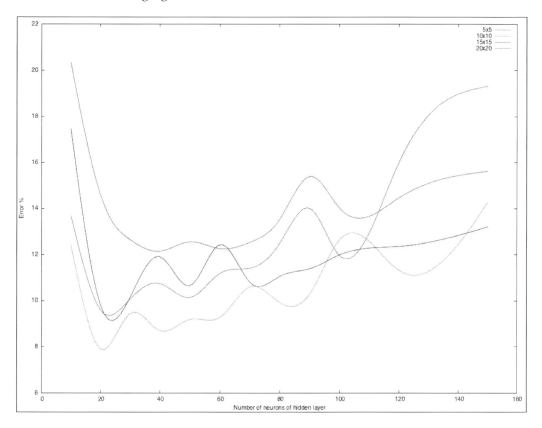

We can see that the lowest error is under 8 percent and is using 20 neurons in a hidden layer and characters' features extracted from a downscaled 10 x 10 image patch.

Summary

In this chapter, we learned how an Automatic License Plate Recognition program works, and its two important steps: plate localization and plate recognition.

In the first step we learned how to segment an image looking for patches where we can have a plate, and how to use a simple heuristics and Support Vector Machine algorithm to make a binary classification for patches with plates and no plates.

In the second step we learned how to segment with the Find Contours algorithm, extract feature vector from each character, and use an Artificial Neural Network to classify each feature in a character class.

We also learned how to evaluate a machine algorithm with training using random samples and evaluate it using different parameters and features.

6
Non-rigid Face Tracking

Non-rigid face tracking, which is the estimation of a quasi-dense set of facial features in each frame of a video stream, is a difficult problem for which modern approaches borrow ideas from a number of related fields, including computer vision, computational geometry, machine learning, and image processing. Non-rigidity here refers to the fact that relative distances between facial features vary between facial expression and across the population, and is distinct from face detection and tracking, which aims only to find the location of the face in each frame, rather than the configuration of facial features. Non-rigid face tracking is a popular research topic that has been pursued for over two decades, but it is only recently that various approaches have become robust enough, and processors fast enough, which makes the building of commercial applications possible.

Although commercial-grade face tracking can be highly sophisticated and pose a challenge even for experienced computer vision scientists, in this chapter we will see that a face tracker that performs reasonably well under constrained settings can be devised using modest mathematical tools and OpenCV's substantial functionality in linear algebra, image processing, and visualization. This is particularly the case when the person to be tracked is known ahead of time, and training data in the form of images and landmark annotations are available. The techniques described henceforth will act as a useful starting point and a guide for further pursuits towards a more elaborate face-tracking system.

An outline of this chapter is as follows:

- **Overview**: This section covers a brief history of face tracking.
- **Utilities**: This section outlines the common structures and conventions used in this chapter. It includes the object-oriented design, data storage and representation, and a tool for data collection and annotation.

- **Geometrical constraints**: This section describes how facial geometry and its variations are learned from the training data and utilized during tracking to constrain the solution. This includes modeling the face as a linear shape model and how global transformations can be integrated into its representation.

- **Facial feature detectors**: This section describes how to learn the appearance of facial features in order to detect them in an image where the face is to be tracked.

- **Face detection and initialization**: This section describes how to use face detection to initialize the tracking process.

- **Face tracking**: This section combines all components described previously into a tracking system through the process of image alignment. A discussion on the settings in which the system can be expected to work best is also carried out.

The following block diagram illustrates the relationships between the various components of the system:

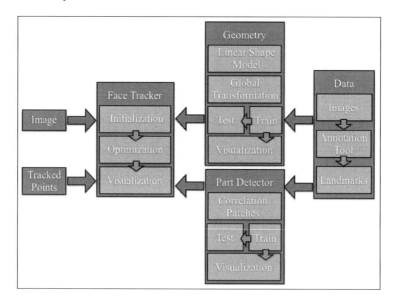

 Note that all methods employed in this chapter follow a data-driven paradigm whereby all models used are learned from data rather than being designed by hand in a rule-based setting. As such, each component of the system will involve two components: training and testing. Training builds the models from data and testing employs these models on new unseen data.

Overview

Non-rigid face tracking was first popularized in the early to mid 90s with the advent of **active shape models (ASM)** by Cootes and Taylor. Since then, a tremendous amount of research has been dedicated to solving the difficult problem of generic face tracking with many improvements over the original method that ASM proposed. The first milestone was the extension of ASM to **active appearance models (AAM)** in 2001, also by Cootes and Taylor. This approach was later formalized though the principled treatment of image warps by Baker and colleges in the the mid 2000s. Another strand of work along these lines was the **3D Morphable Model (3DMM)** by Blanz and Vetter, which like AAM, not only modeled image textures as opposed to profiles along object boundaries as in ASM, but took it one step further by representing the models with a highly dense 3D data learned from laser scans of faces. From the mid to the late 2000s, the focus of research on face tracking shifted away from how the face was parameterized to how the objective of the tracking algorithm was posed and optimized. Various techniques from the machine-learning community were applied with various degrees of success. Since the turn of the century, the focus has shifted once again, this time towards joint parameter and objective design strategies that guarantee global solutions.

Despite the continued intense research into face tracking, there have been relatively few commercial applications that use it. There has also been a lag in uptake by hobbyists and enthusiasts, despite there being a number of freely available source-code packages for a number of common approaches. Nonetheless, in the past two years there has been a renewed interest in the public domain for the potential use of face tracking and commercial-grade products are beginning to emerge.

Utilities

Before diving into the intricacies of face tracking, a number of book-keeping tasks and conventions common to all face-tracking methods must first be introduced. The rest of this section will deal with these issues. An interested reader may want to skip this section at the first reading and go straight to the section on geometrical constraints.

Object-oriented design

As with face detection and recognition, programmatically, face tracking consists of two components: data and algorithms. The algorithms typically perform some kind of operation on the incoming (that is, online) data by referencing prestored (that is, offline) data as a guide. As such, an object-oriented design that couples algorithms with the data they rely on is a convenient design choice.

In OpenCV v2.x, a convenient XML/YAML file storage class was introduced that greatly simplifies the task of organizing offline data for use in the algorithms. To leverage this feature, all classes described in this chapter will implement read-and write-serialization functions. An example of this is shown as follows for an imaginary class `foo`:

```
#include <opencv2/opencv.hpp>
using namespace cv;
class foo{
    public:
        Mat a;
        type_b b;
        void write(FileStorage &fs) const{
            assert(fs.isOpened());
            fs << "{" << "a"  << a << "b"  << b << "}";
        }
        void read(const FileNode& node){
            assert(node.type() == FileNode::MAP);
            node["a"] >> a; node["b"] >> b;
        }
};
```

Here, `Mat` is OpenCV's matrix class and `type_b` is an (imaginary) user-defined class that also has the serialization functionality defined. The I/O functions `read` and `write` implement the serialization. The `FileStorage` class supports two types of data structures that can be serialized. For simplicity, in this chapter all classes will only utilize mappings, where each stored variable creates a `FileNode` object of type `FileNode::MAP`. This requires a unique key to be assigned to each element. Although the choice for this key is arbitrary, we will use the variable name as the label for consistency reasons. As illustrated in the preceding code snippet, the `read` and `write` functions take on a particularly simple form, whereby the streaming operators (`<<` and `>>`) are used to insert and extract data to the `FileStorage` object. Most OpenCV classes have implementations of the `read` and `write` functions, allowing the storage of the data that they contain to be done with ease.

In addition to defining the serialization functions, one must also define two additional functions for the serialization in the `FileStorage` class to work, as follows:

```
void write(FileStorage& fs, const string&, const foo& x){
  x.write(fs);
}
void read(const FileNode& node, foo& x,const foo& default){
  if(node.empty())x = d; else x.read(node);
}
```

As the functionality of these two functions remains the same for all classes we describe in this section, they are templated and defined in the `ft.hpp` header file found in the source code pertaining to this chapter. Finally, to easily save and load user-defined classes that utilize the serialization functionality, templated functions for these are also implemented in the header file as follows:

```
template <class T>
T load_ft(const char* fname){
  T x; FileStorage f(fname,FileStorage::READ);
  f["ft object"] >> x; f.release(); return x;
}
template<class T>
void save_ft(const char* fname,const T& x){
  FileStorage f(fname,FileStorage::WRITE);
  f << "ft object" << x; f.release();
}
```

Note that the label associated with the object is always the same (that is, `ft object`). With these functions defined, saving and loading object data is a painless process. This is shown with the help of the following example:

```
#include "opencv_hotshots/ft/ft.hpp"
#include "foo.hpp"
int main(){
  ...
  foo A; save_ft<foo>("foo.xml",A);
  ...
  foo B = load_ft<foo>("foo.xml");
  ...
}
```

Note that the `.xml` extension results in an XML-formatted data file. For any other extension it defaults to the (more human readable) YAML format.

Data collection: Image and video annotation

Modern face tracking techniques are almost entirely data driven, that is, the algorithms used to detect the locations of facial features in the image rely on models of the appearance of the facial features and the geometrical dependencies between their relative locations from a set of examples. The larger the set of examples, the more robust the algorithms behave, as they become more aware of the gamut of variability that faces can exhibit. Thus, the first step in building a face tracking algorithm is to create an image/video annotation tool, where the user can specify the locations of the desired facial features in each example image.

Training data types

The data for training face tracking algorithms generally consists of four components:

- **Images**: This component is a collection of images (still images or video frames) that contain an entire face. For best results, this collection should be specialized to the types of conditions (that is, identity, lighting, distance from camera, capturing device, among others) in which the tracker is later deployed. It is also crucial that the faces in the collection exhibit the range of head poses and facial expressions that the intended application expects.

- **Annotations**: This component has ordered hand-labeled locations in each image that correspond to every facial feature to be tracked. More facial features often lead to a more robust tracker as the tracking algorithm can use their measurements to reinforce each other. The computational cost of common tracking algorithms typically scales linearly with the number of facial features.

- **Symmetry indices**: This component has an index for each facial feature point that defines its bilaterally symmetrical feature. This can be used to mirror the training images, effectively doubling the training set size and symmetrizing the data along the y axis.

- **Connectivity indices**: This component has a set of index pairs of the annotations that define the semantic interpretation of the facial features. These connections are useful for visualizing the tracking results.

A visualization of these four components is shown in the following image, where from left to right we have the raw image, facial feature annotations, color-coded bilateral symmetry points, mirrored image, and annotations and facial feature connectivity.

To conveniently manage such data, a class that implements storage and access functionality is a useful component. The CvMLData class in the ml module of OpenCV has the functionality for handling general data often used in machine-learning problems. However, it lacks the functionality required from the face-tracking data. As such, in this chapter we will use the ft_data class, declared in the ft_data.hpp header file, which is designed specifically with the peculiarity of face-tracking data in mind. All data elements are defined as public members of the class, as follows:

```
class ft_data{
public:
  vector<int> symmetry;
  vector<Vec2i> connections;
  vector<string> imnames;
  vector<vector<Point2f> > points;
  ...
}
```

The Vec2i and Point2f types are OpenCV classes for vectors of two integers and 2D floating-point coordinates respectively. The symmetry vector has as many components as there are feature points on the face (as defined by the user). Each of the connections define a zero-based index pair of connected facial features. As the training set can potentially be very large, rather than storing the images directly, the class stores the filenames of each image in the imnames member variable (note that this requires the images to be located in the same relative path for the filenames to remain valid). Finally, for each training image, a collection of facial feature locations are stored as vectors of floating-point coordinates in the points member variable.

The ft_data class implements a number of convenience methods for accessing the data. To access an image in the dataset, the get_image function loads the image at the specified index, idx, and optionally mirrors it around the y axis as follows:

```
Mat
ft_data::get_image(
const int idx,    //index of image to load from file
const int flag){ //0=gray,1=gray+flip,2=rgb,3=rgb+flip
  if((idx < 0) || (idx >= (int)imnames.size()))return Mat();
  Mat img,im;
  if(flag < 2)img = imread(imnames[idx],0);
  else        img = imread(imnames[idx],1);
  if(flag % 2 != 0)flip(img,im,1); else im = img;
  return im;
}
```

The $(0,1)$ flag passed to OpenCV's `imread` function specifies whether the image is loaded as a 3-channel color image or as a single-channel grayscale image. The flag passed to OpenCV's `flip` function specifies mirroring around the y axis.

To access a point set corresponding to an image at a particular index, the `get_points` function returns a vector of floating-point coordinates with the option of mirroring their indices as follows:

```
vector<Point2f>
ft_data::get_points(
const int idx,          //index of image corresponding to points
const bool flipped){ //is the image flipped around the y-axis?
  if((idx < 0) || (idx >= (int)imnames.size()))
    return vector<Point2f>();
  vector<Point2f> p = points[idx];
  if(flipped){
    Mat im = this->get_image(idx,0); int n = p.size();
    vector<Point2f> q(n);
    for(int i = 0; i < n; i++){
      q[i].x = im.cols-1-p[symmetry[i]].x;
      q[i].y = p[symmetry[i]].y;
    }return q;
  }else return p;
}
```

Notice that when the mirroring flag is specified, this function calls the `get_image` function. This is required to determine the width of the image in order to correctly mirror the facial feature coordinates. A more efficient method could be devised by simply passing the image width as a variable. Finally, the utility of the `symmetry` member variable is illustrated in this function. The mirrored feature location of a particular index is simply the feature location at the index specified in the `symmetry` variable with its x coordinate flipped and biased.

Both the `get_image` and `get_points` functions return empty structures if the specified index is outside the one that exists for the dataset. It is also possible that not all images in the collection are annotated. Face tracking algorithms can be designed to handle missing data, however, these implementations are often quite involved and are outside the scope of this chapter. The `ft_data` class implements a function for removing samples from its collection that do not have corresponding annotations, as follows:

```
void
ft_data::rm_incomplete_samples(){
  int n = points[0].size(),N = points.size();
  for(int i = 1; i < N; i++)n = max(n,int(points[i].size()));
  for(int i = 0; i < int(points.size()); i++){
```

```
      if(int(points[i].size()) != n){
        points.erase(points.begin()+i);
         imnames.erase(imnames.begin()+i); i--;
      }else{
        int j = 0;
        for(; j < n; j++){
         if((points[i][j].x <= 0) ||
           (points[i][j].y <= 0))break;
        }
        if(j < n){
        points.erase(points.begin()+i);
        imnames.erase(imnames.begin()+i); i--;
        }
      }
    }
  }
}
```

The sample instance that has the most number of annotations is assumed to be the canonical sample. All data instances that have a point set with less than that many number of points are removed from the collection using the vector's `erase` function. Also notice that points with (x, y) coordinates less than one are considered missing in their corresponding image (possibly due to occlusion, poor visibility, or ambiguity).

The `ft_data` class implements the serialization functions `read` and `write`, and can thus be stored and loaded easily. For example, saving a dataset can be done as simply as:

```
ft_data D;                              //instantiate data structure
...                                     //populate data
save_ft<ft_data>("mydata.xml",D); //save data
```

For visualizing the dataset, `ft_data` implements a number of drawing functions. Their use is illustrated in the `visualize_annotations.cpp` file. This simple program loads annotation data stored in the file specified in the command line, removes the incomplete samples, and displays the training images with their corresponding annotations, symmetry, and connections superimposed. A few notable features of OpenCV's `highgui` module are demonstrated here. Although quite rudimentary and not well suited for complex user interfaces, the functionality in OpenCV's `highgui` module is extremely useful for loading and visualizing data and algorithmic outputs in computer vision applications. This is perhaps one of OpenCV's distinguishing qualities compared to other computer vision libraries.

Annotation tool

To aid in generating annotations for use with the code in this chapter, a rudimentary annotation tool can be found in the `annotate.cpp` file. The tool takes as input a video stream, either from a file or from the camera. The procedure for using the tool is listed in the following four steps:

1. **Capture images**: In this first step, the image stream is displayed on the screen and the user chooses the images to annotate by pressing the *S* key. The best set of features to annotate are those that maximally span the range of facial behaviors that the face tracking system will be required to track.

2. **Annotate first image**: In this second step, the user is presented with the first image selected in the previous stage. The user then proceeds to click on the image at the locations pertaining to the facial features that require tracking.

3. **Annotate connectivity**: In this third step, to better visualize a shape, the connectivity structure of points needs to be defined. Here, the user is presented with the same image as in the previous stage, where the task now is to click a set of point pairs, one after the other, to build the connectivity structure for the face model.

4. **Annotate symmetry**: In this step, still with the same image, the user selects pairs of points that exhibit bilateral symmetry.

5. **Annotate remaining images**: In this final step, the procedure here is similar to that of step 2, except that the user can browse through the set of images and annotate them asynchronously.

An interested reader may want to improve on this tool by improving its usability or may even integrate an incremental learning procedure, whereby a tracking model is updated after each additional image is annotated and is subsequently used to initialize the points to reduce the burden of annotation.

Although some publicly available datasets are available for use with the code developed in this chapter (see for example the description in the following section), the annotation tool can be used to build person-specific face tracking models, which often perform far better than their generic, person-independent, counterparts.

Pre-annotated data (The MUCT dataset)

One of the hindering factors of developing face tracking systems is the tedious and error-prone process of manually annotating a large collection of images, each with a large number of points. To ease this process for the purpose of following the work in this chapter, the publicly available MUCT dataset can be downloaded from: `http://www/milbo.org/muct`.

The dataset consists of 3,755 face images annotated with 76-point landmarks. The subjects in the dataset vary in age and ethnicity and are captured under a number of different lighting conditions and head poses.

To use the MUCT dataset with the code in this chapter, perform the following steps:

1. **Download the image set**: In this step, all the images in the dataset can be obtained by downloading the files `muct-a-jpg-v1.tar.gz` to `muct-e-jpg-v1.tar.gz` and uncompressing them. This will generate a new folder in which all the images will be stored.

2. **Download the annotations**: In this step, download the file containing the annotations `muct-landmarks-v1.tar.gz`. Save and uncompress this file in the same folder as the one in which the images were downloaded.

3. **Define connections and symmetry using the annotation tool**: In this step, from the command line, issue the command `./annotate -m $mdir -d $odir`, where `$mdir` denotes the folder where the MUCT dataset was saved and `$odir` denotes the folder to which the `annotations.yaml` file, containing the data stored as a `ft_data` object will be written.

 Usage of the MUCT dataset is encouraged to get a quick introduction to the functionality of the face tracking code described in this chapter.

Geometrical constraints

In face tracking, geometry refers to the spatial configuration of a predefined set of points that correspond to physically consistent locations on the human face (such as eye corners, nose tip, and eyebrow edges). A particular choice of these points is application dependent, with some applications requiring a dense set of over 100 points and others requiring only a sparser selection. However, robustness of face tracking algorithms generally improves with an increased number of points, as their separate measurements can reinforce each other through their relative spatial dependencies. For example, knowing the location of an eye corner is a good indication of where to expect the nose to be located. However, there are limits to improvements in robustness gained by increasing the number of points, where performance typically plateaus after around 100 points. Furthermore, increasing the point set used to describe a face carries with it a linear increase in computational complexity. Thus, applications with strict constraints on computational load may fare better with fewer points.

It is also the case that faster tracking often leads to more accurate tracking in the online setting. This is because, when frames are dropped, the perceived motion between frames increases, and the optimization algorithm used to find the configuration of the face in each frame has to search a larger space of possible configurations of feature points; a process that often fails when displacement between frames becomes too large. In summary, although there are general guidelines on how to best design the selection of facial feature points, to get an optimal performance, this selection should be specialized to the application's domain.

Facial geometry is often parameterized as a composition of two elements: a global (rigid) transformation and a local (non-rigid) deformation. The global transformation accounts for the overall placement of the face in the image, which is often allowed to vary without constraint (that is, the face can appear anywhere in the image). This includes the (x, y) location of the face in the image, the in-plane head rotation, and the size of the face in the image. Local deformations, on the other hand, account for differences between facial shapes across identities and between expressions. In contrast to the global transformation, these local deformations are often far more constrained largely due to the highly structured configuration of facial features. Global transformations are generic functions of 2D coordinates, applicable to any type of object, whereas local deformations are object specific and must be learned from a training dataset.

In this section we will describe the construction of a geometrical model of a facial structure, hereby referred to as the shape model. Depending on the application, it can capture expression variations of a single individual, differences between facial shapes across a population, or a combination of both. This model is implemented in the `shape_model` class that can be found in the `shape_model.hpp` and `shape_model.cpp` files. The following code snippet is a part of the header of the `shape_model` class that highlights its primary functionality:

```
class shape_model{ //2d linear shape model
public:
  Mat p; //parameter vector (kx1) CV_32F
  Mat V; //linear subspace (2nxk) CV_32F
  Mat e; //parameter variance (kx1) CV_32F
  Mat C; //connectivity (cx2) CV_32S
  ...
  void calc_params(
  const vector<Point2f> &pts,  //points to compute parameters
```

```
const Mat &weight = Mat(),      //weight/point (nx1) CV_32F
const float c_factor = 3.0); //clamping factor
...
vector<Point2f>                 //shape described by parameters
calc_shape();
...
void train(
const vector<vector<Point2f> > &p, //N-example shapes
const vector<Vec2i> &con = vector<Vec2i>(),//connectivity
const float frac = 0.95, //fraction of variation to retain
const int kmax = 10);   //maximum number of modes to retain
...
}
```

The model that represents variations in face shapes is encoded in the subspace matrix V and variance vector e. The parameter vector p stores the encoding of a shape with respect to the model. The connectivity matrix C is also stored in this class as it pertains only to visualizing instances of the face's shape. The three functions of primary interest in this class are calc_params, calc_shape, and train. The calc_params function projects a set of points onto the space of plausible face shapes. It optionally provides separate confidence weights for each of the points to be projected. The calc_shape function generates a set of points by decoding the parameter vector p using the face model (encoded by V and e). The train function learns the encoding model from a dataset of face shapes, each of which consists of the same number of points. The parameters frac and kmax are parameters of the training procedure that can be specialized for the data at hand.

The functionality of this class will be elaborated in the sections that follow, where we begin by describing **Procrustes analysis**, a method for rigidly registering a point set, followed by the linear model used to represent local deformations. The programs in the train_shape_model.cpp and visualize_shape_model.cpp files train and visualize the shape model respectively. Their usage will be outlined at the end of this section.

Procrustes analysis

In order to build a deformation model of face shapes, we must first process the raw annotated data to remove components pertaining to global rigid motion. When modeling geometry in 2D, a rigid motion is often represented as a similarity transform; this includes the scale, in-plane rotation and translation. The following image illustrates the set of permissible motion types under a similarity transform. The process of removing global rigid motion from a collection of points is called Procrustes analysis.

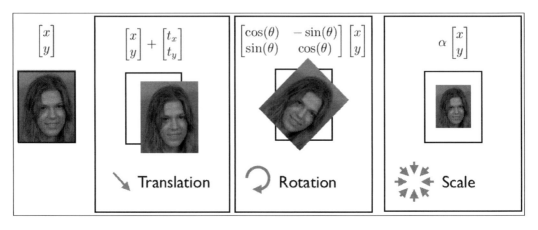

Mathematically, the objective of Procrustes analysis is to simultaneously find a canonical shape and similarity transform each data instance that brings them into alignment with the canonical shape. Here, alignment is measured as the least-squares distance between each transformed shape with the canonical shape. An iterative procedure for fulfilling this objective is implemented in the `shape_model` class as follows:

```
#define fl at<float>
Mat shape_model::procrustes(
const Mat &X,          //interleaved raw shape data as columns
const int itol,        //maximum number of iterations to try
const float ftol)      //convergence tolerance
{
  int N = X.cols,n = X.rows/2; Mat Co,P = X.clone();//copy
  for(int i = 0; i < N; i++){
    Mat p = P.col(i);              //i'th shape
    float mx = 0,my = 0;           //compute centre of mass...
    for(int j = 0; j < n; j++){    //for x and y separately
      mx += p.fl(2*j); my += p.fl(2*j+1);
    }
    mx /= n; my /= n;
```

```
      for(int j = 0; j < n; j++){ //remove center of mass
        p.fl(2*j) -= mx; p.fl(2*j+1) -= my;
      }
    }
    for(int iter = 0; iter < itol; iter++){
      Mat C = P*Mat::ones(N,1,CV_32F)/N; //compute normalized...
      normalize(C,C);                      //canonical shape
      if(iter > 0){if(norm(C,Co) < ftol)break;} //converged?
      Co = C.clone();                //remember current estimate
      for(int i = 0; i < N; i++){
        Mat R = this->rot_scale_align(P.col(i),C);
        for(int j = 0; j < n; j++){ //apply similarity transform
          float x = P.fl(2*j,i),y = P.fl(2*j+1,i);
          P.fl(2*j  ,i) = R.fl(0,0)*x + R.fl(0,1)*y;
          P.fl(2*j+1,i) = R.fl(1,0)*x + R.fl(1,1)*y;
        }
      }
    }return P; //returned procrustes aligned shapes
  }
```

The algorithm begins by subtracting the center of mass of each shape's instance followed by an iterative procedure that alternates between computing the canonical shape, as the normalized average of all shapes, and rotating and scaling each shape to best match the canonical shape. The normalization step of the estimated canonical shape is necessary to fix the scale of the problem and prevent it from shrinking all the shapes to zero. The choice of this anchor scale is arbitrary, here we have chosen to enforce the length of the canonical shape vector c to 1.0, as is the default behavior of OpenCV's `normalize` function. Computing the in-plane rotation and scaling that best aligns each shape's instance to the current estimate of the canonical shape is effected through the `rot_scale_align` function as follows:

```
Mat shape_model::rot_scale_align(
const Mat &src, //[x1;y1;...;xn;yn] vector of source shape
const Mat &dst) //destination shape
{
  //construct linear system
  int n = src.rows/2; float a=0,b=0,d=0;
  for(int i = 0; i < n; i++){
    d+= src.fl(2*i)*src.fl(2*i  )+src.fl(2*i+1)*src.fl(2*i+1);
    a+= src.fl(2*i)*dst.fl(2*i  )+src.fl(2*i+1)*dst.fl(2*i+1);
    b+= src.fl(2*i)*dst.fl(2*i+1)-src.fl(2*i+1)*dst.fl(2*i  );
  }
  a /= d; b /= d;//solve linear system
  return (Mat_<float>(2,2) << a,-b,b,a);
}
```

This function minimizes the following least-squares difference between the rotated and canonical shapes. Mathematically this can be written as:

$$\min_{a,b} \sum_{i=1}^{n} \left\| \begin{bmatrix} a & -b \\ b & a \end{bmatrix} \begin{bmatrix} x_i \\ y_i \end{bmatrix} - \begin{bmatrix} c_x \\ c_y \end{bmatrix} \right\|^2 \rightarrow \begin{bmatrix} a \\ b \end{bmatrix} = \frac{1}{\sum_i (x_i^2 + y_i^2)} \sum_{i=1}^{n} \begin{bmatrix} x_i c_x + y_i c_y \\ x_i c_y - y_i c_x \end{bmatrix}$$

Here the solution to the least-squares problem takes on the closed-form solution shown in the following image on the right-hand side of the equation. Note that rather than solving for the scaling and in-plane rotation, which are nonlinearly related in the scaled 2D rotation matrix, we solve for the variables (a, b). These variables are related to the scale and rotation matrix as follows:

$$\begin{bmatrix} a & -b \\ b & a \end{bmatrix} = \begin{bmatrix} k\cos(\theta) & -k\sin(\theta) \\ k\sin(\theta) & k\cos(\theta) \end{bmatrix}$$

A visualization of the effects of Procrustes analysis on raw annotated shape data is illustrated in the following image . Each facial feature is displayed with a unique color. After translation normalization, the structure of the face becomes apparent, where the locations of facial features cluster around their average locations. After the iterative scale and rotation normalization procedure, the feature clustering becomes more compact and their distribution becomes more representative of the variation induced by facial deformation. This last point is important as it is these deformations that we will attempt to model in the following section. Thus, the role of Procrustes analysis can be thought of as a preprocessing operation on the raw data that will allow better local deformation models of the face to be learned.

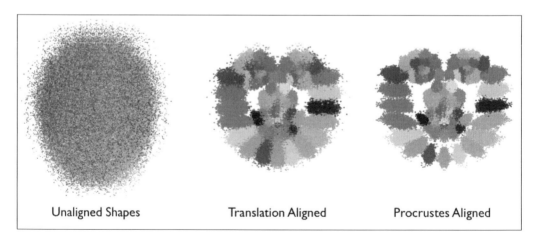

Unaligned Shapes   Translation Aligned   Procrustes Aligned

Linear shape models

The aim of facial-deformation modeling is to find a compact parametric representation of how the face's shape varies across identities and between expressions. There are many ways of achieving this goal with various levels of complexity. The simplest of these is to use a linear representation of facial geometry. Despite its simplicity, it has been shown to accurately capture the space of facial deformations, particularly when the faces in the dataset are largely in a frontal pose. It also has the advantage that inferring the parameters of its representation is an extremely simple and cheap operation, in contrast to its nonlinear counterparts. This plays an important role when deploying it to constrain the search procedure during tracking.

The main idea of linearly modeling facial shapes is illustrated in the following image. Here, a face shape, which consists of N facial features, is modeled as a single point in a $2N$-dimensional space. The aim of linear modeling is to find a low-dimensional hyperplane embedded within this $2N$-dimensional space in which all the face shape points lie (that is, the green points in the image). As this hyperplane spans only a subset of the entire $2N$-dimensional space it is often referred to as the subspace. The lower the dimensionality of the subspace the more compact the representation of the face is and the stronger the constraint that it places on the tracking procedure becomes. This often leads to more robust tracking. However, care should be taken in selecting the subspace's dimension so that it has enough capacity to span the space of all faces but not so much that non-face shapes lie within its span (that is, the red points in the image). It should be noted that when modeling data from a single person, the subspace that captures the face's variability is often far more compact than the one that models multiple identities. This is one of the reasons why person-specific trackers perform much better than generic ones.

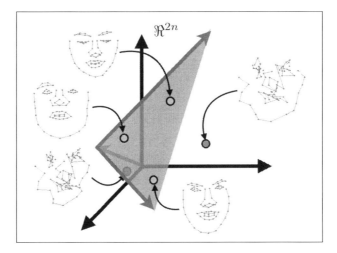

The procedure for finding the best low-dimensional subspace that spans a dataset is called **Principal Component Analysis (PCA)**. OpenCV implements a class for computing PCA, however, it requires the number of preserved subspace dimensions to be prespecified. As this is often difficult to determine a priori, a common heuristic is to choose it based on the fraction of the total amount of variation it accounts for. In the shape_model::train function, PCA is implemented as follows:

```
SVD svd(dY*dY.t());
int m = min(min(kmax,N-1),n-1);
float vsum = 0; for(int i = 0; i < m; i++)vsum += svd.w.fl(i);
float v = 0; int k = 0;
for(k = 0; k < m; k++){
  v += svd.w.fl(k); if(v/vsum >= frac){k++; break;}
}
if(k > m)k = m;
Mat D = svd.u(Rect(0,0,k,2*n));
```

Here, each column of the dY variable denotes the mean-subtracted Procrustes-aligned shape. Thus, **singular value decomposition (SVD)** is effectively applied to the covariance matrix of the shape data (that is, dY.t()*dY). The w member of OpenCV's SVD class stores the variance in the major directions of variability of the data, ordered from largest to smallest. A common approach to choose the dimensionality of the subspace is to choose the smallest set of directions that preserve a fraction frac of the total energy of the data, which is represented by the entries of svd.w. As these entries are ordered from largest to smallest, it suffices to enumerate the subspace selection by greedily evaluating the energy in the top k directions of variability. The directions themselves are stored in the u member of the SVD class. The svd.w and svd.u components are generally referred to as the eigenspectrum and eigenvectors respectively. A visualization of these two components are shown in the following figure:

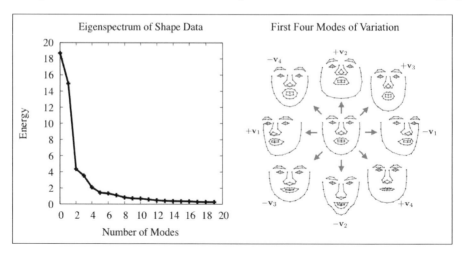

Notice that the eigenspectrum decreases rapidly, which suggests that most of the variation contained in the data can be modeled with a low-dimensional subspace.

A combined local-global representation

A shape in the image frame is generated by the composition of a local deformation and a global transformation. Mathematically, this parameterization can be problematic, as the composition of these transformations results in a nonlinear function that does not admit a closed-form solution. A common way to circumvent this problem is to model the global transformation as a linear subspace and append it to the deformation subspace. For a fixed shape, a similarity transform can be modeled with a subspace as follows:

$$\begin{bmatrix} \begin{bmatrix} a & -b \\ b & a \end{bmatrix} \begin{bmatrix} x_1 \\ y_1 \end{bmatrix} + \begin{bmatrix} t_x \\ t_y \end{bmatrix} \\ \vdots \\ \begin{bmatrix} a & -b \\ b & a \end{bmatrix} \begin{bmatrix} x_n \\ y_n \end{bmatrix} + \begin{bmatrix} t_x \\ t_y \end{bmatrix} \end{bmatrix} = \begin{bmatrix} x_1 & -y_1 & 1 & 0 \\ y_1 & x_1 & 0 & 1 \\ \vdots & \vdots & \vdots & \vdots \\ x_n & -y_n & 1 & 0 \\ y_n & x_n & 0 & 1 \end{bmatrix} \begin{bmatrix} a \\ b \\ t_x \\ t_y \end{bmatrix}$$

In the `shape_model` class, this subspace is generated using the `calc_rigid_basis` function. The shape from which the subspace is generated (that is, the x and y components in the preceding equation) is the mean shape ov++er the Procustes-aligned shape (that is, the canonical shape). In addition to constructing the subspace in the aforementioned form, each column of the matrix is normalized to unit length. In the `shape_model::train` function, the variable dY described in the previous section is computed by projecting out the components of the data that pertain to rigid motion, as follows:

```
Mat R = this->calc_rigid_basis(Y); //compute rigid subspace
Mat P = R.t()*Y; Mat dY = Y - R*P; //project-out rigidity
```

Notice that this projection is implemented as a simple matrix multiplication. This is possible because the columns of the rigid subspace have been length normalized. This does not change the space spanned by the model, and means only that `R.t()*R` equals the identity matrix.

As the directions of variability stemming from rigid transformations have been removed from the data before learning the deformation model, the resulting deformation subspace will be orthogonal to the rigid transformation subspace. Thus, concatenating the two subspaces results in a combined local-global linear representation of facial shapes that is also orthonormal. Concatenation here can be performed by assigning the two subspace matrices to submatrices of the combined subspace matrix through the ROI extraction mechanism implemented in OpenCV's `Mat` class as follows:

```
V.create(2*n,4+k,CV_32F);                    //combined subspace
Mat Vr = V(Rect(0,0,4,2*n)); R.copyTo(Vr); //rigid subspace
Mat Vd = V(Rect(4,0,k,2*n)); D.copyTo(Vd); //nonrigid subspace
```

The orthonormality of the resulting model means that the parameters describing a shape can be computed easily, as is done in the `shape_model::calc_params` function:

```
p = V.t()*s;
```

Here `s` is a vectorized face shape and `p` stores the coordinates in the face subspace that represents it.

A final point to note about linearly modeling facial shapes is how to constrain the subspace coordinates such that shapes generated using it remain valid. In the following image, instances of face shapes that lie within the subspace are shown for an increasing value of the coordinates in one of the directions of variability in increments of four standard deviations. Notice that for small values, the resulting shape remains face-like, but deteriorates as the values become too large.

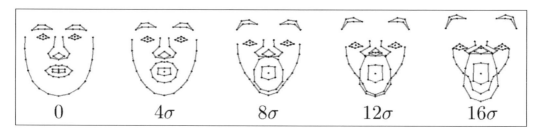

A simple way to prevent such deformation is to clamp the subspace coordinate values to lie within a permissible region as determined from the dataset. A common choice for this is a box constraint within ± 3 standard deviations of the data, which accounts for 99.7 percent of variation in the data. These clamping values are computed in the `shape_model::train` function after the subspace is found, as follows:

```
Mat Q = V.t()*X;                    //project raw data onto subspace
for(int i = 0; i < N; i++){ //normalize coordinates w.r.t scale
   float v = Q.fl(0,i); Mat q = Q.col(i); q /= v;
```

```
    }
    e.create(4+k,1,CV_32F); multiply(Q,Q,Q);
    for(int i = 0; i < 4+k; i++){
        if(i < 4)e.fl(i) = -1; //no clamping for rigid coefficients
        else e.fl(i) = Q.row(i).dot(Mat::ones(1,N,CV_32F))/(N-1);
    }
```

Notice that the variance is computed over the subspace coordinate `Q` after normalizing with respect to the coordinate of the first dimension (that is, scale). This prevents data samples that have relatively large scale from dominating the estimate. Also, notice that a negative value is assigned to the variance of the coordinates of the rigid subspace (that is, the first four columns of v). The clamping function `shape_model::clamp` checks to see if the variance of a particular direction is negative and only applies clamping if it is not, as follows:

```
    void shape_model::clamp(
    const float c){ //clamping as fraction of standard deviation
        double scale = p.fl(0);          //extract scale
        for(int i = 0; i < e.rows; i++){
            if(e.fl(i) < 0)continue;     //ignore rigid components
            float v = c*sqrt(e.fl(i));   //c*standard deviations box
            if(fabs(p.fl(i)/scale) > v){ //preserve sign of coordinate
            if(p.fl(i) > 0)p.fl(i) =  v*scale; //positive threshold
                else p.fl(i) = -v*scale; //negative threshold
            }
        }
    }
```

The reason for this is that the training data is often captured under contrived settings where the face is upright and centered in the image at a particular scale. Clamping the rigid components of the shape model to adhere to the configurations in the training set would then be too restrictive. Finally, as the variance of each deformable coordinate is computed in the scale-normalized frame, the same scaling must be applied to the coordinates during clamping.

Training and visualization

An example program for training a shape model from the annotation data can be found in `train_shape_model.cpp`. With the command-line argument `argv[1]` containing the path to the annotation data, training begins by loading the data into memory and removing incomplete samples, as follows:

```
    ft_data data = load_ft<ft_data>(argv[1]);
    data.rm_incomplete_samples();
```

The annotations for each example, and optionally their mirrored counterparts, are then stored in a vector before passing them to the training function as follows:

```
vector<vector<Point2f> > points;
for(int i = 0; i < int(data.points.size()); i++){
  points.push_back(data.get_points(i,false));
  if(mirror)points.push_back(data.get_points(i,true));
}
```

The shape model is then trained by a single function call to `shape_model::train` as follows:

```
shape_model smodel; smodel.train(points,data.connections,frac,kmax);
```

Here, `frac` (that is, the fraction of variation to retain) and `kmax` (that is, the maximum number of eigenvectors to retain) can be optionally set through command-line options, although the default settings of 0.95 and 20, respectively, tend to work well in most cases. Finally, with the command-line argument `argv[2]` containing the path to save the trained shape model to, saving can be performed by a single function call as follows:

```
save_ft(argv[2],smodel);
```

The simplicity of this step results from defining the `read` and `write` serialization functions for the `shape_model` class.

To visualize the trained shape model, the `visualize_shape_model.cpp` program animates the learned non-rigid deformations of each direction in turn. It begins by loading the shape model into memory as follows:

```
shape_model smodel = load_ft<shape_model>(argv[1]);
```

The rigid parameters that place the model at the center of the display window are computed as follows:

```
int n = smodel.V.rows/2;
float scale = calc_scale(smodel.V.col(0),200);
float tranx =
n*150.0/smodel.V.col(2).dot(Mat::ones(2*n,1,CV_32F));
float trany =
n*150.0/smodel.V.col(3).dot(Mat::ones(2*n,1,CV_32F));
```

Here, the `calc_scale` function finds the scaling coefficient that would generate face shapes with a width of 200 pixels. The translation components are computed by finding the coefficients that generate a translation of 150 pixels (that is, the model is mean-centered and the display window is 300 x 300 pixels in size).

Note that the first column of `shape_model::V` corresponds to scale and the third and fourth columns to x and y translations respectively.

A trajectory of parameter values is then generated, which begins at zero, moves to the positive extreme, moves to the negative extreme, and then back to zero as follows:

```
vector<float> val;
for(int i = 0; i < 50; i++)val.push_back(float(i)/50);
for(int i = 0; i < 50; i++)val.push_back(float(50-i)/50);
for(int i = 0; i < 50; i++)val.push_back(-float(i)/50);
for(int i = 0; i < 50; i++)val.push_back(-float(50-i)/50);
```

Here, each phase of the animation is composed of fifty increments. This trajectory is then used to animate the face model and render the results in a display window as follows:

```
Mat img(300,300,CV_8UC3); namedWindow("shape model");
while(1){
  for(int k = 4; k < smodel.V.cols; k++){
    for(int j = 0; j < int(val.size()); j++){
      Mat p = Mat::zeros(smodel.V.cols,1,CV_32F);
      p.at<float>(0) = scale;
      p.at<float>(2) = tranx;
      p.at<float>(3) = trany;
      p.at<float>(k) = scale*val[j]*3.0*
                      sqrt(smodel.e.at<float>(k));
      p.copyTo(smodel.p); img = Scalar::all(255);
      vector<Point2f> q = smodel.calc_shape();
      draw_shape(img,q,smodel.C);
      imshow("shape model",img);
      if(waitKey(10) == 'q')return 0;
    }
  }
}
```

 Note that the rigid coefficients (that is, those corresponding to the first four columns of `shape_model::V`) are always set to the values computed previously, to place the face at the center of the display window.

Facial feature detectors

Detecting facial features in images bares a strong resemblance to general object detection. OpenCV has a set of sophisticated functions for building general object detectors, the most well-known of which is the cascade of Haar-based feature detectors used in their implementation of the well-known Viola-Jones face detector. There are, however, a few distinguishing factors that make facial feature detection unique. These are as follows:

- **Precision versus robustness**: In generic object detection, the aim is to find the coarse position of the object in the image; facial feature detectors are required to give highly precise estimates of the location of the feature. An error of a few pixels is considered inconsequential in object detection but it can mean the difference between a smile and a frown in facial expression estimation through feature detections.

- **Ambiguity from limited spatial support**: It is common to assume that the object of interest in generic object detection exhibits sufficient image structure such that it can be reliably discriminated from image regions that do not contain the object. This is often not the case for facial features, which typically have limited spatial support. This is because image regions that do not contain the object can often exhibit a very similar structure to facial features. For example, a feature on the periphery of the face, seen from a small bounding box centered at the feature, can be easily confused with any other image patch that contains a strong edge through its center.

- **Computational complexity**: Generic object detection aims to find all instances of the object in an image. Face tracking, on the other hand, requires the locations of all facial features, which often ranges from around 20 to 100 features. Thus, the ability to evaluate each feature detector efficiently is paramount in building a face tracker that can run in real time.

Due to these differences, the facial feature detectors used in face tracking are often specifically designed with that purpose in mind. There are, of course, many instances of generic object-detection techniques being applied to facial feature detectors in face tracking. However, there does not appear to be a consensus in the community about which representation is best suited for the problem.

In this section, we will build facial feature detectors using a representation that is perhaps the simplest model one would consider: a linear image patch. Despite its simplicity, with due care in designing its learning procedure, we will see that this representation can in fact give reasonable estimates of facial feature locations for use in a face tracking algorithm. Furthermore, their simplicity enables an extremely rapid evaluation that makes real-time face tracking possible. Due to their representation as an image patch, the facial feature detectors are hereby referred to as patch models. This model is implemented in the `patch_model` class that can be found in the `patch_model.hpp` and `patch_model.cpp` files. The following code snippet is of the header of the `patch_model` class that highlights its primary functionality:

```
class patch_model{
public:
  Mat P; //normalized patch
  ...
  Mat                            //response map
  calc_response(
  const Mat &im,                 //image patch of search region
  const bool sum2one = false); //normalize to sum-to-one?
  ...
  void
  train(const vector<Mat> &images, //training image patches
  const Size psize,               //patch size
  const float var = 1.0,          //ideal response variance
  const float lambda = 1e-6,      //regularization weight
  const float mu_init = 1e-3,     //initial step size
  const int nsamples = 1000,      //number of samples
  const bool visi = false);       //visualize process?
  ...
};
```

The patch model used to detect a facial feature is stored in the matrix P. The two functions of primary interest in this class are `calc_response` and `train`. The `calc_response` function evaluates the patch model's response at every integer displacements over the search region `im`. The `train` function learns the patch model P of size `psize` that, on an average, yields response maps over the training set that is as close as possible to the ideal response map. The parameters `var`, `lambda`, `mu_init`, and `nsamples` are parameters of the training procedure that can be tuned to optimize performance for the data at hand.

The functionality of this class will be elaborated in this section. We begin by discussing the correlation patch and its training procedure, which will be used to learn the patch model. Next, the `patch_models` class, which is a collection of the patch models for each facial feature and has functionality that accounts for global transformations, will be described. The programs in `train_patch_model.cpp` and `visualize_patch_model.cpp` train and visualize the patch models, respectively, and their usage will be outlined at the end of this section on facial feature detectors.

Correlation-based patch models

In learning detectors, there are two primary competing paradigms: generative and discriminative. Generative methods learn an underlying representation of image patches that can best generate the object appearance in all its manifestations. Discriminative methods, on the other hand, learn a representation that best discriminates instances of the object from other objects that the model will likely encounter when deployed. Generative methods have the advantage that the resulting model encodes properties specific to the object, allowing novel instances of the object to be visually inspected. A popular approach that falls within the paradigm of generative methods is the famous Eigenfaces method. Discriminative methods have the advantage that the full capacity of the model is geared directly towards the problem at hand; discriminating instances of the object from all others. Perhaps the most well-known of all discriminative methods is the support vector machine. Although both paradigms can work well in many situations, we will see that when modeling facial features as an image patch, the discriminative paradigm is far superior.

 Note that the eigenfaces and support vector machine methods were originally developed for classification rather than detection or image alignment. However, their underlying mathematical concepts have been shown to be applicable to the face tracking domain.

Learning discriminative patch models

Given an annotated dataset, the feature detectors can be learned independently from each other. The learning objective of a discriminative patch model is to construct an image patch that, when cross-correlated with an image region containing the facial feature, yields a strong response at the feature location and weak responses everywhere else. Mathematically, this can be expressed as:

$$\min_{\mathbf{P}} \sum_{i=1}^{N} \sum_{x,y} \left[\mathbf{R}(x,y) - \mathbf{P} \cdot \mathbf{I}_i \left(x - \frac{w}{2} : x + \frac{w}{2}, y - \frac{h}{2} : y + \frac{h}{2} \right) \right]^2$$

Here, **P** denotes the patch model, **I** denotes the i'th training image I(a:b, c:d) denotes the rectangular region whose top-left and bottom-right corners are located at (a, c) and (b, d), respectively. The period symbol denotes the inner product operation and **R** denotes the ideal response map. The solution to this equation is a patch model that generates response maps that are, on average, closest to the ideal response map as measured using the least-squares criterion. An obvious choice for the ideal response map, R, is a matrix with zeros everywhere except at the center (assuming the training image patches are centered at the facial feature of interest). In practice, since the images are hand-labeled, there will always be an annotation error. To account for this, it is common to describe R as a decaying function of distance from the center. A good choice is the 2D-Gaussian distribution, which is equivalent to assuming the annotation error is Gaussian distributed. A visualization of this setup is shown in the following figure for the left outer eye corner:

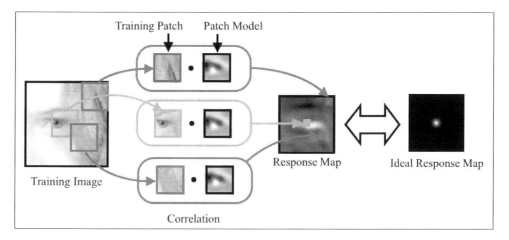

The learning objective as written previously is in a form commonly referred to as linear least squares. As such, it affords a closed-form solution. However, the degrees of freedom of this problem, that is, the number of ways the variables can vary to solve the problem, is equal to the number of pixels in the patch. Thus, the computational cost and memory requirements of solving for the optimal patch model can be prohibitive, even for a moderately sized patch or example, a 40 x 40- patch model has 1,600 degrees of freedom).

An efficient alternative to solving the learning problem as a linear system of equations is a method called stochastic gradient descent. By visualizing the learning objective as an error terrain over the degrees of freedom of the patch model, stochastic gradient descent iteratively makes an approximate estimate of the gradient direction of the terrain and takes a small step in the opposite direction. For our problem, the approximation to gradient can be computed by considering only the gradient of the learning objective for a single, randomly chosen image from the training set:

$$\mathbf{D} = -\sum_{x,y} \left(\mathbf{R}(x,y) - \mathbf{P}\cdot\mathbf{W}\right)\ \mathbf{W} \ \ ; \ \ \mathbf{W} = \mathbf{I}\left(x - \frac{w}{2} : x + \frac{w}{2}, y - \frac{h}{2} : y + \frac{h}{2}\right)$$

In the `patch_model` class, this learning process is implemented in the `train` function:

```
void
patch_model::train(
const vector<Mat> &images,  //featured centered training images
const Size psize,           //desired patch model size
const float var,            //variance of annotation error
const float lambda,         //regularization parameter
const float mu_init,        //initial step size
const int nsamples,         //number of stochastic samples
const bool visi){           //visualise training process
  int N = images.size(),n = psize.width*psize.height;
  int dx = wsize.width-psize.width;    //center of response map
  int dy = wsize.height-psize.height; //...
  Mat F(dy,dx,CV_32F); //ideal response map
  for(int y = 0; y < dy; y++){   float vy = (dy-1)/2 - y;
    for(int x = 0; x < dx; x++){float vx = (dx-1)/2 - x;
      F.fl(y,x) = exp(-0.5*(vx*vx+vy*vy)/var); //Gaussian
    }
  }
  normalize(F,F,0,1,NORM_MINMAX); //normalize to [0:1] range

  //allocate memory
  Mat I(wsize.height,wsize.width,CV_32F);
  Mat dP(psize.height,psize.width,CV_32F);
  Mat O = Mat::ones(psize.height,psize.width,CV_32F)/n;
  P = Mat::zeros(psize.height,psize.width,CV_32F);

  //optimise using stochastic gradient descent
  RNG rn(getTickCount()); //random number generator
  double mu=mu_init,step=pow(1e-8/mu_init,1.0/nsamples);
```

```
for(int sample = 0; sample < nsamples; sample++){
  int i = rn.uniform(0,N); //randomly sample image index
  I = this->convert_image(images[i]); dP = 0.0;
  for(int y = 0; y < dy; y++){ //compute stochastic gradient
    for(int x = 0; x < dx; x++){
    Mat Wi=I(Rect(x,y,psize.width,psize.height)).clone();
    Wi -= Wi.dot(O); normalize(Wi,Wi); //normalize
      dP += (F.fl(y,x) - P.dot(Wi))*Wi;
    }
  }
  P += mu*(dP - lambda*P); //take a small step
  mu *= step;             //reduce step size
  ...
}return;
}
```

The first highlighted code snippet in the preceding code is where the ideal response
map is computed. Since the images are centered on the facial feature of interest, the
response map is the same for all samples. In the second highlighted code snippet, the
decay rate, step, of the step sizes is determined such that after nsamples iterations,
the step size would have decayed to a value close to zero. The third highlighted code
snippet is where the stochastic gradient direction is computed and used to update
the patch model. There are two things to note here. First, the images used in training
are passed to the patch_model::convert_image function, which converts the image
to a single-channel image (if it is a color image) and applies the natural logarithm to
the image pixel intensities:

```
I += 1.0; log(I,I);
```

A bias value of one is added to each pixel before applying the logarithm since the
logarithm of zero is undefined. The reason for performing this pre-processing on the
training images is because log-scale images are more robust against differences in
contrast and changes in illumination conditions. The following figure shows images
of two faces with different degrees of contrast in the facial region. The difference
between the images is much less pronounced in the log-scale images than it is in the
raw images.

Raw　　　　　　　　　　　　　　　　　　　　Log Scale

The second point to note about the update equation is the subtraction of `lambda*P` from the update direction. This effectively regularizes the solution from growing too large; a procedure that is often applied in machine-learning algorithms to promote generalization to unseen data. The scaling factor `lambda` is user defined and is usually problem dependent. However, a small value typically works well for learning patch models for facial feature detection.

Generative versus discriminative patch models

Despite the ease of which discriminative patch models can be learned as described previously, it is worth considering whether generative patch models and their corresponding training regimes are simpler enough to achieve similar results. The generative counterpart of the correlation patch model is the average patch. The learning objective for this model is to construct a single image patch that is as close as possible to all examples of the facial feature as measured via the least-squares criterion:

$$\min_{\mathbf{P}} \sum_{i=1}^{N} \|\mathbf{P} - \mathbf{I}_i\|_F^2$$

The solution to this problem is exactly the average of all the feature-centered training image patches. Thus, in a way, the solution afforded by this objective is far simpler.

In the following figure, a comparison is shown for the response maps obtained by cross-correlating the average and correlation patch models with an example image. The respective average and correlation patch models are also shown, where the range of pixel values are normalized for visualization purposes. Although the two patch model types exhibit some similarities, the response maps they generate differ substantially. While the correlation patch model generates response maps that are highly peaked around the feature location, the response map generated by the average patch model is overly smooth and does not strongly distinguish the feature location from those close by. Inspecting the patch models' appearance, the correlation patch model is mostly gray, which corresponds to zero in the un-normalized pixel range, with strong positive and negative values strategically placed around prominent areas of the facial feature. Thus, it preserves only components of the training patches useful for discriminating it from misaligned configuration, which leads to highly peaked responses. In contrast, the average patch model encodes no knowledge of misaligned data. As a result, it is not well suited to the task of facial feature localization, where the task is to discriminate an aligned image patch from locally shifted versions of itself.

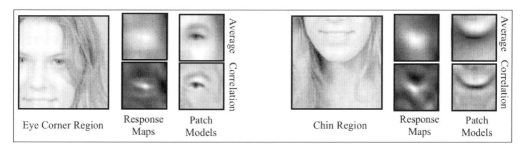

Eye Corner Region   Response Maps   Patch Models   Average Correlation   Chin Region   Response Maps   Patch Models   Average Correlation

Accounting for global geometric transformations

So far, we have assumed that the training images are centered at the facial feature and are normalized with respect to global scale and rotation. In practice, the face can appear at any scale and rotation within the image during tracking. Thus, a mechanism must be devised to account for this discrepancy between the training and testing conditions. One approach is to synthetically perturb the training images in scale and rotation within the ranges one expects to encounter during deployment. However, the simplistic form of the detector as a correlation patch model often lacks the capacity to generate useful response maps for that kind of data. On the other hand, the correlation patch model does exhibit a degree of robustness against small perturbations in scale and rotation. Since motion between consecutive frames in a video sequence is relatively small, one can leverage the estimated global transformation of the face in the previous frame to normalize the current image with respect to scale and rotation. All that is needed to enable this procedure is to select a reference frame in which the correlation patch models are learned.

The `patch_models` class stores the correlation patch models for each facial feature as well as the reference frame in which they are trained. It is the `patch_models` class, rather than the `patch_model` class, that the face tracker code interfaces with directly, to obtain the feature detections. The following code snippet of the declaration of this class highlights its primary functionality:

```
class patch_models{
public:
  Mat reference;          //reference shape [x1;y1;...;xn;yn]
  vector<patch_model> patches; //patch model/facial feature
  ...
  void
  train(ft_data &data,        //annotated image and shape data
  const vector<Point2f> &ref, //reference shape
  const Size psize,           //desired patch size
```

```
        const Size ssize,           //training search window size
        const bool mirror = false,  //use mirrored training data
        const float var = 1.0,      //variance of annotation error
        const float lambda = 1e-6,  //regularisation weight
        const float mu_init = 1e-3, //initial step size
        const int nsamples = 1000,  //number of samples
        const bool visi = false);   //visualise training procedure?
        ...
        vector<Point2f>//location of peak responses/feature in image
        calc_peaks(
        const Mat &im,       //image to detect features in
        const vector<Point2f> &points, //current estimate of shape
        const Size ssize = Size(21,21)); //search window size
        ...
    };
```

The `reference` shape is stored as an interleaved set of (x, y) coordinates that are used to normalize the scale and rotation of the training images, and later during deployment that of the test images. In the `patch_models::train` function, this is done by first computing the similarity transform between the `reference` shape and the annotated shape for a given image using the `patch_models::calc_simil` function, which solves a similar problem to that in the `shape_model::procrustes` function, albeit for a single pair of shapes. Since the rotation and scale is common across all facial features, the image normalization procedure only requires adjusting this similarity transform to account for the centers of each feature in the image and the center of the normalized image patch. In `patch_models::train`, this is implemented as follows:

```
Mat S = this->calc_simil(pt),A(2,3,CV_32F);
A.fl(0,0) = S.fl(0,0); A.fl(0,1) = S.fl(0,1);
A.fl(1,0) = S.fl(1,0); A.fl(1,1) = S.fl(1,1);
A.fl(0,2) = pt.fl(2*i  ) - (A.fl(0,0)*(wsize.width -1)/2 +
                            A.fl(0,1)*(wsize.height-1)/2);
A.fl(1,2) = pt.fl(2*i+1) - (A.fl(1,0)*(wsize.width -1)/2 +
                            A.fl(1,1)*(wsize.height-1)/2);
Mat I; warpAffine(im,I,A,wsize,INTER_LINEAR+WARP_INVERSE_MAP);
```

Here, `wsize` is the total size of the normalized training image, which is the sum of the patch size and the search region size. As just mentioned, that the top-left (2 x 2) block of the similarity transform from the reference shape to the annotated shape `pt`, which corresponds to the scale and rotation component of the transformation, is preserved in the affine transform passed to OpenCV's `warpAffine` function. The last column of the affine transform `A` is an adjustment that will render the i'th facial feature location centered in the normalized image after warping (that is, the normalizing translation). Finally, the `cv::warpAffine` function has the default setting of warping from the image to the reference frame. Since the similarity transform was computed for transforming the `reference` shape to the image-space annotations `pt`, the `WARP_INVERSE_MAP` flag needs to be set to ensure the function applies the warp in the desired direction. Exactly the same procedure is performed in the `patch_models::calc_peaks` function, with the additional step that the computed similarity transform between the reference and the current shape in the image-frame is re-used to un-normalize the detected facial features, placing them appropriately in the image:

```
vector<Point2f>
patch_models::calc_peaks(const Mat &im,
  const vector<Point2f> &points,const Size ssize){
  int n = points.size(); assert(n == int(patches.size()));
  Mat pt = Mat(points).reshape(1,2*n);
  Mat S = this->calc_simil(pt);
  Mat Si = this->inv_simil(S);
  vector<Point2f> pts = this->apply_simil(Si,points);
  for(int i = 0; i < n; i++){
    Size wsize = ssize + patches[i].patch_size();
    Mat A(2,3,CV_32F),I;
    A.fl(0,0) = S.fl(0,0); A.fl(0,1) = S.fl(0,1);
    A.fl(1,0) = S.fl(1,0); A.fl(1,1) = S.fl(1,1);
    A.fl(0,2) = pt.fl(2*i  ) - (A.fl(0,0)*(wsize.width -1)/2 +
                                A.fl(0,1)*(wsize.height-1)/2);
    A.fl(1,2) = pt.fl(2*i+1) - (A.fl(1,0)*(wsize.width -1)/2 +
                                A.fl(1,1)*(wsize.height-1)/2);
    warpAffine(im,I,A,wsize,INTER_LINEAR+WARP_INVERSE_MAP);
    Mat R = patches[i].calc_response(I,false);
    Point maxLoc; minMaxLoc(R,0,0,0,&maxLoc);
    pts[i] = Point2f(pts[i].x + maxLoc.x - 0.5*ssize.width,
                     pts[i].y + maxLoc.y - 0.5*ssize.height);
  }return this->apply_simil(S,pts);
```

In the first highlighted code snippet in the preceding code, both the forward and inverse similarity transforms are computed. The reason why the inverse transform is required here is so that the peaks of the response map for each feature can be adjusted according to the normalized locations of the current shape estimate. This must be performed before reapplying the similarity transform to place the new estimates of the facial feature locations back into the image frame using the `patch_models::apply_simil` function.

Training and visualization

An example program for training the patch models from annotation data can be found in `train_patch_model.cpp`. With the command-line argument `argv[1]` containing the path to the annotation data, training begins by loading the data into memory and removing incomplete samples:

```
ft_data data = load_ft<ft_data>(argv[1]);
data.rm_incomplete_samples();
```

The simplest choice for the reference shape in the `patch_models` class is the average shape of the training set, scaled to a desired size. Assuming that a shape model has previously been trained for this dataset, the reference shape is computed by first loading the shape model stored in `argv[2]` as follows:

```
shape_model smodel = load_ft<shape_model>(argv[2]);
```

This is followed by the computation of the scaled centered average shape:

```
smodel.p = Scalar::all(0.0);
smodel.p.fl(0) = calc_scale(smodel.V.col(0),width);
vector<Point2f> r = smodel.calc_shape();
```

The `calc_scale` function computes the scaling factor to transform the average shape (that is, the first column of `shape_model::V`) to one with a width of `width`. Once the reference shape `r` is defined, training the set of patch models can be done with a single function call:

```
patch_models pmodel; pmodel.train(data,r,Size(psize,psize),Size(ssize
,ssize));
```

The optimal choices for the parameters `width`, `psize`, and `ssize` are application dependent; however, the default values of 100, 11, and 11, respectively, give reasonable results in general.

Although the training process is quite simple, it can still take some time to complete. Depending on the number of facial features, the size of the patches, and the number of stochastic samples in the optimization algorithm, the training process can take anywhere between a few minutes to over an hour. However, since the training of each patch can be performed independently of all others, this process can be sped up substantially by parallelizing the training process across multiple processor-cores or machines.

Once training has been completed, the program in `visualize_patch_model.cpp` can be used to visualize the resulting patch models. As with the `visualize_shape_model.cpp` program, the aim here is to visually inspect the results to verify if anything went wrong during the training process. The program generates a composite image of all the patch models, `patch_model::P`, each centered at their respective feature location in the reference shape, `patch_models::reference`, and displays a bounding rectangle around the patch whose index is currently active. The `cv::waitKey` function is used to get user input for selecting the active patch index and terminating the program. The following image shows three examples of composite patch images learned for patch model with varying spatial support. Despite using the same training data, modifying the spatial support of the patch model appears to change the structure of the patch models substantially. Visually inspecting the results in this way can lend intuition into how to modify the parameters of the training process, or even the training process itself, in order to optimize results for a particular application.

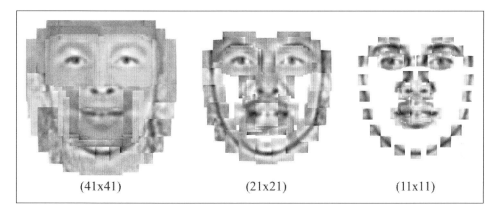

(41x41)   (21x21)   (11x11)

Face detection and initialization

The method for face tracking described thus far has assumed that the facial features in the image are located within a reasonable proximity to the current estimate. Although this assumption is reasonable during tracking, where face motion between frames is often quite small, we are still faced with the dilemma of how to initialize the model in the first frame of the sequence. An obvious choice for this is to use OpenCV's in-built cascade detector to find the face. However, the placement of the model within the detected bounding box will depend on the selection made for the facial features to track. In keeping with the data-driven paradigm we have followed so far in this chapter, a simple solution is to learn the geometrical relationship between the face detection's bounding box and the facial features.

The `face_detector` class implements exactly this solution. A snippet of its declaration that highlights its functionality is given as follows:

```
class face_detector{ //face detector for initialisation
public:
  string detector_fname; //file containing cascade classifier
  Vec3f detector_offset; //offset from center of detection
  Mat reference;         //reference shape
  CascadeClassifier detector; //face detector

  vector<Point2f>  //points describing detected face in image
  detect(const Mat &im,          //image containing face
    const float scaleFactor = 1.1,//scale increment
    const int minNeighbours = 2,  //minimum neighborhood size
    const Size minSize = Size(30,30));//minimum window size

  void
  train(ft_data &data,                //training data
    const string fname,               //cascade detector
    const Mat &ref,                   //reference shape
    const bool mirror = false,        //mirror data?
    const bool visi = false,          //visualize training?
    const float frac = 0.8, //fraction of points in detection
    const float scaleFactor = 1.1, //scale increment
    const int minNeighbours = 2,   //minimum neighbourhood size
    const Size minSize = Size(30,30)); //minimum window size
  ...
};
```

The class has four public member variables: the path to an object of type
`cv::CascadeClassifier` called `detector_fname`, a set of offsets from a detection
bounding box to the location and scale of the face in the image `detector_offset`,
a reference shape to place in the bounding box `reference`, and a face detector
`detector`. The primary function of use to a face tracking system is `face_`
`detector::detect`, which takes an image as the input, along with standard options
for the `cv::CascadeClassifier` class, and returns a rough estimate of the facial
feature locations in the image. Its implementation is as follows:

```
Mat gray; //convert image to grayscale and histogram equalize
if(im.channels() == 1)gray = im;
else cvtColor(im,gray,CV_RGB2GRAY);
Mat eqIm; equalizeHist(gray,eqIm);
vector<Rect> faces; //detect largest face in image
 detector.detectMultiScale(eqIm,faces,scaleFactor,
                        minNeighbours,0
                        |CV_HAAR_FIND_BIGGEST_OBJECT
                        |CV_HAAR_SCALE_IMAGE,minSize);
if(faces.size() < 1){return vector<Point2f>();}

Rect R = faces[0]; Vec3f scale = detector_offset*R.width;
int n = reference.rows/2; vector<Point2f> p(n);
for(int i = 0; i < n; i++){ //predict face placement
  p[i].x = scale[2]*reference.fl(2*i  ) +
         R.x + 0.5 * R.width  + scale[0];
  p[i].y = scale[2]*reference.fl(2*i+1) +
         R.y + 0.5 * R.height + scale[1];
}return p;
```

The face is detected in the image in the usual way, except that the `CV_HAAR_FIND_`
`BIGGEST_OBJECT` flag is set so as to enable tracking the most prominent face in the
image. The highlighted code is where the reference shape is placed in the image in
accordance with the detected face's bounding box. The `detector_offset` member
variable consists of three components: an (x, y) offset of the center of the face from
the center of the detection's bounding box, and the scaling factor that resizes the
reference shape to best fit the face in the image. All three components are a linear
function of the bounding box's width.

The linear relationship between the bounding box's width and the `detector_offset`
variable is learned from the annotated dataset in the `face_detector::train`
function. The learning process is started by loading the training data into memory
and assigning the reference shape:

```
detector.load(fname.c_str()); detector_fname = fname; reference = ref.
clone();
```

As with the reference shape in the `patch_models` class, a convenient choice for the reference shape is the normalized average face shape in the dataset. The `cv::CascadeClassifier` is then applied to each image (and optionally its mirrored counterpart) in the dataset and the resulting detection is checked to ensure that enough annotated points lie within the detected bounding box (see the figure towards the end of this section) to prevent learning from misdetections:

```
if(this->enough_bounded_points(pt,faces[0],frac)){
    Point2f center = this->center_of_mass(pt);
    float w = faces[0].width;
    xoffset.push_back((center.x -
                      (faces[0].x+0.5*faces[0].width ))/w);
    yoffset.push_back((center.y -
                      (faces[0].y+0.5*faces[0].height))/w);
    zoffset.push_back(this->calc_scale(pt)/w);
}
```

If more than a fraction of `frac` of the annotated points lie within the bounding box, the linear relationship between its width and the offset parameters for that image are added as a new entry in an STL `vector` class object. Here, the `face_detector::center_of_mass` function computes the center of mass of the annotated point set for that image and the `face_detector::calc_scale` function computes the scaling factor for transforming the reference shape to the centered annotated shape. Once all images have been processed, the `detector_offset` variable is set to the median over all of the image-specific offsets:

```
Mat X = Mat(xoffset),Xsort,Y = Mat(yoffset),Ysort,Z =
Mat(zoffset),Zsort;
cv::sort(X,Xsort,CV_SORT_EVERY_COLUMN|CV_SORT_ASCENDING);
int nx = Xsort.rows;
cv::sort(Y,Ysort,CV_SORT_EVERY_COLUMN|CV_SORT_ASCENDING);
int ny = Ysort.rows;
cv::sort(Z,Zsort,CV_SORT_EVERY_COLUMN|CV_SORT_ASCENDING);
int nz = Zsort.rows;
detector_offset =
    Vec3f(Xsort.fl(nx/2),Ysort.fl(ny/2),Zsort.fl(nz/2));
```

As with the shape and patch models, the simple program in `train_face_detector.cpp` is an example of how a `face_detector` object can be built and saved for later use in the tracker. It first loads the annotation data and the shape model, and sets the reference shape as the mean-centered average of the training data (that is, the identity shape of the `shape_model` class):

```
ft_data data = load_ft<ft_data>(argv[2]);
shape_model smodel = load_ft<shape_model>(argv[3]);
smodel.set_identity_params();
vector<Point2f> r = smodel.calc_shape();
Mat ref = Mat(r).reshape(1,2*r.size());
```

Training and saving the face detector, then, consists of two function calls:

```
face_detector detector;
detector.train(data,argv[1],ref,mirror,true,frac);
save_ft<face_detector>(argv[4],detector);
```

To test the performance of the resulting shape-placement procedure, the program in `visualize_face_detector.cpp` calls the `face_detector::detect` function for each image in the video or camera input stream and draws the results on screen. An example of the results using this approach is shown in the following figure Although the placed shape does not match the individual in the image, its placement is close enough so that face tracking can proceed using the approach described in the following section:

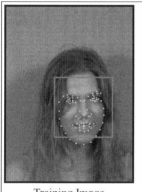
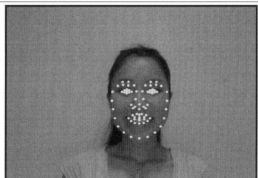

Training Image   Test Image

Face tracking

The problem of face tracking can be posed as that of finding an efficient and robust way to combine the independent detections of various facial features with the geometrical dependencies they exhibit in order to arrive at an accurate estimate of facial feature locations in each image of a sequence. With this in mind, it is perhaps worth considering whether geometrical dependencies are at all necessary. In the following figure, the results of detecting the facial features with and without geometrical constraints are shown. These results clearly highlight the benefit of capturing the spatial interdependencies between facial features. The relative performance of these two approaches is typical, whereby relying strictly on the detections leads to overly noisy solutions. The reason for this is that the response maps for each facial feature cannot be expected to always peak at the correct location. Whether due to image noise, lighting changes, or expression variation, the only way to overcome the limitations of facial feature detectors is by leveraging the geometrical relationship they share with each other.

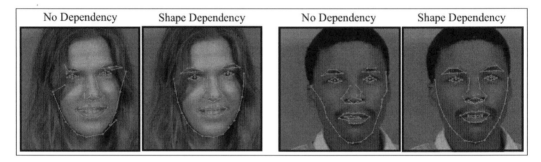

A particularly simple, but surprisingly effective, way to incorporate facial geometry into the tracking procedure is by projecting the output of the feature detections onto the linear shape model's subspace. This amounts to minimizing the distance between the original points and its closest plausible shape that lies on the subspace. Thus, when the spatial noise in the feature detections is close to being Gaussian distributed, the projection yields the maximum likely solution. In practice, the distribution of detection errors on occasion does not follow a Gaussian distribution and additional mechanisms need to be introduced to account for this.

Face tracker implementation

An implementation of the face tracking algorithm can be found in the `face_tracker` class (see `face_tracker.cpp` and `face_tracker.hpp`). The following code is a snippet of its header that highlights its primary functionality:

```
class face_tracker{
public:
  bool tracking;          //are we in tracking mode?
  fps_timer timer;        //frames/second timer
  vector<Point2f> points; //current tracked points
  face_detector detector; //detector for initialisation
  shape_model smodel;     //shape model
  patch_models pmodel;    //feature detectors

  face_tracker(){tracking = false;}

  int                              //0 = failure
  track(const Mat &im,             //image containing face
  const face_tracker_params &p =   //fitting parameters
  face_tracker_params());          //default tracking parameters

  void
  reset(){                              //reset tracker
    tracking = false; timer.reset();
  }
  ...
protected:
  ...
  vector<Point2f>   //points for fitted face in image
  fit(const Mat &image,//image containing face
      const vector<Point2f> &init,    //initial point estimates
      const Size ssize = Size(21,21),//search region size
      const bool robust = false,      //use robust fitting?
      const int itol = 10,    //maximum number of iterations
      const float ftol = 1e-3);       //convergence tolerance
};
```

The class has public member instances of the `shape_model`, `patch_models`, and `face_detector` classes. It uses the functionality of these three classes to effect tracking. The `timer` variable is an instance of the `fps_timer` class that keeps track of the frame-rate at which the `face_tracker::track` function is called and is useful for analyzing the effects patch and shape model configurations on the computational complexity of the algorithm. The `tracking` member variable is a flag to indicate the current state of the tracking procedure. When this flag is set to `false`, as it is in the constructor and the `face_tracker::reset` function, the tracker enters a Detection mode whereby the `face_detector::detect` function is applied to the next incoming image to initialize the model. When in the tracking mode, the initial estimate used for inferring facial feature locations in the next incoming image is simply their location in the previous frame. The complete tracking algorithm is implemented simply as follows:

```
int face_tracker::
track(const Mat &im,const face_tracker_params &p){
  Mat gray; //convert image to grayscale
  if(im.channels()==1)gray=im;
  else cvtColor(im,gray,CV_RGB2GRAY);
  if(!tracking) //initialize
    points = detector.detect(gray,p.scaleFactor,
                             p.minNeighbours,p.minSize);
  if((int)points.size() != smodel.npts())return 0;
  for(int level = 0; level < int(p.ssize.size()); level++)
    points = this->fit(gray,points,p.ssize[level],
                       p.robust,p.itol,p.ftol);
  tracking = true; timer.increment();   return 1;
}
```

Other than bookkeeping operations, such as setting the appropriate `tracking` state and incrementing the tracking time, the core of the tracking algorithm is the multi-level fitting procedure, which is highlighted in the preceding code snippet. The fitting algorithm, implemented in the `face_tracker::fit` function, is applied multiple times with the different search window sizes stored in `face_tracker_params::ssize`, where the output of the previous stage is used as input to the next. In its simplest setting, the `face_tracker_params::ssize` function performs the facial feature detection around the current estimate of the shape in the image:

```
smodel.calc_params(init);
vector<Point2f> pts = smodel.calc_shape();
vector<Point2f> peaks = pmodel.calc_peaks(image,pts,ssize);
```

It also projects the result onto the face shape's subspace:

```
smodel.calc_params(peaks);
pts = smodel.calc_shape();
```

To account for gross outliers in the facial features' detected locations, a robust model's fitting procedure can be employed instead of a simple projection by setting the `robust` flag to `true`. However, in practice, when using a decaying search window size (that is, as set in `face_tracker_params::ssize`), this is often unnecessary as gross outliers typically remain far from its corresponding point in the projected shape, and will likely lie outside the search region of the next level of the fitting procedure. Thus, the rate at which the search region size is reduced acts as an incremental outlier rejection scheme.

Training and visualization

Unlike the other classes detailed in this chapter, training a `face_tracker` object does not involve any learning process. It is implemented in `train_face_tracker.cpp` simply as:

```
face_tracker tracker;
tracker.smodel = load_ft<shape_model>(argv[1]);
tracker.pmodel = load_ft<patch_models>(argv[2]);
tracker.detector = load_ft<face_detector>(argv[3]);
save_ft<face_tracker>(argv[4],tracker);
```

Here `arg[1]` to `argv[4]` contain the paths to the `shape_model`, `patch_model`, `face_detector`, and `face_tracker` objects, respectively. The visualization for the face tracker in `visualize_face_tracker.cpp` is equally simple. Obtaining its input image stream either from a camera or video file, through the `cv::VideoCapture` class, the program simply loops until the end of the stream or until the user presses the *Q* key, tracking each frame as it comes in. The user also has the option of resetting the tracker by pressing the *D* key at any time.

Generic versus person-specific models

There are a number of variables in the training and tracking process that can be tweaked to optimize the performance for a given application. However, one of the primary determinants of tracking quality is the range of shape and appearance variability the tracker has to model. As a case in point, consider the generic versus person-specific case. A generic model is trained using annotated data from multiple identities, expressions, lighting conditions, and other sources of variability. In contrast, person-specific models are trained specifically for a single individual. Thus, the amount of variability it needs to account for is far smaller. As a result, person-specific tracking is often more accurate than its generic counter part by a large magnitude.

An illustration of this is shown in the following image. Here the generic model was trained using the MUCT dataset. The person-specific model was learned from data generated using the annotation tool described earlier in this chapter. The results clearly show a substantially better tracking offered by the person-specific model, capable of capturing complex expressions and head-pose changes, whereas the generic model appears to struggle even for some of the simpler expressions:

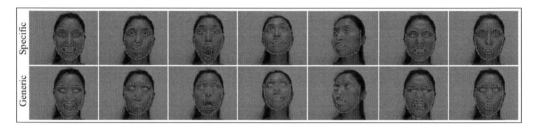

It should be noted that the method for face tracking described in this chapter is a bare-bones approach that serves to highlight the various components utilized in most non-rigid face tracking algorithms. The numerous approaches to remedy some of the drawbacks of this method are beyond the scope of this book and require specialized mathematical tools that are not yet supported by OpenCV's functionality. The relatively few commercial-grade face-tracking software packages available is testament to the difficulty of this problem in the general setting. Nonetheless, the simple approach described in this chapter can work remarkably well in constrained settings.

Summary

In this chapter we have built a simple face tracker that can work reasonably in constrained settings using only modest mathematical tools and OpenCV's substantial functionality for basic image processing and linear algebraic operations. Improvements to this simple tracker can be achieved by employing more sophisticated techniques in each of the three components of the tracker: the shape model, the feature detectors, and the fitting algorithm. The modular design of the tracker described in this section should allow these three components to be modified without substantial disruptions to the functionality of the others.

References

- *Procrustes Problems, Gower, John C. and Dijksterhuis, Garmt B, Oxford University Press, 2004.*

3D Head Pose Estimation Using AAM and POSIT

A good computer vision algorithm can't be complete without great, robust capabilities as well as wide generalization and a solid math foundation. All these features accompany the work mainly developed by Tim Cootes with Active Appearance Models. This chapter will teach you how to create an **Active Appearance Model** of your own using OpenCV as well as how to use it to search for the closest position your model is located at in a given frame. Besides, you will learn how to use the POSIT algorithm and how to fit your 3D model in the "posed" image. With all these tools, you will be able to track a 3D model in a video, in real time; ain't it great? Although the examples focus on head pose, virtually any deformable model could use the same approach.

As you read the sections, you will come across the following topics:

- Active Appearance Models overview
- Active Shape Models overview
- Model instantiation—playing with the Active Appearance Model
- AAM search and fitting
- POSIT

The following list has an explanation of the terms that you will come across in the chapter:

- **Active Appearance Model (AAM)**: An object model containing statistical information of its shape and texture. It is a powerful way of capturing shape and texture variation from objects.

- **Active Shape Model (ASM)**: A statistical model of the shape of an object. It is very useful for learning shape variation.

- **Principal Component Analysis (PCA)**: An orthogonal linear transformation that transforms the data to a new coordinate system such that the greatest variance by any projection of the data comes to lie on the first coordinate (called the first principal component), the second greatest variance on the second coordinate, and so on. This procedure is often used in dimensionality reduction. When reducing the dimension of the original problem, one can use a faster-fitting algorithm.

- **Delaunay Triangulation (DT)**: For a set of P points in a plane, it is a triangulation such that no point in P is inside the circumcircle of any triangle in the triangulation. It tends to avoid skinny triangles. The triangulation is required for texture mapping.

- **Affine transformation**: Any transformation that can be expressed in the form of a matrix multiplication followed by a vector addition. This can be used for texture mapping.

- **Pose from Orthography and Scaling with Iterations (POSIT)**: A computer vision algorithm that performs 3D pose estimation.

Active Appearance Models overview

In few words, Active Appearance Models are a nice model parameterization of combined texture and shape coupled to an efficient search algorithm that can tell exactly where and how a model is located in a picture frame. In order to do that, we will start with the *Active Shape Models* section and will see that they are more closely related to landmark positions. A principal component analysis and some hands-on experience will be better described in the following sections. Then, we will be able to get some help from OpenCV's Delaunay functions and learn some triangulation. From that we will evolve to applying piecewise affine warps in the triangle texture warping section, where we can get information from an object's texture.

As we get enough background to build a good model, we can play with the techniques in the model instantiation section. We will then be able to solve the inverse problem through AAM search and fitting. These by themselves are already very useful algorithms for 2D and maybe even 3D image matching. But when one is able to get it to work, why not bridge it to **POSIT (Pose from Orthography and Scaling with Iterations)**, another rock solid algorithm for 3D model fitting? Diving into the POSIT section will give us enough background to work with it in OpenCV, and we will then learn how to couple a head model to it, in the following section. This way, we can use a 3D model to fit the already matched 2D frame. And if a sharp reader wants to know where this will take us, it is just a matter of combining AAM and Posit in a frame-by-frame fashion to get real-time 3D tracking by detection for deformable models! These details will be covered in the tracking from webcam or video file section.

It is said that a picture is worth a thousand words; imagine if we get *N* pictures. This way, what we previously mentioned is easily tracked in the following screenshot:

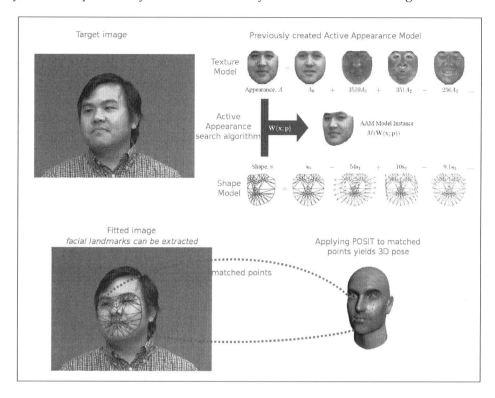

Overview of the chapter algorithms: Given an image (upper-left image in the preceding screenshot), we can use an Active Appearance search algorithm to find the 2D pose of the human head. The upper-right side figure in the screenshot shows a previously trained Active Appearance model used in the search algorithm. After a pose has been found, POSIT can be applied to extend the result to a 3D pose. If the procedure is applied to a video sequence, 3D tracking by detection will be obtained.

Active Shape Models

As mentioned previously, AAMs require a shape model, and this role is played by Active Shape Models (ASMs). In the coming sections, we will create an ASM that is a statistical model of shape variation. The shape model is generated through the combination of shape variations. A training set of labeled images is required, as described in the article *Active Shape Models – Their Training and Application*, by Timothy Cootes. In order to build a face-shape model, several images marked with points on key positions of a face are required to outline the main features. The following screenshot shows such an example:

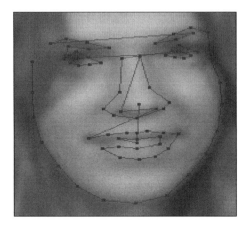

There are 76 landmarks on a face, which are taken from the MUCT dataset. These landmarks are usually marked up by hand and they outline several face features, such as mouth contour, nose, eyes, eyebrows, and face shape, since they are easier to track.

 Procrustes Analysis: A form of statistical shape analysis used to analyze the distribution of a set of shapes. Procrustes superimposition is performed by optimally translating, rotating, and uniformly scaling the objects.

If we have the previously mentioned set of images, we can generate a statistical model of shape variation. Since the labeled points on an object describe the shape of that object, we firstly align all the sets of points into a coordinate frame using Procrustes Analysis, if required, and represent each shape by a vector, x. Then, we apply Principal Component Analysis (PCA) to the data. We can then approximate any example using the following formula:

x = x + Ps bs

In the preceding formula, x is the mean shape, Ps is a set of orthogonal modes of variation, and bs is a set of shape parameters. Well, in order to understand that better, we will create a simple application in the rest of this section, which will show us how to deal with PCA and shape models.

Why use PCA at all? Because PCA is going to really help us when it comes to reducing the number of parameters of our model. We will also see how much that helps when searching for it in a given image later in this chapter. A web page URL should be given for the following quote (`http://en.wikipedia.org/wiki/Principal_component_analysis`):

> *PCA can supply the user with a lower-dimensional picture, a "shadow" of this object when viewed from its (in some sense) most informative viewpoint. This is done by using only the first few principal components so that the dimensionality of the transformed data is reduced.*

This becomes clear when we see a screenshot such as the following:

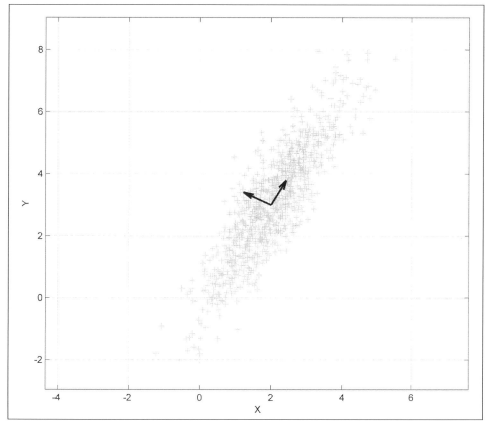

Image source: `http://en.wikipedia.org/wiki/File:GaussianScatterPCA.png`

The preceding screenshot shows the PCA of a multivariate Gaussian distribution centered at (2,3). The vectors shown are the eigenvectors of the covariance matrix, shifted so their tails are at the mean.

This way, if we wanted to represent our model with a single parameter, taking the direction from the eigenvector that points to the upper-right part of the screenshot would be a good idea. Besides, by varying the parameter a bit, we can extrapolate data and get values similar to the ones we are looking for.

Getting the feel of PCA

In order to get a feeling of how PCA could help us with our face model, we will start with an active shape model and test some parameters.

Since face detection and tracking has been studied for a while, several face databases are available online for research purposes. We are going to use a couple of samples from the IMM database.

First, let's understand how the PCA class works in OpenCV. We can conclude from the documentation that the PCA class is used to compute a special basis for a set of vectors, which consists of eigenvectors of the covariance matrix computed from the input set of vectors. This class can also transform vectors to and from the new coordinate space, using `project` and `backproject` methods. This new coordinate system can be quite accurately approximated by taking just the first few of its components. This means we can represent the original vector from a high-dimensional space with a much shorter vector consisting of the projected vector's coordinates in the subspace.

Since we want a parameterization in terms of a few scalar values, the main method we will use from the class is the `backproject` method. It takes principal component coordinates of projected vectors and reconstructs the original ones. We could retrieve the original vectors if we retained all the components, but the difference will be very small if we just use a couple of components; that's one of the reasons for using PCA. Since we want some variability around the original vectors, our parameterized scalars will be able to extrapolate the original data.

Besides, the PCA class can transform vectors to and from the new coordinate space, defined by the basis. Mathematically, it means that we compute projection of the vector to a subspace formed by a few eigenvectors corresponding to the dominant eigenvalues of the covariance matrix, as one can see from the documentation.

Our approach will be annotating our face images with landmarks yielding a training set for our **point distribution model (PDM)**. If we have k aligned landmarks in two dimensions, our shape description becomes:

X = { x1, y1, x2, y2, ..., xk, yk}

It's important to note that we need consistent labeling across all image samples. So, for instance, if the left part of the mouth is landmark number 3 in the first image, it will need to be number 3 in all other images.

These sequences of landmarks will now form the shape outlines, and a given training shape can be defined as a vector. We generally assume this scattering is Gaussian in this space, and we use PCA to compute normalized eigenvectors and eigenvalues of the covariance matrix across all training shapes. Using the top-center eigenvectors, we create a matrix of dimensions $2k * m$, which we will call P. This way, each eigenvector describes a principal mode of variation along the set.

Now we can define a new shape through the following equation:

$X' = X' + Pb$

Here, X' is the mean shape across all training images — we just average each of the landmarks — and b is a vector of scaling values for each principal component. This leads us to create a new shape modifying the value of b. It's common to set b to vary within three standard deviations so that the generated shape can fall inside the training set.

The following screenshot shows point-annotated mouth landmarks for three different pictures:

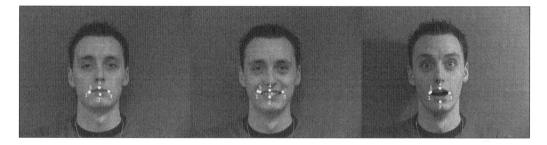

As can be seen in the preceding screenshot, the shapes are described by their landmark sequences. One could use a program like GIMP or ImageJ as well as building a simple application in OpenCV, in order to annotate the training images. We will assume the user has completed this process and saved the points as sequences of x and y landmark positions for all training images in a text file, which will be used in our PCA analysis. We will then add two parameters to the first line of this file, which is the number of training images and the number of read columns. So, for k 2D points, this number will be $2*k$.

In the following data, we have an instance of this file, which was obtained through the annotation of three images from IMM database, in which *k* is equal to 5:

```
3 10
265 311 303 321 337 310 302 298 265 311
255 315 305 337 346 316 305 309 255 315
262 316 303 342 332 315 298 299 262 316
```

Now that we have annotated images, let's turn this data into our shape model. Firstly, load this data into a matrix. This will be achieved through the function `loadPCA`. The following code snippet shows the use of the `loadPCA` function:

```
PCA loadPCA(char* fileName, int& rows, int& cols,Mat& pcaset){
    FILE* in = fopen(fileName,"r");
    int a;
    fscanf(in,"%d%d",&rows,&cols);

    pcaset = Mat::eye(rows,cols,CV_64F);
    int i,j;


    for(i=0;i<rows;i++){
      for(j=0;j<cols;j++){
        fscanf(in,"%d",&a);
        pcaset.at<double>(i,j) = a;
      }
    }


    PCA pca(pcaset, // pass the data
      Mat(), // we do not have a pre-computed mean vector,
      // so let the PCA engine compute it
      CV_PCA_DATA_AS_ROW, // indicate that the vectors
      // are stored as matrix rows
      // (use CV_PCA_DATA_AS_COL if the vectors are
      // the matrix columns)
      pcaset.cols// specify, how many principal components to retain
      );
    return pca;
}
```

Note that our matrix is created in the line `pcaset = Mat::eye(rows,cols,CV_64F)` and that enough space is allocated for *2*k* values. After the two *for* loops load the data into the matrix, the PCA constructor is called with the data—an empty matrix— that could be our precomputed mean vector, if we wish to make it only once. We also indicate that our vectors will be stored as matrix rows and that we wish to keep the same number of given rows as the number of components, though we could use just a few ones.

Now that we have filled our PCA object with our training set, it has everything it needs to backproject our shape according to given parameters. We do so by invoking `PCA.backproject`, passing the parameters as a row vector, and receiving the backprojected vector into the second argument.

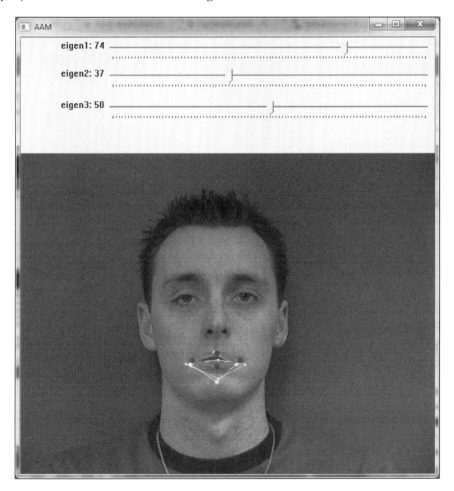

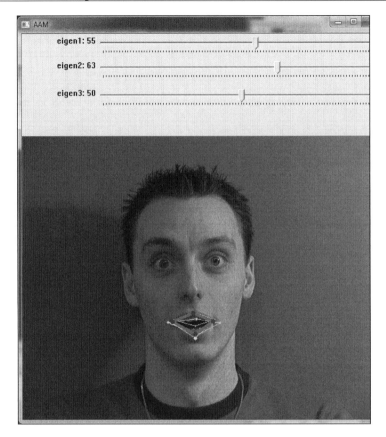

The two previous screenshots show two different shape configurations according to the selected parameters chosen from the slider. The yellow and green shapes show training data, while the red one reflects the shape generated from the chosen parameters.

A sample program can be used to experiment with active shape models, as it allows the user to try different parameters for the model. One is able to note that varying only the first two scalar values through the slider (which correspond to the first and second modes of variation) we can achieve a shape that is very close to the trained ones. This variability will help us when searching for a model in AAM, since it provides interpolated shapes. We will discuss triangulation, texturing, AAM, and AAM-search in the following sections.

Triangulation

As the shape we are looking for might be distorted, such as an open mouth for instance, we are required to map our texture back to a mean shape and then apply PCA to this normalized texture. In order to do that, we will use triangulation. The concept is very simple: we will create triangles including our annotated points and then map from one triangle to another. OpenCV comes with a handy function called `cvCreateSubdivDelaunay2D`, which creates an empty Delaunay triangulation. You can just consider this a good triangulation that will avoid skinny triangles.

> In mathematics and computational geometry, a **Delaunay triangulation** for a set *P* of points in a plane is a triangulation DT(P) such that no point in *P* is inside the circumcircle of any triangle in DT(P). Delaunay triangulations maximize the minimum angle of all the angles of the triangles in the triangulation; they tend to avoid skinny triangles. The triangulation is named after Boris Delaunay for his work on this topic from 1934 onwards.

After a Delaunay subdivision has been initialized, one will use `cvSubdivDelaunay2DInsert` to populate points into the subdivision. The following lines of code will elucidate what a direct use of triangulation would be like:

```
CvMemStorage* storage;
CvSubdiv2D* subdiv;
CvRect rect = { 0, 0, 640, 480 };

storage = cvCreateMemStorage(0);
subdiv = cvCreateSubdivDelaunay2D(rect,storage);

std::vector<CvPoint> points;

//initialize points somehow
...

//iterate through points inserting them in the subdivision
for(int i=0;i<points.size();i++){
  float x = points.at(i).x;
  float y = points.at(i).y;
  CvPoint2D32f floatingPoint = cvPoint2D32f(x, y);
  cvSubdivDelaunay2DInsert( subdiv, floatingPoint );
}
```

Note that our points are going to be inside a rectangular frame that is passed as a parameter to `cvCreateSubdivDelaunay2D`. In order to create a subdivision, we also need to create and initialize a memory storage structure. This can be seen in the first five lines of the preceding code. Then, in order to create the triangulation, we need to insert points using the `cvSubdivDelaunay2DInsert` function. This happens inside the *for* loop in the preceding code. Please note that the points should already have been initialized, since they are the ones we'll usually be using as inputs. The following screenshot shows what the triangulation could look like:

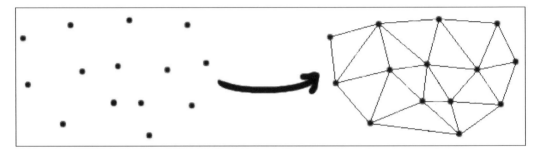

This screenshot is the output of the preceding code for a set of points that yield the triangulation using Delaunay algorithm.

Although subdivision creation is a very handy function of OpenCV, it might not be very easy iterating through all the triangles. The following code shows how to iterate through the edges of a subdivision:

```
void iterate(CvSubdiv2D* subdiv, CvNextEdgeType triangleDirection){

    CvSeqReader reader;
    CvPoint buf[3];

    int i, j, total = subdiv->edges->total;
    int elem_size = subdiv->edges->elem_size;
    cvStartReadSeq((CvSeq*)(subdiv->edges), &reader, 0);

    for(i = 0; i < total; i++){
        CvQuadEdge2D* edge = (CvQuadEdge2D*)(reader.ptr);

        if(CV_IS_SET_ELEM(edge)){

            CvSubdiv2DEdge t = (CvSubdiv2DEdge)edge;

            for(j=0;j<3;j++){

                CvSubdiv2DPoint* pt = cvSubdiv2DEdgeOrg(t);
```

```
        if(!pt) break;
        buf[j] = cvPoint(cvRound(pt->pt.x), cvRound(pt->pt.y));
        t = cvSubdiv2DGetEdge(t, triangleDirection);
      }
    }
    CV_NEXT_SEQ_ELEM(elem_size, reader);
  }
}
```

Given a subdivision, we initialize its edge reader calling the `cvStartReadSeq`
function. From OpenCV's documentation, we have the following quoted definition:

> *The function initializes the reader state. After that, all the sequence elements from
> the first one down to the last one can be read by subsequent calls of the macro
> CV_READ_SEQ_ELEM(read_elem, reader) in the case of forward reading and
> by using CV_REV_READ_SEQ_ELEM(read_elem, reader) in the case of reverse
> reading. Both macros put the sequence element to read_elem and move the reading
> pointer toward the next element.*

An alternative way of getting the following element is by using the macro `CV_NEXT_SEQ_ELEM( elem_size, reader )`, which is preferred if sequence elements are large. In this case, we use `CvQuadEdge2D* edge = (CvQuadEdge2D*)(reader.ptr)` to access the edge, which is just a cast from a reader pointer to a `CvQuadEdge2D` pointer. The macro `CV_IS_SET_ELEM` only checks whether the specified edge is occupied or not. Given an edge, for us to get the source point we need to call the `cvSubdiv2DEdgeOrg` function. In order to run around a triangle, we repeatedly call `cvSubdiv2DGetEdge` and pass the triangle direction, which could be `CV_NEXT_AROUND_LEFT` or `CV_NEXT_AROUND_RIGHT`, for instance.

Triangle texture warping

Now that we've been able to iterate through the triangles of a subdivision, we are able to warp one triangle from an original annotated image into a generated distorted one. This is useful for mapping the texture from the original shape to a distorted one. The following piece of code will guide the process:

```
void warpTextureFromTriangle(Point2f srcTri[3], Mat originalImage,
Point2f dstTri[3], Mat warp_final){

  Mat warp_mat(2, 3, CV_32FC1);
  Mat warp_dst, warp_mask;
  CvPoint trianglePoints[3];
  trianglePoints[0] = dstTri[0];
  trianglePoints[1] = dstTri[1];
```

```
    trianglePoints[2] = dstTri[2];
    warp_dst = Mat::zeros(originalImage.rows, originalImage.cols,
originalImage.type());
    warp_mask = Mat::zeros(originalImage.rows, originalImage.cols,
originalImage.type());

    /// Get the Affine Transform
    warp_mat = getAffineTransform(srcTri, dstTri);

    /// Apply the Affine Transform to the src image
    warpAffine(originalImage, warp_dst, warp_mat, warp_dst.size());
    cvFillConvexPoly(new IplImage(warp_mask), trianglePoints, 3, CV_
RGB(255,255,255), CV_AA, 0);
    warp_dst.copyTo(warp_final, warp_mask);


}
```

The preceding code assumes we have the triangle vertices packed in the `srcTri` array and the destination one packed in the `dstTri` array. The 2 x 3 `warp_mat` matrix is used to get the affine transformation from the source triangles to the destination ones. More information can be quoted from OpenCV's *cvGetAffineTransform* documentation:

The function `cvGetAffineTransform` calculates the matrix of an affine transform such that:

$$\begin{bmatrix} x'_i \\ y'_i \end{bmatrix} = \texttt{mapMatrix} \cdot \begin{bmatrix} x_i \\ y_i \\ 1 \end{bmatrix}$$

In the preceding equation, destination *(i)* is equal to (x'_i, y'_i), source *(i)* is equal to (x_i, y_i), and *i* is equal to 0, 1, 2.

After retrieving the affine matrix, we can apply the affine transformation to the source image. This is done through the `warpAffine` function. Since we don't want to do it in the entire image—we want to focus on our triangle—a mask can be used for this task. This way, the last line copies only the triangle from our original image with our just-created mask, which was made through a `cvFillConvexPoly` call.

The following screenshot shows the result of applying this procedure to every triangle in an annotated image. Note that the triangles are mapped back to the alignment frame, which faces toward the viewer. This procedure is used to create the statistical texture of the AAM.

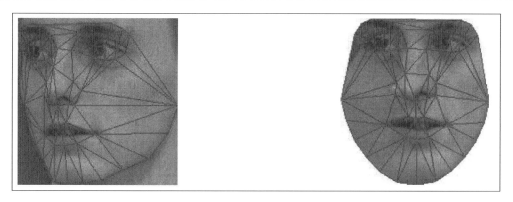

The preceding screenshot shows the result of warping all the mapped triangles in the left image to a mean reference frame.

Model Instantiation – playing with the Active Appearance Model

An interesting aspect of AAMs is their ability to easily interpolate the model that we trained our images on. We can get used to their amazing representational power through the adjustment of a couple of shape or model parameters. As we vary shape parameters, the destination of our warp changes according to the trained shape data. On the other hand, while appearance parameters are modified, the texture on the base shape is modified. Our warp transforms will take every triangle from the base shape to the modified destination shape so we can synthesize a closed mouth on top of an open mouth, as shown in the following screenshot:

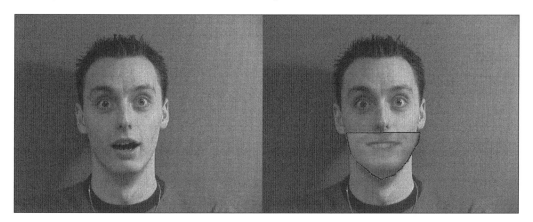

This preceding screenshot shows a synthesized closed mouth obtained through active appearance model instantiation on top of another image. It shows how one could combine a smiling mouth with an admired face, extrapolating the trained images.

The preceding screenshot was obtained by changing only three parameters for shape and three for the texture, which is the goal of AAMs. A sample application has been developed and is available at `http://www.packtpub.com/` for the reader to try out AAM. Instantiating a new model is just a question of sliding the equation parameters, as defined in the section *Getting the feel of PCA*. You should note that AAM search and fitting rely on this flexibility to find the best match for a given captured frame of our model in a different position from the trained ones. We will see this in the next section.

AAM search and fitting

With our fresh new combined shape and texture model, we have found a nice way to describe how a face could change not only in shape but also in appearance. Now we want to find which set of p shape and λ appearance parameters will bring our model as close as possible to a given input image $I(x)$. We could naturally calculate the error between our instantiated model and the given input image in the coordinate frame of $I(x)$, or map the points back to the base appearance and calculate the difference there. We are going to use the latter approach. This way, we want to minimize the following function:

$$\sum_{\mathbf{x} \in s_0} \left[A_0(\mathbf{x}) + \sum_{i=1}^{m} \lambda_i A_i(\mathbf{x}) - I(\mathbf{W}(\mathbf{x}; \mathbf{p})) \right]^2$$

In the preceding equation, *S0* denotes the set of pixels x is equal to $(x,y)T$ that lie inside the AAMs base mesh, $A_0(x)$ is our base mesh texture, $A_i(x)$ is appearance images from PCA, and $W(x;p)$ is the warp that takes pixels from the input image back to the base mesh frame.

Several approaches have been proposed for this minimization through years of studying. The first idea was use an additive approach, in which Δp_i and $\Delta \lambda_i$ were calculated as linear functions of the error image and then shape parameter p and appearance λ were updated as $p_i \leftarrow p_i + \Delta p_i$ and $\lambda_i \leftarrow \lambda_i + \Delta \lambda_i$, in the *i-th* iteration. Although convergence can occur sometimes, the delta doesn't always depend on current parameters, and this might lead to divergence. Another approach—which was studied based on the gradient descent algorithms—was very slow, so another way of finding convergence was sought. Instead of updating the parameters, the whole warp could be updated. This way, a compositional approach was proposed by Ian Mathews and Simon Baker in a famous paper called *Active Appearance Models Revisited*. More details can be found in the paper, but the important contribution it gave to fitting was that it brought the most intensive computation to a pre-compute step, as seen in the following screenshot:

Pre-compute:

   (3) Evaluate the gradient ∇A_0 of the template $A_0(\mathbf{x})$

   (4) Evaluate the Jacobian $\frac{\partial \mathbf{W}}{\partial \mathbf{p}}$ at $(\mathbf{x}; 0)$

   (5) Compute the modified steepest descent images using Equation (41)

   (6) Compute the Hessian matrix using modified steepest descent images

Iterate:

   (1) Warp I with $\mathbf{W}(\mathbf{x}; \mathbf{p})$ to compute $I(\mathbf{W}(\mathbf{x}; \mathbf{p}))$

   (2) Compute the error image $I(\mathbf{W}(\mathbf{x}; \mathbf{p})) - A_0(\mathbf{x})$

   (7) Compute dot product of modified steepest descent images with error image

   (8) Compute $\Delta \mathbf{p}$ by multiplying by inverse Hessian

   (9) Update the warp $\mathbf{W}(\mathbf{x}; \mathbf{p}) \leftarrow \mathbf{W}(\mathbf{x}; \mathbf{p}) \circ \mathbf{W}(\mathbf{x}; \Delta \mathbf{p})^{-1}$

Post-computation:

   (10) Compute λ_i using Equation (40). [Optional step]

Note that the update occurs in terms of a compositional step as seen in step **(9)** (see the previous screenshot). Equations **(40)** and **(41)** from the paper can be seen in the following screenshots:

$$\lambda_i = \sum_{\mathbf{x} \in s_0} A_i(\mathbf{x}) \cdot [I(\mathbf{W}(\mathbf{x}; \mathbf{p})) - A_0(\mathbf{x})], \tag{40}$$

$$SD_j(\mathbf{x}) = \nabla A_0 \frac{\partial \mathbf{W}}{\partial p_j} - \sum_{i=1}^{m} \left[\sum_{\mathbf{x} \in s_0} A_i(\mathbf{x}) \cdot \nabla A_0 \frac{\partial \mathbf{W}}{\partial p_j} \right] A_i(\mathbf{x}) \tag{41}$$

Although the algorithm just mentioned will mostly converge very well from a position near the final one, this might not be the case when there's a big difference in rotation, translation, or scale. We can bring more information to the convergence through the parameterization of a global 2D similarity transform. This is equation *42* in the paper and is shown as follows:

$$\mathbf{N(x; q)} = \begin{pmatrix} (1+a) & -b \\ b & (1+a) \end{pmatrix} \begin{pmatrix} x \\ y \end{pmatrix} + \begin{pmatrix} t_x \\ t_y \end{pmatrix}$$

In the preceding equation, the four parameters $q = (a, b, t_x, t_y)$T have the following interpretations. The first pair (a, b) are related to the scale k and rotation θ: a is equal to k cos θ - 1, and b = k sin θ. The second pair (t_x, t_y) are the x and y translations, as proposed in the Active Appearance Models Revisited paper.

With a bit more of math transformations, one can finally use the preceding algorithm to find the best image fit with a global 2D transform.

As the warp compositional algorithm has several performance advantages, we will use the one described in the AAM Revisited paper, the inverse compositional project-out algorithm. Remember that in this method, the effects of appearance variation during fitting can be precomputed — or projected out — improving AAM fitting performance.

The following screenshot shows convergence for different images from the MUCT dataset using the inverse compositional project-out AAM fitting algorithm.

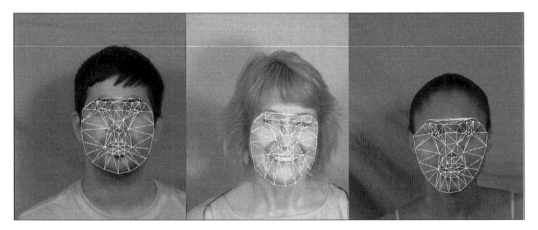

The preceding screenshot shows successful convergences—over faces outside the AAM training set—using the inverse compositional project-out AAM fitting algorithm.

POSIT

After we have found the 2D position of our landmark points, we can derive the 3D pose of our model using the POSIT. The pose P of a 3D object is defined as the 3 x 3 rotation matrix R and the 3D translation vector T, hence P is equal to $[R \mid T]$.

 Most of this section is based on the *OpenCV POSIT* tutorial by Javier Barandiaran.

As the name implies, POSIT uses the **Pose from Orthography and Scaling (POS)** algorithm in several iterations, so it is an acronym for POS with Iterations. The hypothesis for its working is that we can detect and match in the image four or more non-coplanar feature points of the object and that we know their relative geometry on the object.

The main idea of the algorithm is that we can find a good approximation to the object pose, supposing that all the model points are in the same plane, since their depths are not very different from one another if compared to the distance from the camera to a face. After the initial pose is obtained, the rotation matrix and translation vector of the object are found by solving a linear system. Then, the approximate pose is iteratively used to better compute scaled orthographic projections of the feature points, followed by POS application to these projections instead of the original ones. For more information, you can refer to the paper by DeMenton, *Model-Based Object Pose in 25 Lines of Code*.

Diving into POSIT

In order for POSIT to work, you need at least four non-coplanar 3D model points and their respective matchings in the 2D image. We add to that a termination criteria—since POSIT is an iterative algorithm—which generally is a number of iterations or a distance parameter. We then call the function cvPOSIT, which yields the rotation matrix and the translation vector.

As an example, we will follow the tutorial from Javier Barandiaran, which uses POSIT to obtain the pose of a cube. The model is created with four points. It is initialized with the following code:

```
float cubeSize = 10.0;
std::vector<CvPoint3D32f> modelPoints;
```

```
modelPoints.push_back(cvPoint3D32f(0.0f, 0.0f, 0.0f));
modelPoints.push_back(cvPoint3D32f(0.0f, 0.0f, cubeSize));
modelPoints.push_back(cvPoint3D32f(cubeSize, 0.0f, 0.0f));
modelPoints.push_back(cvPoint3D32f(0.0f, cubeSize, 0.0f));
CvPOSITObject *positObject = cvCreatePOSITObject( &modelPoints[0],
static_cast<int>(modelPoints.size()) );
```

Note that the model itself is created with the `cvCreatePOSITObject` method, which returns a `CvPOSITObject` method that will be used in the `cvPOSIT` function. Be aware that the pose will be calculated referring to the first model point, which makes it a good idea to put it at the origin.

We then need to put the 2D image points in another vector. Remember that they must be put in the array in the same order that the model points were inserted in; this way, the i'th 2D image point matches the i'th 3D model point. A catch here is that the origin for the 2D image points is located at the center of the image, which might require you to translate them. You can insert the following 2D image points (of course, they will vary according to the user's matching):

```
std::vector<CvPoint2D32f> srcImagePoints;
srcImagePoints.push_back( cvPoint2D32f( -48, -224 ) );
srcImagePoints.push_back( cvPoint2D32f( -287, -174 ) );
srcImagePoints.push_back( cvPoint2D32f( 132, -153 ) );
srcImagePoints.push_back( cvPoint2D32f( -52, 149 ) );
```

Now, you only need to allocate memory for the matrixes and create termination criteria, followed by a call to `cvPOSIT`, as shown in the following code snippet:

```
//Estimate the pose
CvMatr32f rotation_matrix = new float[9];
CvVect32f translation_vector = new float[3];
CvTermCriteria criteria = cvTermCriteria(CV_TERMCRIT_EPS | CV_
TERMCRIT_ITER, 100, 1.0e-4f);
cvPOSIT( positObject, &srcImagePoints[0], FOCAL_LENGTH, criteria,
rotation_matrix, translation_vector );
```

After the iterations, `cvPOSIT` will store the results in `rotation_matrix` and `translation_vector`. The following screenshot shows the inserted `srcImagePoints` with white circles as well as a coordinate axis showing the rotation and translation results:

With reference to the preceding screenshot, let's see the input points and results of running the POSIT algorithm:

- The white circles show input points, while the coordinate axes show the resulting model pose.

- Make sure you use the focal length of your camera as obtained through a calibration process. You might want to check one of the calibration procedures available in the *Camera calibration* section in *Chapter 2, Marker-based Augmented Reality on iPhone or iPad*. The current implementation of POSIT will only allow square pixels, so there won't be room for focal length in the x and y axes.

- Expect the rotation matrix in the following format:

  [rot[0] rot[1] rot[2]]

  [rot[3] rot[4] rot[5]]

  [rot[6] rot[7] rot[8]]

- The translation vector will be in the following format:

  [trans[0]]

  [trans[1]]

  [trans[2]]

POSIT and head model

In order to use POSIT as a tool for head pose, you will need to use a 3D head model. There is one available from the Institute of Systems and Robotics of the University of Coimbra and can be found at `http://aifi.isr.uc.pt/Downloads/OpenGL/ glAnthropometric3DModel.cpp`. Note that the model can be obtained from where it says:

```
float Model3D[58][3]= {{-7.308957,0.913869,0.000000}, ...
```

The model can be seen in the following screenshot:

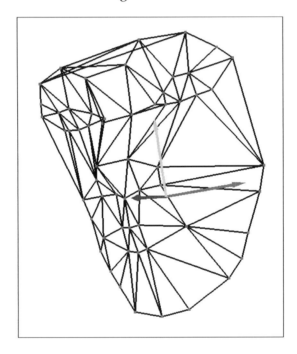

The preceding screenshot shows a 58-point 3D head model available for POSIT.

In order to get POSIT to work, the point corresponding to the 3D head model must be matched accordingly. Note that at least four non-coplanar 3D points and their corresponding 2D projections are required for POSIT to work, so these must be passed as parameters, pretty much as described in the *Diving into POSIT* section. Note that this algorithm is linear in terms of the number of matched points. The following screenshot shows how matching should be done:

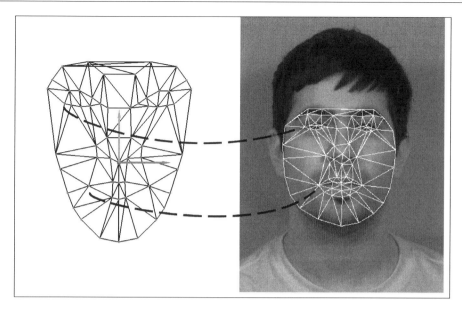

The preceding screenshot shows the correctly matched points of a 3D head model and an AAM mesh.

Tracking from webcam or video file

Now that all the tools have been assembled to get 6 degrees of freedom head tracking, we can apply it to a camera stream or video file. OpenCV provides the `VideoCapture` class that can be used in the following manner (see the *Accessing the webcam* section in *Chapter 1, Cartoonifier and Skin Changer for Android*, for more details):

```
#include "cv.h"
#include "highgui.h"

using namespace cv;

int main(int, char**)
{
    VideoCapture cap(0);// opens the default camera, could use a
                        // video file path instead

    if(!cap.isOpened()) // check if we succeeded
          return -1;

    AAM aam = loadPreviouslyTrainedAAM();
    HeadModel headModel = load3DHeadModel();
```

```
Mapping mapping = mapAAMLandmarksToHeadModel();

Pose2D pose = detectFacePosition();


while(1)
{
Mat frame;
cap >> frame; // get a new frame from camera

Pose2D new2DPose = performAAMSearch(pose, aam);
Pose3D new3DPose = applyPOSIT(new2DPose, headModel, mapping);

if(waitKey(30) >= 0) break;
}

// the camera will be deinitialized automatically in VideoCapture
// destructor
return 0;
}
```

The algorithm works like this. A video capture is initialized through `VideoCapture cap(0)`, so that the default webcam is used. Now that we have video capture working, we also need to load our trained active appearance model, which will occurs in the pseudocode `loadPreviouslyTrainedAAM` mapping. We also load the 3D head model for POSIT and the mapping of landmark points to 3D head points in our mapping variable.

After everything we need has been loaded, we will need to initialize the algorithm from a known pose, which is a known 3D position, known rotation, and a known set of AAM parameters. This could be made automatically through OpenCV's highly documented Haar features classifier face detector (more details in the *Face Detection* section of *Chapter 6, Non-rigid Face Tracking*, or in OpenCV's cascade classifier documentation), or we could manually initialize the pose from a previously annotated frame. A brute-force approach, which would be to run an AAM fitting for every rectangle, could also be used, since it would be very slow only during the first frame. Note that by initialization we mean finding the 2D landmarks of the AAM through their parameters.

When everything is loaded, we can iterate through the main loop delimited by the *while* loop. In this loop, we first query the next grabbed frame, and we then run an active appearance model fit so that we can find landmarks on the next frame. Since the current position is very important at this step, we pass it as a parameter to the pseudocode function `performAAMSearch(pose,aam)`. If we find the current pose, which is signaled through error image convergence, we will get the next landmark positions so we can provide them to POSIT. This happens in the following line, `applyPOSIT(new2DPose, headModel, mapping)`, where the new 2D pose is passed as a parameter, as also our previously loaded `headModel` and the mapping. After that, we can render any 3D model in the obtained pose like a coordinate axis or an augmented reality model. As we have landmarks, more interesting effects can be obtained through model parameterization, such as opening a mouth or changing eyebrow position.

As this procedure relies on previous pose for next estimation, we could accumulate errors and diverge from head position. A workaround could be to reinitialize the procedure every time it happens, checking a given error image threshold. Another factor to pay attention to is the use of filters when tracking, since jittering can occur. A simple mean filter for each of the translation and rotation coordinates can give reasonable results.

Summary

In this chapter, we have discussed how active appearance models can be combined with the POSIT algorithm in order to obtain a 3D head pose. An overview on how to create, train, and manipulate AAMs has been given and the reader can use this background for any other field, such as medical, imaging, or industry. Besides dealing with AAMs, we got familiar to Delaunay subdivisions and learned how to use such an interesting structure as a triangulated mesh. We also showed how to perform texture mapping in the triangles using OpenCV functions. Another interesting topic was approached in AAM fitting. Although only the inverse compositional project-out algorithm was described, we could easily obtain the results of years of research by simply using its output.

After enough theory and practice of AAMs, we dived into the details of POSIT in order to couple 2D measurements to 3D ones explaining how to fit a 3D model using matchings between model points. We concluded the chapter by showing how to use all the tools in an online face tracker by detection, which yields 6 degrees of freedom head pose—3 degrees for rotation— and 3 for translation. The complete code for this chapter can be downloaded from `http://www.packtpub.com/`.

References

- *Active Appearance Models, T.F. Cootes, G. J. Edwards, and C. J. Taylor, ECCV, 2:484–498, 1998* (`http://www.cs.cmu.edu/~efros/courses/AP06/Papers/cootes-eccv-98.pdf`)

- *Active Shape Models – Their Training and Application, T.F. Cootes, C.J. Taylor, D.H. Cooper, and J. Graham, Computer Vision and Image Understanding, (61): 38–59, 1995* (`http://www.wiau.man.ac.uk/~bim/Papers/cviu95.pdf`)

- *The MUCT Landmarked Face Database, S. Milborrow, J. Morkel, and F. Nicolls, Pattern Recognition Association of South Africa, 2010* (`http://www.milbo.org/muct/`)

- *The IMM Face Database – An Annotated Dataset of 240 Face Images, Michael M. Nordstrom, Mads Larsen, Janusz Sierakowski, and Mikkel B. Stegmann, Informatics and Mathematical Modeling, Technical University of Denmark, 2004,* (`http://www2.imm.dtu.dk/~aam/datasets/datasets.html`)

- *Sur la sphère vide, B. Delaunay, Izvestia Akademii Nauk SSSR, Otdelenie Matematicheskikh i Estestvennykh Nauk, 7:793–800, 1934*

- *Active Appearance Models for Facial Expression Recognition and Monocular Head Pose Estimation Master Thesis, P. Martins, 2008*

- *Active Appearance Models Revisited, International Journal of Computer Vision, Vol. 60, No. 2, pp. 135 - 164, I. Mathews and S. Baker, November, 2004* (`http://www.ri.cmu.edu/pub_files/pub4/matthews_iain_2004_2/matthews_iain_2004_2.pdf`)

- *POSIT Tutorial, Javier Barandiaran* (`http://opencv.willowgarage.com/wiki/Posit`)

- *Model-Based Object Pose in 25 Lines of Code, International Journal of Computer Vision, 15, pp. 123-141, Dementhon and L.S Davis, 1995* (`http://www.cfar.umd.edu/~daniel/daniel_papersfordownload/Pose25Lines.pdf`)

8
Face Recognition using Eigenfaces or Fisherfaces

This chapter will introduce concepts in face detection and face recognition and provide a project to detect faces and recognize them when it sees them again. Face recognition is both a popular and a difficult topic, and many researchers devote years to the field of face recognition. So this chapter will explain simple methods of face recognition, giving the reader a good start if they want to explore more complex methods.

In this chapter, we cover the following:

- Face detection
- Face preprocessing
- Training a machine-learning algorithm from collected faces
- Face recognition
- Finishing touches

Introduction to face recognition and face detection

Face recognition is the process of putting a label to a known face. Just like humans learn to recognize their family, friends and celebrities just by seeing their face, there are many techniques for a computer to learn to recognize a known face. These generally involve four main steps:

1. **Face detection**: It is the process of locating a face region in an image (a large rectangle near the center of the following screenshot). This step does not care who the person is, just that it is a human face.

2. **Face preprocessing**: It is the process of adjusting the face image to look more clear and similar to other faces (a small grayscale face in the top-center of the following screenshot).

3. **Collect and learn faces**: It is the process of saving many preprocessed faces (for each person that should be recognized), and then learning how to recognize them.

4. **Face recognition**: It is the process that checks which of the collected people are most similar to the face in the camera (a small rectangle on the top-right of the following screenshot).

 Note that the phrase face recognition is often used by the general public for finding positions of faces (that is, face detection, as described in step 1), but this book will use the formal definition of face recognition referring to step 4 and face detection referring to step 1.

The following screenshot shows the final WebcamFaceRec project, including a small rectangle at the top-right corner highlighting the recognized person. Also notice the confidence bar that is next to the preprocessed face (a small face at the top-center of the rectangle marking the face), which in this case shows roughly 70 percent confidence that it has recognized the correct person.

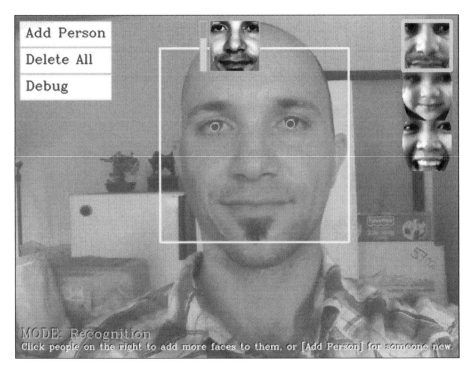

The current face detection techniques are quite reliable in real-world conditions, whereas current face recognition techniques are much less reliable when used in real-world conditions. For example, it is easy to find research papers showing face recognition accuracy rates above 95 percent, but when testing those same algorithms yourself, you may often find that accuracy is lower than 50 percent. This comes from the fact that current face recognition techniques are very sensitive to exact conditions in the images, such as the type of lighting, direction of lighting and shadows, exact orientation of the face, expression of the face, and the current mood of the person. If they are all kept constant when training (collecting images) as well as when testing (from the camera image), then face recognition should work well, but if the person was standing to the left-hand side of the lights in a room when training, and then stood to the right-hand side while testing with the camera, it may give quite bad results. So the dataset used for training is very important.

Face preprocessing (step 2) aims to reduce these problems, such as by making sure the face always appears to have similar brightness and contrast, and perhaps makes sure the features of the face will always be in the same position (such as aligning the eyes and/or nose to certain positions). A good face preprocessing stage will help improve the reliability of the whole face recognition system, so this chapter will place some emphasis on face preprocessing methods.

Despite the big claims about face recognition for security in the media, it is unlikely that the current face recognition methods alone are reliable enough for any true security system, but they can be used for purposes that don't need high reliability, such as playing personalized music for different people entering a room or a robot that says your name when it sees you. There are also various practical extensions to face recognition, such as gender recognition, age recognition, and emotion recognition.

Step 1: Face detection

Until year 2000, there were many different techniques used for finding faces, but all of them were either very slow, very unreliable, or both. A major change came in 2001 when Viola and Jones invented the Haar-based cascade classifier for object detection, and in 2002 when it was improved by Lienhart and Maydt. The result is an object detector that is both fast (can detect faces in real time on a typical desktop with a VGA webcam) and reliable (detects approximately 95 percent of frontal faces correctly). This object detector revolutionized the field of face recognition (as well as that of robotics and computer vision in general), as it finally allowed real-time face detection and face recognition, especially as Lienhart himself wrote the object detector that comes free with OpenCV! It works not only for frontal faces but also side-view faces (referred to as profile faces), eyes, mouths, noses, company logos, and many other objects.

This object detector was extended in OpenCV v2.0 to also use LBP features for detection based on work by Ahonen, Hadid and Pietikäinen in 2006, as LBP-based detectors are potentially several times faster than Haar-based detectors, and don't have the licensing issues that many Haar detectors have.

The basic idea of the Haar-based face detector is that if you look at most frontal faces, the region with the eyes should be darker than the forehead and cheeks, and the region with the mouth should be darker than cheeks, and so on. It typically performs about 20 stages of comparisons like this to decide if it is a face or not, but it must do this at each possible position in the image and for each possible size of the face, so in fact it often does thousands of checks per image. The basic idea of the LBP-based face detector is similar to the Haar-based one, but it uses histograms of pixel intensity comparisons, such as edges, corners, and flat regions.

Rather than have a person decide which comparisons would best define a face, both Haar- and LBP-based face detectors can be automatically trained to find faces from a large set of images, with the information stored as XML files to be used later. These cascade classifier detectors are typically trained using at least 1,000 unique face images and 10,000 non-face images (for example, photos of trees, cars, and text), and the training process can take a long time even on a multi-core desktop (typically a few hours for LBP but one week for Haar!). Luckily, OpenCV comes with some pretrained Haar and LBP detectors for you to use! In fact you can detect frontal faces, profile (side-view) faces, eyes, or noses just by loading different cascade classifier XML files to the object detector, and choose between the Haar or LBP detector, based on which XML file you choose.

Implementing face detection using OpenCV

As mentioned previously, OpenCV v2.4 comes with various pretrained XML detectors that you can use for different purposes. The following table lists some of the most popular XML files:

Type of cascade classifier	XML filename
Face detector (default)	`haarcascade_frontalface_default.xml`
Face detector (fast Haar)	`haarcascade_frontalface_alt2.xml`
Face detector (fast LBP)	`lbpcascade_frontalface.xml`
Profile (side-looking) face detector	`haarcascade_profileface.xml`
Eye detector (separate for left and right)	`haarcascade_lefteye_2splits.xml`
Mouth detector	`haarcascade_mcs_mouth.xml`
Nose detector	`haarcascade_mcs_nose.xml`
Whole person detector	`haarcascade_fullbody.xml`

Haar-based detectors are stored in the folder data\haarcascades and LBP-based detectors are stored in the folder data\lbpcascades of the OpenCV root folder, such as C:\opencv\data\lbpcascades\.

For our face recognition project, we want to detect frontal faces, so let's use the LBP face detector because it is the fastest and doesn't have patent licensing issues. Note that this pretrained LBP face detector that comes with OpenCV v2.x is not tuned as well as the pretrained Haar face detectors, so if you want more reliable face detection then you may want to train your own LBP face detector or use a Haar face detector.

Loading a Haar or LBP detector for object or face detection

To perform object or face detection, first you must load the pretrained XML file using OpenCV's CascadeClassifier class as follows:

```
CascadeClassifier faceDetector;
faceDetector.load(faceCascadeFilename);
```

This can load Haar or LBP detectors just by giving a different filename. A very common mistake when using this is to provide the wrong folder or filename, but depending on your build environment, the load() method will either return false or generate a C++ exception (and exit your program with an assert error). So it is best to surround the load() method with a try/catch block and display a nice error message to the user if something went wrong. Many beginners skip checking for errors, but it is crucial to show a help message to the user when something did not load correctly, otherwise you may spend a very long time debugging other parts of your code before eventually realizing something did not load. A simple error message can be displayed as follows:

```
CascadeClassifier faceDetector;
try {
    faceDetector.load(faceCascadeFilename);
} catch (cv::Exception e) {}
if ( faceDetector.empty() ) {
    cerr << "ERROR: Couldn't load Face Detector (";
    cerr << faceCascadeFilename << ")!" << endl;
    exit(1);
}
```

Accessing the webcam

To grab frames from a computer's webcam or even from a video file, you can simply call the `VideoCapture::open()` function with the camera number or video filename, then grab the frames using the C++ stream operator, as mentioned in the section *Accessing the webcam* in *Chapter 1, Cartoonifier and Skin Changer for Android*.

Detecting an object using the Haar or LBP Classifier

Now that we have loaded the classifier (just once during initialization), we can use it to detect faces in each new camera frame. But first we should do some initial processing of the camera image just for face detection, by performing the following steps:

1. **Grayscale color conversion**: Face detection only works on grayscale images. So we should convert the color camera frame to grayscale.

2. **Shrinking the camera image**: The speed of face detection depends on the size of the input image (it is very slow for large images but fast for small images), and yet detection is still fairly reliable even at low resolutions. So we should shrink the camera image to a more reasonable size (or use a large value for `minFeatureSize` in the detector, as explained shortly).

3. **Histogram equalization**: Face detection is not as reliable in low-light conditions. So we should perform histogram equalization to improve the contrast and brightness.

Grayscale color conversion

We can easily convert an RGB color image to grayscale using the `cvtColor()` function. But we should only do this if we know we have a color image (that is, it is not a grayscale camera), and we must specify the format of our input image (usually 3-channel BGR on desktop or 4-channel BGRA on mobile). So we should allow three different input color formats, as shown in the following code:

```
Mat gray;
if (img.channels() == 3) {
    cvtColor(img, gray, CV_BGR2GRAY);
}
else if (img.channels() == 4) {
    cvtColor(img, gray, CV_BGRA2GRAY);
}
else {
    // Access the grayscale input image directly.
    gray = img;
}
```

Shrinking the camera image

We can use the `resize()` function to shrink an image to a certain size or scale factor. Face detection usually works quite well for any image size greater than 240 x 240 pixels (unless you need to detect faces that are far away from the camera), because it will look for any faces larger than the `minFeatureSize` (typically 20 x 20 pixels). So let's shrink the camera image to be 320 pixels wide; it doesn't matter if the input is a VGA webcam or a 5 mega pixel HD camera. It is also important to remember and enlarge the detection results, because if you detect faces in a shrunk image then the results will also be shrunk. Note that instead of shrinking the input image, you could use a large `minFeatureSize` value in the detector instead. We must also ensure the image does not become fatter or thinner. For example, a widescreen 800 x 400 image when shrunk to 300 x 200 would make a person look thin. So we must keep the aspect ratio (the ratio of width to height) of the output same as the input. Let's calculate how much to shrink the image width by, then apply the same scale factor to the height as well, as follows:

```
const int DETECTION_WIDTH = 320;
// Possibly shrink the image, to run much faster.
Mat smallImg;
float scale = img.cols / (float) DETECTION_WIDTH;
if (img.cols > DETECTION_WIDTH) {
    // Shrink the image while keeping the same aspect ratio.
    int scaledHeight = cvRound(img.rows / scale);
    resize(img, smallImg, Size(DETECTION_WIDTH, scaledHeight));
}
else {
    // Access the input directly since it is already small.
    smallImg = img;
}
```

Histogram equalization

We can easily perform histogram equalization to improve the contrast and brightness of an image, using the `equalizeHist()` function (as explained in *Learning OpenCV: Computer Vision with the OpenCV Library*). Sometimes this will make the image look strange, but in general it should improve the brightness and contrast and help face detection. The `equalizeHist()` function is used as follows:

```
// Standardize the brightness & contrast, such as
// to improve dark images.
Mat equalizedImg;
equalizeHist(inputImg, equalizedImg);
```

Detecting the face

Now that we have converted the image to grayscale, shrunk the image, and equalized the histogram, we are ready to detect the faces using the `CascadeClassifier::detectMultiScale()` function! There are many parameters that we pass to this function:

- `minFeatureSize`: This parameter determines the minimum face size that we care about, typically 20 x 20 or 30 x 30 pixels but this depends on your use case and image size. If you are performing face detection on a webcam or smartphone where the face will always be very close to the camera, you could enlarge this to 80 x 80 to have much faster detections, or if you want to detect far away faces, such as on a beach with friends, then leave this as 20 x 20.

- `searchScaleFactor`: The parameter determines how many different sizes of faces to look for; typically it would be `1.1` for good detection, or `1.2` for faster detection that does not find the face as often.

- `minNeighbors`: This parameter determines how sure the detector should be that it has detected a face, typically a value of `3` but you can set it higher if you want more reliable faces, even if many faces are not detected.

- `flags`: This parameter allows you to specify whether to look for all faces (default) or only look for the largest face (`CASCADE_FIND_BIGGEST_OBJECT`). If you only look for the largest face, it should run faster. There are several other parameters you can add to make the detection about one percent or two percent faster, such as `CASCADE_DO_ROUGH_SEARCH` or `CASCADE_SCALE_IMAGE`.

The output of the `detectMultiScale()` function will be a `std::vector` of the `cv::Rect` type object. For example, if it detects two faces then it will store an array of two rectangles in the output. The `detectMultiScale()` function is used as follows:

```
int flags = CASCADE_SCALE_IMAGE; // Search for many faces.
Size minFeatureSize(20, 20);     // Smallest face size.
float searchScaleFactor = 1.1f;  // How many sizes to search.
int minNeighbors = 4;            // Reliability vs many faces.

// Detect objects in the small grayscale image.
std::vector<Rect> faces;
faceDetector.detectMultiScale(img, faces, searchScaleFactor,
            minNeighbors, flags, minFeatureSize);
```

We can see if any faces were detected by looking at the number of elements stored in our vector of rectangles, that is by using the `objects.size()` function.

As mentioned earlier, if we gave a shrunken image to the face detector, the results will also be shrunk, so we need to enlarge them if we want to know the face regions for the original image. We also need to make sure faces on the border of the image stay completely within the image, as OpenCV will now raise an exception if this happens, as shown by the following code:

```
// Enlarge the results if the image was temporarily shrunk.
if (img.cols > scaledWidth) {
    for (int i = 0; i < (int)objects.size(); i++ ) {
        objects[i].x = cvRound(objects[i].x * scale);
        objects[i].y = cvRound(objects[i].y * scale);
        objects[i].width = cvRound(objects[i].width * scale);
        objects[i].height = cvRound(objects[i].height * scale);
    }
}
// If the object is on a border, keep it in the image.
for (int i = 0; i < (int)objects.size(); i++ ) {
    if (objects[i].x < 0)
        objects[i].x = 0;
    if (objects[i].y < 0)
        objects[i].y = 0;
    if (objects[i].x + objects[i].width > img.cols)
        objects[i].x = img.cols - objects[i].width;
    if (objects[i].y + objects[i].height > img.rows)
        objects[i].y = img.rows - objects[i].height;
}
```

Note that the preceding code will look for all faces in the image, but if you only care about one face, then you could change the flag variable as follows:

```
int flags = CASCADE_FIND_BIGGEST_OBJECT |
            CASCADE_DO_ROUGH_SEARCH;
```

The WebcamFaceRec project includes a wrapper around OpenCV's Haar or LBP detector, to make it easier to find a face or eye within an image. For example:

```
Rect faceRect;    // Stores the result of the detection, or -1.
int scaledWidth = 320; // Shrink the image before detection.
detectLargestObject(cameraImg, faceDetector, faceRect,
            scaledWidth);
if (faceRect.width > 0)
    cout << "We detected a face!" << endl;
```

Now that we have a face rectangle, we can use it in many ways, such as to extract or crop the face image from the original image. The following code allows us to access the face:

```
// Access just the face within the camera image.
Mat faceImg = cameraImg(faceRect);
```

The following image shows the typical rectangular region given by the face detector:

Step 2: Face preprocessing

As mentioned earlier, Face recognition is extremely vulnerable to changes in lighting conditions, face orientation, face expression, and so on, so it is very important to reduce these differences as much as possible. Otherwise the face recognition algorithm will often think there is more similarity between faces of two different people in the same conditions than between two faces of the same person.

The easiest form of face preprocessing is just to apply histogram equalization using the equalizeHist() function, like we just did for face detection. This may be sufficient for some projects where the lighting and positional conditions won't change by much. But for reliability in real-world conditions, we need many sophisticated techniques, including facial feature detection (for example, detecting eyes, nose, mouth and eyebrows). For simplicity, this chapter will just use eye detection and ignore other facial features such as the mouth and nose, which are less useful. The following image shows an enlarged view of a typical preprocessed face, using the techniques that will be covered in this section:

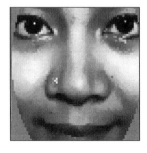

Eye detection

Eye detection can be very useful for face preprocessing, because for frontal faces you can always assume a person's eyes should be horizontal and on opposite locations of the face and should have a fairly standard position and size within a face, despite changes in facial expressions, lighting conditions, camera properties, distance to camera, and so on. It is also useful to discard false positives when the face detector says it has detected a face and it is actually something else. It is rare that the face detector and two eye detectors will all be fooled at the same time, so if you only process images with a detected face and two detected eyes then it will not have many false positives (but will also give fewer faces for processing, as the eye detector will not work as often as the face detector).

Some of the pretrained eye detectors that come with OpenCV v2.4 can detect an eye whether it is open or closed, whereas some of them can only detect open eyes.

Eye detectors that detect open or closed eyes are as follows:

- `haarcascade_mcs_lefteye.xml` (and `haarcascade_mcs_righteye.xml`)
- `haarcascade_lefteye_2splits.xml` (and `haarcascade_righteye_2splits.xml`)

Eye detectors that detect open eyes only are as follows:

- `haarcascade_eye.xml`
- `haarcascade_eye_tree_eyeglasses.xml`

As the open or closed eye detectors specify which eye they are trained on, you need to use a different detector for the left and the right eye, whereas the detectors for just open eyes can use the same detector for left or right eyes.

The detector `haarcascade_eye_tree_eyeglasses.xml` can detect the eyes if the person is wearing glasses, but is not reliable if they don't wear glasses.

If the XML filename says "left eye", it means the actual left eye of the person, so in the camera image it would normally appear on the right-hand side of the face, not on the left-hand side!

The list of four eye detectors mentioned is ranked in approximate order from most reliable to least reliable, so if you know you don't need to find people with glasses then the first detector is probably the best choice.

Eye search regions

For eye detection, it is important to crop the input image to just show the approximate eye region, just like doing face detection and then cropping to just a small rectangle where the left eye should be (if you are using the left eye detector) and the same for the right rectangle for the right eye detector. If you just do eye detection on a whole face or whole photo then it will be much slower and less reliable. Different eye detectors are better suited to different regions of the face, for example, the `haarcascade_eye.xml` detector works best if it only searches in a very tight region around the actual eye, whereas the `haarcascade_mcs_lefteye.xml` and `haarcascade_lefteye_2splits.xml` detectors work best when there is a large region around the eye.

The following table lists some good search regions of the face for different eye detectors (when using the LBP face detector), using relative coordinates within the detected face rectangle:

Cascade Classifier	EYE_SX	EYE_SY	EYE_SW	EYE_SH
haarcascade_eye.xml	0.16	0.26	0.30	0.28
haarcascade_mcs_lefteye.xml	0.10	0.19	0.40	0.36
haarcascade_lefteye_2splits.xml	0.12	0.17	0.37	0.36

Here is the source code to extract the left-eye and right-eye regions from a detected face:

```
int leftX = cvRound(face.cols * EYE_SX);
int topY = cvRound(face.rows * EYE_SY);
int widthX = cvRound(face.cols * EYE_SW);
int heightY = cvRound(face.rows * EYE_SH);
int rightX = cvRound(face.cols * (1.0-EYE_SX-EYE_SW));

Mat topLeftOfFace = faceImg(Rect(leftX, topY, widthX,
                heightY));
Mat topRightOfFace = faceImg(Rect(rightX, topY, widthX,
                heightY));
```

The following image shows the ideal search regions for the different eye detectors, where `haarcascade_eye.xml` and `haarcascade_eye_tree_eyeglasses.xml` are best with the small search region, while `haarcascade_mcs_*eye.xml` and `haarcascade_*eye_2splits.xml` are best with larger search regions. Note that the detected face rectangle is also shown, to give an idea of how large the eye search regions are compared to the detected face rectangle:

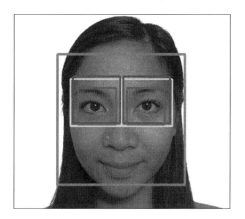

When using the eye search regions given in the preceding table, here are the approximate detection properties of the different eye detectors:

Cascade Classifier	Reliability*	Speed**	Eyes found	Glasses
`haarcascade_mcs_lefteye.xml`	80%	18 msec	Open or closed	no
`haarcascade_lefteye_2splits.xml`	60%	7 msec	Open or closed	no
`haarcascade_eye.xml`	40%	5 msec	Open only	no
`haarcascade_eye_tree_eyeglasses.xml`	15%	10 msec	Open only	yes

* Reliability values show how often both eyes will be detected after LBP frontal face detection when no eyeglasses are worn and both eyes are open. If eyes are closed then the reliability may drop, or if eyeglasses are worn then both reliability and speed will drop.

** Speed values are in milliseconds for images scaled to the size of 320 x 240 pixels on an Intel Core i7 2.2 GHz (averaged across 1,000 photos). Speed is typically much faster when eyes are found than when eyes are not found, as it must scan the entire image, but the `haarcascade_mcs_lefteye.xml` is still much slower than the other eye detectors.

For example, if you shrink a photo to 320 x 240 pixels, perform a histogram equalization on it, use the LBP frontal face detector to get a face, then extract the left-eye-region and right-eye-region from the face using the `haarcascade_mcs_lefteye.xml` values, then perform a histogram equalization on each eye region. Then if you the `haarcascade_mcs_lefteye.xml` detector on the left eye (which is actually on the top-right side of your image) and use the `haarcascade_mcs_righteye.xml` detector on the right eye (the top-left part of your image), each eye detector should work in roughly 90 percent of photos with LBP-detected frontal faces. So if you want both eyes detected then it should work in roughly 80 percent of photos with LBP-detected frontal faces.

Note that while it is recomended to shrink the camera image before detecting faces, you should detect eyes at the full camera resolution because eyes will obviously be much smaller than faces, so you need as much resolution as you can get.

Based on the table, it seems that when choosing an eye detector to use, you should decide whether you want to detect closed eyes or only open eyes. And remember that you can even use one eye detector, and if it does not detect an eye then you can try with another one.

For many tasks, it is useful to detect eyes whether they are opened or closed, so if speed is not crucial, it is best to search with the mcs_*eye detector first, and if it fails then search with the eye_2splits detector.

But for face recognition, a person will appear quite different if their eyes are closed, so it is best to search with the plain haarcascade_eye detector first, and if it fails then search with the haarcascade_eye_tree_eyeglasses detector.

We can use the same `detectLargestObject()` function we used for face detection to search for eyes, but instead of asking to shrink the images before eye detection, we specify the full eye region width to get a better eye detection. It is easy to search for the left eye using one detector, and if it fails then try another detector (same for right eye). The eye detection is done as follows:

```
CascadeClassifier eyeDetector1("haarcascade_eye.xml");
CascadeClassifier
        eyeDetector2("haarcascade_eye_tree_eyeglasses.xml");
...
Rect leftEyeRect;    // Stores the detected eye.
// Search the left region using the 1st eye detector.
detectLargestObject(topLeftOfFace, eyeDetector1, leftEyeRect,
        topLeftOfFace.cols);
// If it failed, search the left region using the 2nd eye
// detector.
if (leftEyeRect.width <= 0)
```

```
    detectLargestObject(topLeftOfFace, eyeDetector2,
            leftEyeRect, topLeftOfFace.cols);
// Get the left eye center if one of the eye detectors worked.
Point leftEye = Point(-1,-1);
if (leftEyeRect.width <= 0) {
    leftEye.x = leftEyeRect.x + leftEyeRect.width/2 + leftX;
    leftEye.y = leftEyeRect.y + leftEyeRect.height/2 + topY;
}


// Do the same for the right-eye
...


// Check if both eyes were detected.
if (leftEye.x >= 0 && rightEye.x >= 0) {
    ...
}
```

With the face and both eyes detected, we'll perform face preprocessing by combining:

- **Geometrical transformation and cropping**: This process would include scaling, rotating, and translating the images so that the eyes are aligned, followed by the removal of the forehead, chin, ears, and background from the face image.

- **Separate histogram equalization for left and right sides**: This process standardizes the brightness and contrast on both the left- and right-hand sides of the face independently.

- **Smoothing**: This process reduces the image noise using a bilateral filter.

- **Elliptical mask**: The elliptical mask removes some remaining hair and background from the face image.

The following image shows the face preprocessing steps 1 to 4 applied to a detected face. Notice how the final image has good brightness and contrast on both sides of the face, whereas the original does not:

Geometrical transformation

It is important that the faces are all aligned together, otherwise the face recognition algorithm might be comparing part of a nose with part of an eye, and so on. The output of face detection just seen will give aligned faces to some extent, but it is not very accurate (that is, the face rectangle will not always be starting from the same point on the forehead).

To have better alignment we will use eye detection to align the face so the positions of the two detected eyes line up perfectly in desired positions. We will do the geometrical transformation using the `warpAffine()` function, which is a single operation that will do four things:

- Rotate the face so that the two eyes are horizontal.

- Scale the face so that the distance between the two eyes is always the same.

- Translate the face so that the eyes are always centered horizontally and at a desired height.

- Crop the outer parts of the face, since we want to crop away the image background, hair, forehead, ears, and chin.

Affine Warping takes an affine matrix that transforms the two detected eye locations to the two desired eye locations, and then crops to a desired size and position. To generate this affine matrix, we will get the center between the eyes, calculate the angle at which the two detected eyes appear, and look at their distance apart as follows:

```
// Get the center between the 2 eyes.
Point2f eyesCenter;
eyesCenter.x = (leftEye.x + rightEye.x) * 0.5f;
eyesCenter.y = (leftEye.y + rightEye.y) * 0.5f;

// Get the angle between the 2 eyes.
double dy = (rightEye.y - leftEye.y);
double dx = (rightEye.x - leftEye.x);
double len = sqrt(dx*dx + dy*dy);
// Convert Radians to Degrees.
double angle = atan2(dy, dx) * 180.0/CV_PI;

// Hand measurements shown that the left eye center should
// ideally be roughly at (0.16, 0.14) of a scaled face image.
const double DESIRED_LEFT_EYE_X = 0.16;
const double DESIRED_RIGHT_EYE_X = (1.0f - 0.16);
// Get the amount we need to scale the image to be the desired
// fixed size we want.
```

```
const int DESIRED_FACE_WIDTH = 70;
const int DESIRED_FACE_HEIGHT = 70;
double desiredLen = (DESIRED_RIGHT_EYE_X - 0.16);
double scale = desiredLen * DESIRED_FACE_WIDTH / len;
```

Now we can transform the face (rotate, scale, and translate) to get the two detected eyes to be in the desired eye positions in an ideal face as follows:

```
// Get the transformation matrix for the desired angle & size.
Mat rot_mat = getRotationMatrix2D(eyesCenter, angle, scale);
// Shift the center of the eyes to be the desired center.
double ex = DESIRED_FACE_WIDTH * 0.5f - eyesCenter.x;
double ey = DESIRED_FACE_HEIGHT * DESIRED_LEFT_EYE_Y -
                eyesCenter.y;
rot_mat.at<double>(0, 2) += ex;
rot_mat.at<double>(1, 2) += ey;
// Transform the face image to the desired angle & size &
// position! Also clear the transformed image background to a
// default grey.
Mat warped = Mat(DESIRED_FACE_HEIGHT, DESIRED_FACE_WIDTH,
                CV_8U, Scalar(128));
warpAffine(gray, warped, rot_mat, warped.size());
```

Separate histogram equalization for left and right sides

In real-world conditions, it is common to have strong lighting on one half of the face and weak lighting on the other. This has an enormous effect on the face recognition algorithm, as the left- and right-hand sides of the same face will seem like very different people. So we will perform histogram equalization separately on the left and right halves of the face, to have standardized brightness and contrast on each side of the face.

If we simply applied histogram equalization on the left half and then again on the right half, we would see a very distinct edge in the middle because the average brightness is likely to be different on the left and the right side, so to remove this edge, we will apply the two histogram equalizations gradually from the left-or right-hand side towards the center and mix it with a whole-face histogram equalization, so that the far left-hand side will use the left histogram equalization, the far right-hand side will use the right histogram equalization, and the center will use a smooth mix of left or right value and the whole-face equalized value.

The following image shows how the left-equalized, whole-equalized, and right-equalized images are blended together:

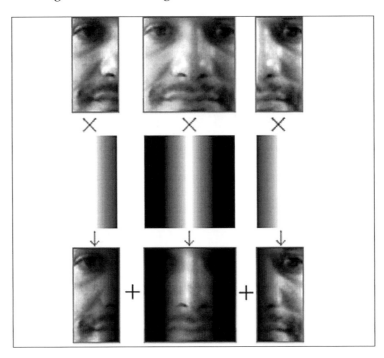

To perform this, we need copies of the whole face equalized as well as the left half equalized and the right half equalized, which is done as follows:

```
int w = faceImg.cols;
int h = faceImg.rows;
Mat wholeFace;
equalizeHist(faceImg, wholeFace);
int midX = w/2;
Mat leftSide = faceImg(Rect(0,0, midX,h));
Mat rightSide = faceImg(Rect(midX,0, w-midX,h));
equalizeHist(leftSide, leftSide);
equalizeHist(rightSide, rightSide);
```

Now we combine the three images together. As the images are small, we can easily access pixels directly using the image.at<uchar>(y,x) function even if it is slow; so let's merge the three images by directly accessing pixels in the three input images and output images, as follows:

```
for (int y=0; y<h; y++) {
    for (int x=0; x<w; x++) {
        int v;
        if (x < w/4) {
            // Left 25%: just use the left face.
            v = leftSide.at<uchar>(y,x);
        }
        else if (x < w*2/4) {
            // Mid-left 25%: blend the left face & whole face.
            int lv = leftSide.at<uchar>(y,x);
            int wv = wholeFace.at<uchar>(y,x);
            // Blend more of the whole face as it moves
            // further right along the face.
            float f = (x - w*1/4) / (float)(w/4);
            v = cvRound((1.0f - f) * lv + (f) * wv);
        }
        else if (x < w*3/4) {
            // Mid-right 25%: blend right face & whole face.
            int rv = rightSide.at<uchar>(y,x-midX);
            int wv = wholeFace.at<uchar>(y,x);
            // Blend more of the right-side face as it moves
            // further right along the face.
            float f = (x - w*2/4) / (float)(w/4);
            v = cvRound((1.0f - f) * wv + (f) * rv);
        }
        else {
            // Right 25%: just use the right face.
            v = rightSide.at<uchar>(y,x-midX);
        }
        faceImg.at<uchar>(y,x) = v;
    }// end x loop
}//end y loop
```

This separated histogram equalization should significantly help reduce the effect of different lighting on the left- and right-hand sides of the face, but we must understand that it won't completely remove the effect of one-sided lighting, since the face is a complex 3D shape with many shadows.

Smoothing

To reduce the effect of pixel noise, we will use a bilateral filter on the face, as a bilateral filter is very good at smoothing most of an image while keeping edges sharp. Histogram equalization can significantly increase the pixel noise, so we will make the filter strength 20 to cover heavy pixel noise, but use a neighborhood of just two pixels as we want to heavily smooth the tiny pixel noise but not the large image regions, as follows:

```
Mat filtered = Mat(warped.size(), CV_8U);
bilateralFilter(warped, filtered, 0, 20.0, 2.0);
```

Elliptical mask

Although we have already removed most of the image background and forehead and hair when we did the geometrical transformation, we can apply an elliptical mask to remove some of the corner region such as the neck, which might be in shadow from the face, particularly if the face is not looking perfectly straight towards the camera. To create the mask, we will draw a black-filled ellipse onto a white image. One ellipse to perform this has a horizontal radius of 0.5 (that is, it covers the face width perfectly), a vertical radius of 0.8 (as faces are usually taller than they are wide), and centered at the coordinates 0.5, 0.4, as shown in the following image, where the elliptical mask has removed some unwanted corners from the face:

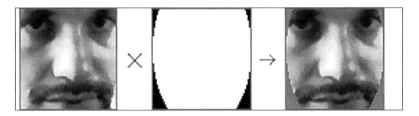

We can apply the mask when calling the cv::setTo() function, which would normally set a whole image to a certain pixel value, but as we will give a mask image, it will only set some parts to the given pixel value. We will fill the image in gray so that it should have less contrast to the rest of the face:

```
// Draw a black-filled ellipse in the middle of the image.
// First we initialize the mask image to white (255).
Mat mask = Mat(warped.size(), CV_8UC1, Scalar(255));
double dw = DESIRED_FACE_WIDTH;
double dh = DESIRED_FACE_HEIGHT;
Point faceCenter = Point( cvRound(dw * 0.5),
                cvRound(dh * 0.4) );
Size size = Size( cvRound(dw * 0.5), cvRound(dh * 0.8) );
ellipse(mask, faceCenter, size, 0, 0, 360, Scalar(0),
```

```
            CV_FILLED);

    // Apply the elliptical mask on the face, to remove corners.
    // Sets corners to gray, without touching the inner face.
    filtered.setTo(Scalar(128), mask);
```

The following enlarged image shows a sample result from all the face preprocessing stages. Notice it is much more consistent for face recognition in different brightness, face rotations, angle from camera, backgrounds, positions of lights, and so on. This preprocessed face will be used as input to the face recognition stages, both when collecting faces for training, and when trying to recognize input faces:

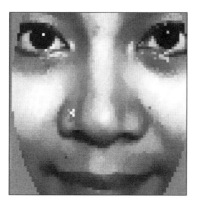

Step 3: Collecting faces and learning from them

Collecting faces can be just as simple as putting each newly preprocessed face into an array of preprocessed faces from the camera, as well as putting a label into an array (to specify which person the face was taken from). For example, you could use 10 preprocessed faces of the first person and 10 preprocessed faces of a second person, so the input to the face recognition algorithm will be an array of 20 preprocessed faces and an array of 20 integers (where the first 10 numbers are 0 and the next 10 numbers are 1).

The face recognition algorithm will then learn how to distinguish between the faces of the different people. This is referred to as the training phase and the collected faces are referred to as the training set. After the face recognition algorithm has finished training, you could then save the generated knowledge to a file or memory and later use it to recognize which person is seen in front of the camera. This is referred to as the testing phase. If you used it directly from a camera input then the preprocessed face would be referred to as the test image, and if you tested with many images (such as from a folder of image files), it would be referred to as the testing set.

It is important that you provide a good training set that covers the types of variations you expect to occur in your testing set. For example, if you will only test with faces that are looking perfectly straight ahead (such as ID photos), then you only need to provide training images with faces that are looking perfectly straight ahead. But if the person might be looking to the left or up, then you should make sure the training set will also include faces of that person doing this, otherwise the face recognition algorithm will have trouble recognizing them, as their face will appear quite different. This also applies to other factors such as facial expression (for example, if the person is always smiling in the training set but not smiling in the testing set) or lighting direction (for example, a strong light is to the left-hand side in the training set but to the right-hand side in the testing set), then the face recognition algorithm will have difficulty recognizing them. The face preprocessing steps that we just saw will help reduce these issues, but it certainly won't remove these factors, particularly the direction in which the face is looking, as it has a large effect on the position of all elements in the face.

One way to obtain a good training set that will cover many different real-world conditions is for each person to rotate their head from looking left, to up, to right, to down then looking directly straight. Then the person tilts their head sideways and then up and down, while also changing their facial expression, such as alternating between smiling, looking angry, and having a neutral face. If each person follows a routine such as this while collecting faces, then there is a much better chance of recognizing everyone in the real-world conditions.

For even better results, it should be performed again with one or two more locations or directions, such as by turning the camera around by 180 degrees and walking in the opposite direction of the camera then repeating the whole routine, so that the training set would include many different lighting conditions.

So in general, having 100 training faces for each person is likely to give better results than having just 10 training faces for each person, but if all 100 faces look almost identical then it will still perform badly because it is more important that the training set has enough variety to cover the testing set, rather than to just have a large number of faces. So to make sure the faces in the training set are not all too similar, we should add a noticeable delay between each collected face. For example, if the camera is running at 30 frames per second, then it might collect 100 faces in just several seconds when the person has not had time to move around, so it is better to collect just one face per second, while the person moves their face around. Another simple method to improve the variation in the training set is to only collect a face if it is noticeably different from the previously collected face.

Collecting preprocessed faces for training

To make sure there is at least a one-second gap between collecting new faces, we need to measure how much time has passed. This is done as follows:

```
// Check how long since the previous face was added.
double current_time = (double)getTickCount();
double timeDiff_seconds = (current_time -
                old_time) / getTickFrequency();
```

To compare the similarity of two images, pixel by pixel, you can find the relative L2 error, which just involves subtracting one image from the other, summing the squared value of it, and then getting the square root of it. So if the person had not moved at all, subtracting the current face with the previous face should give a very low number at each pixel, but if they had just moved slightly in any direction, subtracting the pixels would give a large number and so the L2 error will be high. As the result is summed over all pixels, the value will depend on the image resolution. So to get the mean error we should divide this value by the total number of pixels in the image. Let's put this in a handy function, getSimilarity(), as follows:

```
double getSimilarity(const Mat A, const Mat B) {
    // Calculate the L2 relative error between the 2 images.
    double errorL2 = norm(A, B, CV_L2);
    // Scale the value since L2 is summed across all pixels.
    double similarity = errorL2 / (double)(A.rows * A.cols);
    return similarity;
}

...

// Check if this face looks different from the previous face.
double imageDiff = MAX_DBL;
if (old_prepreprocessedFaceprepreprocessedFace.data) {
    imageDiff = getSimilarity(preprocessedFace,
                        old_prepreprocessedFace);
}
```

This similarity will often be less than 0.2 if the image did not move much, and higher than 0.4 if the image did move, so let's use 0.3 as our threshold for collecting a new face.

There are many tricks we can play to obtain more training data, such as using mirrored faces, adding random noise, shifting the face by a few pixels, scaling the face by a percentage, or rotating the face by a few degrees (even though we specifically tried to remove these effects when preprocessing the face!) Let's add mirrored faces to the training set, so that we have both, a larger training set as well as a reduction in the problems of asymmetrical faces or if a user is always oriented slightly to the left or right during training but not testing. This is done as follows:

```cpp
// Only process the face if it's noticeably different from the
// previous frame and there has been a noticeable time gap.
if ((imageDiff > 0.3) && (timeDiff_seconds > 1.0)) {
    // Also add the mirror image to the training set.
    Mat mirroredFace;
    flip(preprocessedFace, mirroredFace, 1);

    // Add the face & mirrored face to the detected face lists.
    preprocessedFaces.push_back(preprocessedFace);
    preprocessedFaces.push_back(mirroredFace);
    faceLabels.push_back(m_selectedPerson);
    faceLabels.push_back(m_selectedPerson);

    // Keep a copy of the processed face,
    // to compare on next iteration.
    old_preprocessedFace = preprocessedFace;
    old_time = current_time;
}
```

This will collect the `std::vector` arrays `preprocessedFaces` and `faceLabels` for a preprocessed face as well as the label or ID number of that person (assuming it is in the integer `m_selectedPerson` variable).

To make it more obvious to the user that we have added their current face to the collection, you could provide a visual notification by either displaying a large white rectangle over the whole image or just displaying their face for just a fraction of a second so they realize a photo was taken. With OpenCV's C++ interface, you can use the + overloaded `cv::Mat` operator to add a value to every pixel in the image and have it clipped to 255 (using `saturate_cast`, so it doesn't overflow from white back to black!) Assuming `displayedFrame` will be a copy of the color camera frame that should be shown, insert this after the preceding code for face collection:

```cpp
// Get access to the face region-of-interest.
Mat displayedFaceRegion = displayedFrame(faceRect);
// Add some brightness to each pixel of the face region.
displayedFaceRegion += CV_RGB(90,90,90);
```

Training the face recognition system from collected faces

After you have collected enough faces for each person to recognize, you must train the system to learn the data using a machine-learning algorithm suited for face recognition. There are many different face recognition algorithms in literature, the simplest of which are Eigenfaces and Artificial Neural Networks. Eigenfaces tends to work better than ANNs, and despite its simplicity, it tends to work almost as well as many more complex face recognition algorithms, so it has become very popular as the basic face recognition algorithm for beginners as well as for new algorithms to be compared to.

Any reader who wishes to work further on face recognition is recommended to read the theory behind:

- Eigenfaces (also referred to as **Principal Component Analysis (PCA)**
- Fisherfaces (also referred to as **Linear Discriminant Analysis (LDA)**
- Other classic face recognition algorithms (many are available at `http://www.face-rec.org/algorithms/`)
- Newer face recognition algorithms in recent Computer Vision research papers (such as CVPR and ICCV at `http://www.cvpapers.com/`), as there are hundreds of face recognition papers published each year

However, you don't need to understand the theory of these algorithms in order to use them as shown in this book. Thanks to the OpenCV team and Philipp Wagner's `libfacerec` contribution, OpenCV v2.4.1 provided `cv::Algorithm` as a simple and generic method to perform face recognition using one of several different algorithms (even selectable at runtime) without necessarily understanding how they are implemented. You can find the available algorithms in your version of OpenCV by using the `Algorithm::getList()` function, such as with this code:

```
vector<string> algorithms;
Algorithm::getList(algorithms);
cout << "Algorithms: " << algorithms.size() << endl;
for (int i=0; i<algorithms.size(); i++) {
    cout << algorithms[i] << endl;
}
```

Here are the three face recognition algorithms available in OpenCV v2.4.1:

- `FaceRecognizer.Eigenfaces`: Eigenfaces, also referred to as PCA, first used by Turk and Pentland in 1991.

- `FaceRecognizer.Fisherfaces`: Fisherfaces, also referred to as LDA, invented by Belhumeur, Hespanha and Kriegman in 1997.

- `FaceRecognizer.LBPH`: Local Binary Pattern Histograms, invented by Ahonen, Hadid and Pietikäinen in 2004.

 More information on these face recognition algorithm implementations can be found with documentation, samples, and Python equivalents for each of them on Philipp Wagner's website at `http://bytefish.de/blog` and `http://bytefish.de/dev/libfacerec/`.

These face recognition algorithms are available through the `FaceRecognizer` class in OpenCV's `contrib` module. Due to dynamic linking, it is possible that your program is linked to the `contrib` module but it is not actually loaded at runtime (if it was deemed as not required). So it is recommended to call the `cv::initModule_contrib()` function before trying to access the `FaceRecognizer` algorithms. This function is only available from OpenCV v2.4.1, so it also ensures that the face recognition algorithms are at least available to you at compile time:

```
// Load the "contrib" module is dynamically at runtime.
bool haveContribModule = initModule_contrib();
if (!haveContribModule) {
    cerr << "ERROR: The 'contrib' module is needed for ";
    cerr << "FaceRecognizer but hasn't been loaded to OpenCV!";
    cerr << endl;
    exit(1);
}
```

To use one of the face recognition algorithms, we must create a `FaceRecognizer` object using the `cv::Algorithm::create<FaceRecognizer>()` function. We pass the name of the face recognition algorithm we want to use, as a string to this create function. This will give us access to that algorithm if it is available in the OpenCV version. So it may be used as a runtime error check to ensure the user has OpenCV v2.4.1 or newer. For example:

```
string facerecAlgorithm = "FaceRecognizer.Fisherfaces";
Ptr<FaceRecognizer> model;
// Use OpenCV's new FaceRecognizer in the "contrib" module:
model = Algorithm::create<FaceRecognizer>(facerecAlgorithm);
if (model.empty()) {
```

```
    cerr << "ERROR: The FaceRecognizer [" << facerecAlgorithm;
    cerr << "] is not available in your version of OpenCV. ";
    cerr << "Please update to OpenCV v2.4.1 or newer." << endl;
    exit(1);
}
```

Once we have loaded the `FaceRecognizer` algorithm, we simply call the `FaceRecognizer::train()` function with our collected face data as follows:

```
// Do the actual training from the collected faces.
model->train(preprocessedFaces, faceLabels);
```

This one line of code will run the whole face recognition training algorithm that you selected (for example, Eigenfaces, Fisherfaces, or potentially other algorithms). If you have just a few people with less than 20 faces, then this training should return very quickly, but if you have many people with many faces, it is possible that `train()` function will take several seconds or even minutes to process all the data.

Viewing the learned knowledge

While it is not necessary, it is quite useful to view the internal data structures that the face recognition algorithm generated when learning your training data, particularly if you understand the theory behind the algorithm you selected and want to verify if it worked or find why it is not working as you hoped. The internal data structures can be different for different algorithms, but luckily they are the same for Eigenfaces and Fisherfaces, so let's just look at those two. They are both based on 1D eigenvector matrices that appear somewhat like faces when viewed as 2D images, therefore it is common to refer eigenvectors as eigenfaces when using the Eigenface algorithm or as fisherfaces when using the Fisherface algorithm.

In simple terms, the basic principle of Eigenfaces is that it will calculate a set of special images (eigenfaces) and blending ratios (eigenvalues), which when combined in different ways can generate each of the images in the training set but can also be used to differentiate the many face images in the training set from each other. For example, if some of the faces in the training set had a moustache and some did not, then there would be at least one eigenface that shows a moustache, and so the training faces with a moustache would have a high blending ratio for that eigenface to show that it has a moustache, and the faces without a moustache would have a low blending ratio for that eigenvector. If the training set had 5 people with 20 faces for each person, then there would be 100 eigenfaces and eigenvalues to differentiate the 100 total faces in the training set, and in fact these would be sorted so the first few eigenfaces and eigenvalues would be the most critical differentiators, and the last few eigenfaces and eigenvalues would just be random pixel noises that don't actually help to differentiate the data. So it is common practice to discard some of the last eigenfaces and just keep the first 50 or so eigenfaces.

In comparison, the basic principle of Fisherfaces is that instead of calculating a special eigenvector and eigenvalue for each image in the training set, it only calculates one special eigenvector and eigenvalue for each person. So in the preceding example that has 5 people with 20 faces for each person, the Eigenfaces algorithm would use 100 eigenfaces and eigenvalues whereas the Fisherfaces algorithm would use just 5 fisherfaces and eigenvalues.

To access the internal data structures of the Eigenfaces and Fisherfaces algorithms, we must use the `cv::Algorithm::get()` function to obtain them at runtime, as there is no access to them at compile time. The data structures are used internally as part of mathematical calculations rather than for image processing, so they are usually stored as floating-point numbers typically ranging between 0.0 and 1.0, rather than 8-bit uchar pixels ranging from 0 to 255, similar to pixels in regular images. Also, they are often either a 1D row or column matrix or they make up one of the many 1D rows or columns of a larger matrix. So before you can display many of these internal data structures, you must reshape them to be the correct rectangular shape, and convert them to 8-bit uchar pixels between 0 and 255. As the matrix data might range from 0.0 to 1.0 or -1.0 to 1.0 or anything else, you can use the `cv::normalize()` function with the `cv::NORM_MINMAX` option to make sure it outputs data ranging between 0 and 255 no matter what the input range may be. Let's create a function to perform this reshaping to a rectangle and conversion to 8-bit pixels for us as follows:

```
// Convert the matrix row or column (float matrix) to a
// rectangular 8-bit image that can be displayed or saved.
// Scales the values to be between 0 to 255.
Mat getImageFrom1DFloatMat(const Mat matrixRow, int height)
{
    // Make a rectangular shaped image instead of a single row.
    Mat rectangularMat = matrixRow.reshape(1, height);
    // Scale the values to be between 0 to 255 and store them
    // as a regular 8-bit uchar image.
    Mat dst;
    normalize(rectangularMat, dst, 0, 255, NORM_MINMAX,
                 CV_8UC1);
    return dst;
}
```

To make it easier to debug OpenCV code and even more so when internally debugging the `cv::Algorithm` data structure, we can use the `ImageUtils.cpp` and `ImageUtils.h` files to display information about a `cv::Mat` structure easily as follows:

```
Mat img = ...;
printMatInfo(img, "My Image");
```

You will see something similar to the following printed to your console:

My Image: 640w480h 3ch 8bpp, range[79,253][20,58][18,87]

This tells you that it is 640 elements wide and 480 high (that is, a 640 x 480 image or a 480 x 640 matrix, depending on how you view it), with three channels per pixel that are 8-bits each (that is, a regular BGR image), and it shows the min and max value in the image for each of the color channels.

> It is also possible to print the actual contents of an image or matrix by using the `printMat()` function instead of the `printMatInfo()` function. This is quite handy for viewing matrices and multichannel-float matrices as these can be quite tricky to view for beginners.
>
> The ImageUtils code is mostly for OpenCV's C interface, but is gradually including more of the C++ interface over time. The the most recent version can always be found at `http://shervinemami.info/openCV.html`.

Average face

Both the Eigenfaces and Fisherfaces algorithms first calculate the average face that is the mathematical average of all the training images, so they can subtract the average image from each facial image to have better face recognition results. So let's view the average face from our training set. The average face is named mean in the Eigenfaces and Fisherfaces implementations, shown as follows:

```
Mat averageFace = model->get<Mat>("mean");
printMatInfo(averageFace, "averageFace (row)");
// Convert a 1D float row matrix to a regular 8-bit image.
averageFace = getImageFrom1DFloatMat(averageFace, faceHeight);
printMatInfo(averageFace, "averageFace");
imshow("averageFace", averageFace);
```

You should now see an average face image on your screen similar to the following (enlarged) image that is a combination of a man, a woman, and a baby. You should also see similar text shown on your console:

averageFace (row): 4900w1h 1ch 64bpp, range[5.21,251.47]

averageFace: 70w70h 1ch 8bpp, range[0,255]

The image would appear as shown in the following screenshot:

Notice that **averageFace (row)** was a single row matrix of 64-bit floats, whereas **averageFace** is a rectangular image with 8-bit pixels covering the full range from 0 to 255.

Eigenvalues, Eigenfaces, and Fisherfaces

Let's view the actual component values in the eigenvalues (as text):

```
Mat eigenvalues = model->get<Mat>("eigenvalues");
printMat(eigenvalues, "eigenvalues");
```

For Eigenfaces, there is one eigenvalue for each face, so if we have three people with four faces each, we get a column vector with 12 eigenvalues sorted from best to worst as follows:

```
eigenvalues: 1w18h 1ch 64bpp, range[4.52e+04,2.02836e+06]
2.03e+06
1.09e+06
5.23e+05
4.04e+05
2.66e+05
2.31e+05
1.85e+05
1.23e+05
9.18e+04
7.61e+04
6.91e+04
4.52e+04
```

For Fisherfaces, there is just one eigenvalue for each extra person, so if there are three people with four faces each, we just get a row vector with two eigenvalues as follows:

```
eigenvalues: 2w1h 1ch 64bpp, range[152.4,316.6]
317, 152
```

To view the eigenvectors (as Eigenface or Fisherface images), we must extract them as columns from the big eigenvectors matrix. As data in OpenCV and C/C++ is normally stored in matrices using row-major order, it means that to extract a column, we should use the `Mat::clone()` function to ensure the data will be continuous, otherwise we can't reshape the data to a rectangle. Once we have a continuous column Mat, we can display the eigenvectors using the `getImageFrom1DFloatMat()` function just like we did for the average face:

```
// Get the eigenvectors
Mat eigenvectors = model->get<Mat>("eigenvectors");
printMatInfo(eigenvectors, "eigenvectors");

// Show the best 20 eigenfaces
for (int i = 0; i < min(20, eigenvectors.cols); i++) {
    // Create a continuous column vector from eigenvector #i.
    Mat eigenvector = eigenvectors.col(i).clone();

    Mat eigenface = getImageFrom1DFloatMat(eigenvector,
                              faceHeight);
    imshow(format("Eigenface%d", i), eigenface);
}
```

The following figure displays eigenvectors as images. You can see that for three people with four faces, there are 12 Eigenfaces (left-hand side of the figure) or two Fisherfaces (right-hand side).

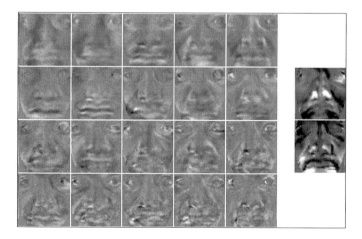

Notice that both Eigenfaces and Fisherfaces seem to have the resemblance of some facial features but they don't really look like faces. This is simply because the average face was subtracted from them, so they just show the differences for each Eigenface from the average face. The numbering shows which Eigenface it is, because they are always ordered from the most significant Eigenface to the least significant Eigenface, and if you have 50 or more Eigenfaces then the later Eigenfaces will often just show random image noise and therefore should be discarded.

Step 4: Face recognition

Now that we have trained the Eigenfaces or Fisherfaces machine-learning algorithm with our set of training images and face labels, we are finally ready to figure out who a person is, just from a facial image! This last step is referred to as face recognition or face identification.

Face identification: Recognizing people from their face

Thanks to OpenCV's `FaceRecognizer` class, we can identify the person in a photo simply by calling the `FaceRecognizer::predict()` function on a facial image as follows:

```
int identity = model->predict(preprocessedFace);
```

This `identity` value will be the label number that we originally used when collecting faces for training. For example, 0 for the first person, 1 for the second person, and so on.

The problem with this identification is that it will always predict one of the given people, even if the input photo is of an unknown person or of a car. It would still tell you which person is the most likely person in that photo, so it can be difficult to trust the result! The solution is to obtain a confidence metric so we can judge how reliable the result is, and if it seems that the confidence is too low then we assume it is an unknown person.

Face verification: Validating that it is the claimed person

To confirm if the result of the prediction is reliable or whether it should be taken as an unknown person, we perform face verification (also referred to as face authentication), to obtain a confidence metric showing whether the single face image is similar to the claimed person (as opposed to face identification, which we just performed, comparing the single face image with many people).

OpenCV's `FaceRecognizer` class can return a confidence metric when you call the `predict()` function but unfortunately the confidence metric is simply based on the distance in eigen-subspace, so it is not very reliable. The method we will use is to reconstruct the facial image using the eigenvectors and eigenvalues, and compare this reconstructed image with the input image. If the person had many of their faces included in the training set, then the reconstruction should work quite well from the learnt eigenvectors and eigenvalues, but if the person did not have any faces in the training set (or did not have any that have similar lighting and facial expressions as the test image), then the reconstructed face will look very different from the input face, signaling that it is probably an unknown face.

Remember we said earlier that the Eigenfaces and Fisherfaces algorithms are based on the notion that an image can be roughly represented as a set of eigenvectors (special face images) and eigenvalues (blending ratios). So if we combine all the eigenvectors with the eigenvalues from one of the faces in the training set then we should obtain a fairly close replica of that original training image. The same applies with other images that are similar to the training set — if we combine the trained eigenvectors with the eigenvalues from a similar test image, we should be able to reconstruct an image that is somewhat a replica to the test image.

Once again, OpenCV's `FaceRecognizer` class makes it quite easy to generate a reconstructed face from any input image, by using the `subspaceProject()` function to project onto the eigenspace and the `subspaceReconstruct()` function to go back from eigenspace to image space. The trick is that we need to convert it from a floating-point row matrix to a rectangular 8-bit image (like we did when displaying the average face and eigenfaces), but we don't want to normalize the data, as it is already in the ideal scale to compare with the original image. If we normalized the data, it would have a different brightness and contrast from the input image, and it would become difficult to compare the image similarity just by using the L2 relative error. This is done as follows:

```
// Get some required data from the FaceRecognizer model.
Mat eigenvectors = model->get<Mat>("eigenvectors");
Mat averageFaceRow = model->get<Mat>("mean");

// Project the input image onto the eigenspace.
Mat projection = subspaceProject(eigenvectors, averageFaceRow,
                    preprocessedFace.reshape(1,1));

// Generate the reconstructed face back from the eigenspace.
Mat reconstructionRow = subspaceReconstruct(eigenvectors,
                    averageFaceRow, projection);

// Make it a rectangular shaped image instead of a single row.
```

```
Mat reconstructionMat = reconstructionRow.reshape(1,
                    faceHeight);
// Convert the floating-point pixels to regular 8-bit uchar.
Mat reconstructedFace = Mat(reconstructionMat.size(), CV_8U);
reconstructionMat.convertTo(reconstructedFace, CV_8U, 1, 0);
```

The following image shows two typical reconstructed faces. The face on the left-hand side was reconstructed well because it was from a known person, whereas the face on the right-hand side was reconstructed badly because it was from an unknown person or a known person but with unknown lighting conditions/facial expression/ face direction.

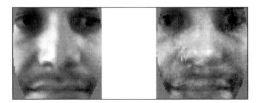

We can now calculate how similar this reconstructed face is to the input face by using the same `getSimilarity()` function we created previously for comparing two images, where a value less than 0.3 implies that the two images are very similar. For Eigenfaces, there is one eigenvector for each face, so reconstruction tends to work well and therefore we can typically use a threshold of 0.5, but Fisherfaces has just one eigenvector for each person, so reconstruction will not work as well and therefore it needs a higher threshold, say 0.7. This is done as follows:

```
similarity = getSimilarity(preprocessedFace,
                        reconstructedFace);
if (similarity > UNKNOWN_PERSON_THRESHOLD) {
    identity = -1;      // Unknown person.
}
```

Now you can just print the identity to the console, or use it for wherever your imagination takes you! Remember that this face recognition method and this face verification method are only reliable in the certain conditions that you train it for. So to obtain good recognition accuracy, you will need to ensure that the training set of each person covers the full range of lighting conditions, facial expressions, and angles that you expect to test with. The face preprocessing stage helped reduce some differences with lighting conditions and in-plane rotation (if the person tilts their head towards their left or right shoulder), but for other differences such as out-of-plane rotation (if the person turns their head towards the left-hand side or right-hand side), it will only work if it is covered well in your training set.

Finishing touches: Saving and loading files

You could potentially add a command-line based method that processes input files and saves them to the disk, or even perform face detection, face preprocessing and/ or face recognition as a web service, and so on. For these types of projects, it is quite easy to add the desired functionality by using the `save` and `load` functions of the `FaceRecognizer` class. You may also want to save the trained data and then load it on the program's start up.

Saving the trained model to an XML or YML file is very easy:

```
model->save("trainedModel.yml");
```

You may also want to save the array of preprocessed faces and labels, if you will want to add more data to the training set later.

For example, here is some sample code for loading the trained model from a file. Note that you must specify the face recognition algorithm (for example `FaceRecognizer.Eigenfaces` or `FaceRecognizer.Fisherfaces`) that was originally used to create the trained model:

```
string facerecAlgorithm = "FaceRecognizer.Fisherfaces";
model = Algorithm::create<FaceRecognizer>(facerecAlgorithm);
Mat labels;
try {
    model->load("trainedModel.yml");
    labels = model->get<Mat>("labels");
} catch (cv::Exception &e) {}
if (labels.rows <= 0) {
    cerr << "ERROR: Couldn't load trained data from "
            "[trainedModel.yml]!" << endl;
    exit(1);
}
```

Finishing touches: Making a nice and interactive GUI

While the code given so far in this chapter is sufficient for a whole face recognition system, there still needs to be a way to put the data into the system and a way to use it. Many face recognition systems for research will choose the ideal input to be text files listing where the static image files are stored on the computer, as well as other important data such as the true name or identity of the person and perhaps true pixel coordinates of regions of the face (such as ground truth of where the face and eye centers actually are). This would either be collected manually by another face recognition system.

The ideal output would then be a text file comparing the recognition results with the ground truth, so that statistics may be obtained for comparing the face recognition system with other face recognition systems.

However, as the face recognition system in this chapter is designed for learning as well as practical fun purposes, rather than competing with the latest research methods it is useful to have an easy-to-use GUI that allows face collection, training, and testing, interactively from the webcam in real time. So this section will provide an interactive GUI providing these features. The reader is expected to either use this provided GUI that comes with this book, or to modify the GUI for their own purposes, or to ignore this GUI and design their own GUI to perform the face recognition techniques discussed so far.

As we need the GUI to perform multiple tasks, let's create a set of modes or states that the GUI will have, with buttons or mouse clicks for the user to change modes:

- **Startup**: This state loads and initializes the data and webcam.
- **Detection**: This state detects faces and shows them with preprocessing, until the user clicks on the **Add Person** button.
- **Collection**: This state collects faces for the current person, until the user clicks anywhere in the window. This also shows the most recent face of each person. User clicks either one of the existing people or the **Add Person** button, to collect faces for different people.
- **Training**: In this state, the system is trained with the help of all the collected faces of all the collected people.
- **Recognition**: This consists of highlighting the recognized person and showing a confidence meter. The user clicks either one of the people or the **Add Person** button, to return to mode 2 (Collection).

To quit, the user can hit Escape in the window at any time. Let's also add a **Delete All** mode that restarts a new face recognition system, and a **Debug** button that toggles the display of extra debug info. We can create an enumerated mode variable to show the current mode.

Drawing the GUI elements

To display the current mode on the screen, let's create a function to draw text easily. OpenCV comes with a `cv::putText()` function with several fonts and anti-aliasing, but it can be tricky to place the text in the correct location that you want. Luckily, there is also a `cv::getTextSize()` function to calculate the bounding box around the text, so we can create a wrapper function to make it easier to place text. We want to be able to place text along any edge of the window and make sure it is completely visible and also to allow placing multiple lines or words of text next to each other without overwriting each other. So here is a wrapper function to allow you to specify either left-justified or right-justified, as well as to specify top-justified or bottom-justified, and return the bounding box, so we can easily draw multiple lines of text on any corner or edge of the window:

```
// Draw text into an image. Defaults to top-left-justified
// text, so give negative x coords for right-justified text,
// and/or negative y coords for bottom-justified text.
// Returns the bounding rect around the drawn text.
Rect drawString(Mat img, string text, Point coord, Scalar
            color, float fontScale = 0.6f, int thickness = 1,
            int fontFace = FONT_HERSHEY_COMPLEX);
```

Now to display the current mode on the GUI, as the background of the window will be the camera feed, it is quite possible that if we simply draw text over the camera feed, it might be the same color as the camera background! So let's just draw a black shadow of text that is just 1 pixel apart from the foreground text we want to draw. Let's also draw a line of helpful text below it, so the user knows the steps to follow. Here is an example of how to draw some text using the `drawString()` function:

```
string msg = "Click [Add Person] when ready to collect faces.";
// Draw it as black shadow & again as white text.
float txtSize = 0.4;
int BORDER = 10;
drawString(displayedFrame, msg, Point(BORDER, -BORDER-2),
            CV_RGB(0,0,0), txtSize);
Rect rcHelp = drawString(displayedFrame, msg, Point(BORDER+1,
            -BORDER-1), CV_RGB(255,255,255), txtSize);
```

The following partial screenshot shows the mode and info at the bottom of the GUI window, overlaid on top of the camera image:

We mentioned that we want a few GUI buttons, so let's create a function to draw a GUI button easily as follows:

```
// Draw a GUI button into the image, using drawString().
// Can give a minWidth to have several buttons of same width.
// Returns the bounding rect around the drawn button.
Rect drawButton(Mat img, string text, Point coord,
                int minWidth = 0)
{
    const int B = 10;
    Point textCoord = Point(coord.x + B, coord.y + B);
    // Get the bounding box around the text.
    Rect rcText = drawString(img, text, textCoord,
                CV_RGB(0,0,0));
    // Draw a filled rectangle around the text.
    Rect rcButton = Rect(rcText.x - B, rcText.y - B,
                rcText.width + 2*B, rcText.height + 2*B);
    // Set a minimum button width.
    if (rcButton.width < minWidth)
        rcButton.width = minWidth;
    // Make a semi-transparent white rectangle.
    Mat matButton = img(rcButton);
    matButton += CV_RGB(90, 90, 90);
    // Draw a non-transparent white border.
    rectangle(img, rcButton, CV_RGB(200,200,200), 1, CV_AA);

    // Draw the actual text that will be displayed.
    drawString(img, text, textCoord, CV_RGB(10,55,20));

    return rcButton;
}
```

Now we create several clickable GUI buttons using the `drawButton()` function, which will always be shown at the top-left of the GUI, as shown in the following partial screenshot:

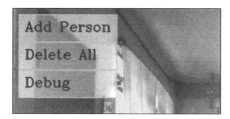

As we mentioned, the GUI program has some modes that it switches between (as a finite state machine), beginning with the Startup mode. We will store the current mode as the `m_mode` variable.

Startup mode

In Startup mode, we just need to load the XML detector files to detect the face and eyes and initialize the webcam, which we've already covered. Let's also create a main GUI window with a mouse callback function that OpenCV will call whenever the user moves or clicks their mouse in our window. It may also be desirable to set the camera resolution to something reasonable, for example, 640 x 480, if the camera supports it. This is done as follows:

```
// Create a GUI window for display on the screen.
namedWindow(windowName);
// Call "onMouse()" when the user clicks in the window.
setMouseCallback(windowName, onMouse, 0);

// Set the camera resolution. Only works for some systems.
videoCapture.set(CV_CAP_PROP_FRAME_WIDTH, 640);
videoCapture.set(CV_CAP_PROP_FRAME_HEIGHT, 480);

// We're already initialized, so let's start in Detection mode.
m_mode = MODE_DETECTION;
```

Detection mode

In Detection mode, we want to continuously detect faces and eyes, draw rectangles or circles around them to show the detection result, and show the current preprocessed face. In fact we will want these to be displayed no matter which mode we are in. The only thing special about Detection mode is that it will change to the next mode (Collection) when the user clicks the **Add Person** button.

If you remember from the detection step previously in this chapter, the output of our detection stage will be:

- `Mat preprocessedFace`: The preprocessed face (if face and eyes were detected)
- `Rect faceRect`: The detected face region coordinates
- `Point leftEye, rightEye`: The detected left and right eye center coordinates

So we should check if a preprocessed face was returned and draw a rectangle and circles around the face and eyes if they were detected as follows:

```
bool gotFaceAndEyes = false;
if (preprocessedFace.data)
    gotFaceAndEyes = true;

if (faceRect.width > 0) {
    // Draw an anti-aliased rectangle around the detected face.
    rectangle(displayedFrame, faceRect, CV_RGB(255, 255, 0), 2,
            CV_AA);

    // Draw light-blue anti-aliased circles for the 2 eyes.
    Scalar eyeColor = CV_RGB(0,255,255);
    if (leftEye.x >= 0) {    // Check if the eye was detected
        circle(displayedFrame, Point(faceRect.x + leftEye.x,
                faceRect.y + leftEye.y), 6, eyeColor, 1,
                CV_AA);
    }
    if (rightEye.x >= 0) {    // Check if the eye was detected
        circle(displayedFrame, Point(faceRect.x + rightEye.x,
                faceRect.y + rightEye.y), 6, eyeColor, 1,
                CV_AA);
    }
}
```

We will overlay the current preprocessed face at the top-center of the window as follows:

```
int cx = (displayedFrame.cols - faceWidth) / 2;
if (preprocessedFace.data) {
    // Get a BGR version of the face, since the output is BGR.
    Mat srcBGR = Mat(preprocessedFace.size(), CV_8UC3);
    cvtColor(preprocessedFace, srcBGR, CV_GRAY2BGR);

    // Get the destination ROI.
    Rect dstRC = Rect(cx, BORDER, faceWidth, faceHeight);
```

```
    Mat dstROI = displayedFrame(dstRC);

    // Copy the pixels from src to dst.
    srcBGR.copyTo(dstROI);
}
// Draw an anti-aliased border around the face.
rectangle(displayedFrame, Rect(cx-1, BORDER-1, faceWidth+2,
            faceHeight+2), CV_RGB(200,200,200), 1, CV_AA);
```

The following screenshot shows the displayed GUI when in Detection mode.
The preprocessed face is shown at the top-center, and the detected face and
eyes are marked:

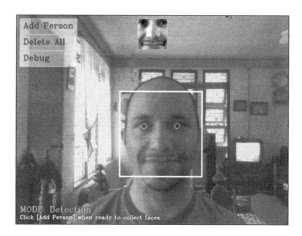

Collection mode

We enter Collection mode when the user clicks on the **Add Person** button to
signal that they want to begin collecting faces for a new person. As mentioned
previously, we have limited the face collection to one face per second and then only
if it has changed noticeably from the previously collected face. And remember, we
decided to collect not only the preprocessed face but also the mirror image of the
preprocessed face.

In Collection mode, we want to show the most recent face of each known person and
let the user click on one of those people to add more faces to them or click the **Add
Person** button to add a new person to the collection. The user must click somewhere
in the middle of the window to continue to the next (Training) mode.

So first we need to keep a reference to the latest face that was collected for each person. We'll do this by updating the m_latestFaces array of integers, which just stores the array index of each person, from the big preprocessedFaces array (that is, the collection of all faces of all the people). As we also store the mirrored face in that array, we want to reference the second last face, not the last face. This code should be appended to the code that adds a new face (and mirrored face) to the preprocessedFaces array as follows:

```
// Keep a reference to the latest face of each person.
m_latestFaces[m_selectedPerson] = preprocessedFaces.size() - 2;
```

We just have to remember to always grow or shrink the m_latestFaces array whenever a new person is added or deleted (for example, due to the user clicking on the **Add Person** button). Now let's display the most recent face for each of the collected people, on the right-hand side of the window (both in Collection mode and Recognition mode later) as follows:

```
m_gui_faces_left = displayedFrame.cols - BORDER - faceWidth;
m_gui_faces_top = BORDER;
for (int i=0; i<m_numPersons; i++) {
    int index = m_latestFaces[i];
    if (index >= 0 && index < (int)preprocessedFaces.size()) {
        Mat srcGray = preprocessedFaces[index];
        if (srcGray.data) {
            // Get a BGR face, since the output is BGR.
            Mat srcBGR = Mat(srcGray.size(), CV_8UC3);
            cvtColor(srcGray, srcBGR, CV_GRAY2BGR);

            // Get the destination ROI
            int y = min(m_gui_faces_top + i * faceHeight,
                        displayedFrame.rows - faceHeight);
            Rect dstRC = Rect(m_gui_faces_left, y, faceWidth,
                        faceHeight);
            Mat dstROI = displayedFrame(dstRC);

            // Copy the pixels from src to dst.
            srcBGR.copyTo(dstROI);
        }
    }
}
```

We also want to highlight the current person being collected, using a thick red border around their face. This is done as follows:

```
if (m_mode == MODE_COLLECT_FACES) {
    if (m_selectedPerson >= 0 &&
                m_selectedPerson < m_numPersons) {
        int y = min(m_gui_faces_top + m_selectedPerson *
                faceHeight, displayedFrame.rows -
                faceHeight);
        Rect rc = Rect(m_gui_faces_left, y, faceWidth,
                faceHeight);
        rectangle(displayedFrame, rc, CV_RGB(255,0,0), 3,
                CV_AA);
    }
}
```

The following partial screenshot shows the typical display when faces for several people have been collected. The user can click any of the people at the top-right to collect more faces for that person.

Training mode

When the user finally clicks in the middle of the window, the face recognition algorithm will begin training on all the collected faces. But it is important to make sure there have been enough faces or people collected, otherwise the program may crash. In general, this just requires making sure there is at least one face in the training set (which implies there is at least one person). But the Fisherfaces algorithm looks for comparisons between people, so if there are less than two people in the training set, it will also crash. So we must check whether the selected face recognition algorithm is Fisherfaces. If it is, then we require at least two people with faces, otherwise we require at least one person with a face. If there isn't enough data, then the program goes back to Collection mode so the user can add more faces before training.

To check if there are at least two people with collected faces, we can make sure that when a user clicks on the **Add Person** button, a new person is only added if there isn't any empty person (that is, a person that was added but does not have any collected faces yet). We can then also make sure that if there are just two people and we are using the Fisherfaces algorithm, then we must make sure an m_latestFaces reference was set for the last person during the collection mode. m_latestFaces[i] is initialized to -1 when there still haven't been any faces added to that person, and then it becomes 0 or higher once faces for that person have been added. This is done as follows:

```
// Check if there is enough data to train from.
bool haveEnoughData = true;
if (!strcmp(facerecAlgorithm, "FaceRecognizer.Fisherfaces")) {
    if ((m_numPersons < 2) ||
              (m_numPersons == 2 && m_latestFaces[1] < 0) ) {
        cout << "Fisherfaces needs >= 2 people!" << endl;
        haveEnoughData = false;
    }
}
if (m_numPersons < 1 || preprocessedFaces.size() <= 0 ||
          preprocessedFaces.size() != faceLabels.size()) {
    cout << "Need data before it can be learnt!" << endl;
    haveEnoughData = false;
}

if (haveEnoughData) {
    // Train collected faces using Eigenfaces or Fisherfaces.
    model = learnCollectedFaces(preprocessedFaces, faceLabels,
              facerecAlgorithm);

    // Now that training is over, we can start recognizing!
    m_mode = MODE_RECOGNITION;
}
else {
    // Not enough training data, go back to Collection mode!
    m_mode = MODE_COLLECT_FACES;
}
```

The training may take a fraction of a second or it may take several seconds or even minutes, depending on how much data is collected. Once the training of collected faces is complete, the face recognition system will automatically enter Recognition mode.

Recognition mode

In Recognition mode, a confidence meter is shown next to the preprocessed face, so the user knows how reliable the recognition is. If the confidence level is higher than the unknown threshold, it will draw a green rectangle around the recognized person to show the result easily. The user can add more faces for further training if they click on the **Add Person** button or one of the existing people, which causes the program to return to the Collection mode.

Now we have obtained the recognized identity and the similarity with the reconstructed face as mentioned earlier. To display the confidence meter, we know that the L2 similarity value is generally between 0 to 0.5 for high confidence and between 0.5 to 1.0 for low confidence, so we can just subtract it from 1.0 to get the confidence level between 0.0 to 1.0. Then we just draw a filled rectangle using the confidence level as the ratio shown as follows:

```
int cx = (displayedFrame.cols - faceWidth) / 2;
Point ptBottomRight = Point(cx - 5, BORDER + faceHeight);
Point ptTopLeft = Point(cx - 15, BORDER);

// Draw a gray line showing the threshold for "unknown" people.
Point ptThreshold = Point(ptTopLeft.x, ptBottomRight.y -
                (1.0 - UNKNOWN_PERSON_THRESHOLD) * faceHeight);
rectangle(displayedFrame, ptThreshold, Point(ptBottomRight.x,
            ptThreshold.y), CV_RGB(200,200,200), 1, CV_AA);

// Crop the confidence rating between 0 to 1 to fit in the bar.
double confidenceRatio = 1.0 - min(max(similarity, 0.0), 1.0);
Point ptConfidence = Point(ptTopLeft.x, ptBottomRight.y -
                confidenceRatio * faceHeight);

// Show the light-blue confidence bar.
rectangle(displayedFrame, ptConfidence, ptBottomRight,
            CV_RGB(0,255,255), CV_FILLED, CV_AA);
// Show the gray border of the bar.
rectangle(displayedFrame, ptTopLeft, ptBottomRight,
            CV_RGB(200,200,200), 1, CV_AA);
```

To highlight the recognized person, we draw a green rectangle around their face as follows:

```
if (identity >= 0 && identity < 1000) {
    int y = min(m_gui_faces_top + identity * faceHeight,
                displayedFrame.rows - faceHeight);
    Rect rc = Rect(m_gui_faces_left, y, faceWidth, faceHeight);
    rectangle(displayedFrame, rc, CV_RGB(0,255,0), 3, CV_AA);
}
```

The following partial screenshot shows a typical display when running in Recognition mode, showing the confidence meter next to the preprocessed face at the top-center, and highlighting the recognized person in the top-right corner.

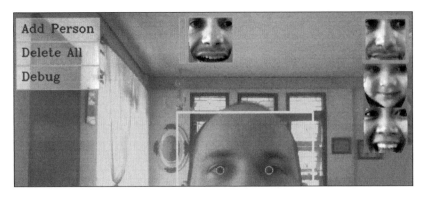

Checking and handling mouse clicks

Now that we have all our GUI elements drawn, we just need to process mouse events. When we initialized the display window, we told OpenCV that we want a mouse event callback to our onMouse function. We don't care about mouse movement, only the mouse clicks, so first we skip the mouse events that aren't for the left-mouse-button click as follows:

```
void onMouse(int event, int x, int y, int, void*)
{
    if (event != CV_EVENT_LBUTTONDOWN)
        return;

    Point pt = Point(x,y);

    ... (handle mouse clicks) ...

}
```

As we obtained the drawn rectangle bounds of the buttons when drawing them, we just check if the mouse click location is in any of our button regions by calling OpenCV's inside() function. Now we can check for each button we have created.

When the user clicks on the **Add Person** button, we just add 1 to the m_numPersons variable, allocate more space in the m_latestFaces variable, select the new person for collection, and begin Collection mode (no matter which mode we were previously in).

But there is one complication; to ensure that we have at least one face for each person when training, we will only allocate space for a new person if there isn't already a person with zero faces. This will ensure that we can always check the value of m_latestFaces[m_numPersons-1] to see if a face has been collected for every person. This is done as follows:

```
if (pt.inside(m_btnAddPerson)) {
    // Ensure there isn't a person without collected faces.
    if ((m_numPersons==0) ||
            (m_latestFaces[m_numPersons-1] >= 0)) {
        // Add a new person.
        m_numPersons++;
        m_latestFaces.push_back(-1);
    }
    m_selectedPerson = m_numPersons - 1;
    m_mode = MODE_COLLECT_FACES;
}
```

This method can be used to test for other button clicks, such as toggling the debug flag as follows:

```
else if (pt.inside(m_btnDebug)) {
    m_debug = !m_debug;
}
```

To handle the **Delete All** button, we need to empty various data structures that are local to our main loop (that is, not accessible from the mouse event callback function), so we change to the **Delete All** mode and then we can delete everything from inside the main loop. We also must deal with the user clicking the main window (that is, not a button). If they clicked on one of the people on the right-hand side, then we want to select that person and change to Collection mode. Or if they clicked in the main window while in Collection mode, then we want to change to Training mode. This is done as follows:

```
else {
    // Check if the user clicked on a face from the list.
    int clickedPerson = -1;
    for (int i=0; i<m_numPersons; i++) {
        if (m_gui_faces_top >= 0) {
            Rect rcFace = Rect(m_gui_faces_left,
                        m_gui_faces_top + i * faceHeight,
                        faceWidth, faceHeight);
            if (pt.inside(rcFace)) {
                clickedPerson = i;
                break;
```

```
            }
        }
    }
    // Change the selected person, if the user clicked a face.
    if (clickedPerson >= 0) {
        // Change the current person & collect more photos.
        m_selectedPerson = clickedPerson;
        m_mode = MODE_COLLECT_FACES;
    }
    // Otherwise they clicked in the center.
    else {
        // Change to training mode if it was collecting faces.
        if (m_mode == MODE_COLLECT_FACES) {
            m_mode = MODE_TRAINING;
        }
    }
}
```

Summary

This chapter has shown you all the steps required to create a real time face recognition app, with enough preprocessing to allow some differences between the training set conditions and the testing set conditions, just using basic algorithms. We used face detection to find the location of a face within the camera image, followed by several forms of face preprocessing to reduce the effects of different lighting conditions, camera and face orientations, and facial expressions. We then trained an Eigenfaces or Fisherfaces machine-learning system with the preprocessed faces we collected, and finally we performed face recognition to see who the person is with face verification providing a confidence metric in case it is an unknown person.

Rather than providing a command-line tool that processes image files in an offline manner, we combined all the preceding steps into a self-contained real time GUI program to allow immediate use of the face recognition system. You should be able to modify the behavior of the system for your own purposes, such as to allow an automatic login of your computer, or if you are interested in improving the recognition reliability then you can read conference papers about recent advances in face recognition to potentially improve each step of the program until it is reliable enough for your specific needs. For example, you could improve the face preprocessing stages, or use a more advanced machine-learning algorithm, or an even better face verification algorithm, based on methods at http://www.face-rec.org/algorithms/ and http://www.cvpapers.com.

References

- *Rapid Object Detection using a Boosted Cascade of Simple Features, P. Viola and M.J. Jones, Proceedings of the IEEE Transactions on CVPR 2001, Vol. 1, pp. 511-518*

- *An Extended Set of Haar-like Features for Rapid Object Detection, R. Lienhart and J. Maydt, Proceedings of the IEEE Transactions on ICIP 2002, Vol. 1, pp. 900-903*

- *Face Description with Local Binary Patterns: Application to Face Recognition, T. Ahonen, A. Hadid and M. Pietikäinen, Proceedings of the IEEE Transactions on PAMI 2006, Vol. 28, Issue 12, pp. 2037-2041*

- *Learning OpenCV: Computer Vision with the OpenCV Library, G. Bradski and A. Kaehler, pp. 186-190, O'Reilly Media.*

- *Eigenfaces for recognition, M. Turk and A. Pentland, Journal of Cognitive Neuroscience 3, pp. 71-86*

- *Eigenfaces vs. Fisherfaces: Recognition using class specific linear projection, P.N. Belhumeur, J. Hespanha and D. Kriegman, Proceedings of the IEEE Transactions on PAMI 1997, Vol. 19, Issue 7, pp. 711–720*

- *Face Recognition with Local Binary Patterns, T. Ahonen, A. Hadid and M. Pietikäinen, Computer Vision - ECCV 2004, pp. 469–48*

Index

Symbols

3D
  marker, placing in 76
3D Morphable Model (3DMM) 191
3D point clouds
  visualizing, with PCL 155-157
3D virtual object
  rendering 82
3D visualization
  support, enabling in OpenCV 116, 117
.pch file 51

A

AAM
  about 191, 235
  model instantiation 249, 250
  overview 236
  search 250-252
active appearance models. *See* **AAM**
Active Shape Model. *See* **ASM**
addRawViewOutput function 60
algorithms, for descriptor matching
  brute force matcher 98
  flann-based matcher 99
alien mode
  generating, skin detection used 16
ALPR 161
Android
  program, porting from desktop to 24
Android 2.2 (Froyo) 24
Android app
  Frames Per Second, displaying for 43
  reviewing 30

Android Cartoonifier app
  customizing 44, 45
Android Emulator 24
Android gallery
  about 33
  image, saving to 33-36
Android menu bar
  cartoon modes, modifying through 37-40
Android NDK app
  cartoonifier code, adding to 28-30
Android notification message
  displaying, for saved image 36, 37
Android project
  color format, inputting from camera 25
  color formats, used for image processing 25
  output color format, for display 26-28
  setting up 24, 25
Android tablet
  Cartoonifier app, running on 8
ANN algorithm 182
annotation tool
  using 198
ANPR
  about 161
  overview 162
ANPR algorithm
  about 163, 164
  pattern recognition steps 164, 165
  plate detection 166
  plate recognition 176
application architecture 52
application infrastructure
  about 114
  ARPipeline.cpp 115
  ARPipeline.hpp 115

flags parameter 268
flann-based matcher 99
floodFill() function 19, 170, 171
Frames Per Second speed
  displaying, of Android app 43
FREAK algorithm 97
ft_data class 195

G

geometrical constraints
  about 199-201
  combined local-global
      representation 207-209
  linear shape models 205-207
  procrustes analysis 202-204
  training 209-211
  visualization 209-211
getList() function 285
getResult method 53
getSimilarity() function 294
getStructuringElement function 168
grayscale conversion 64
GUI
  creating 296
  elements, drawing 297
  modes, creating 296
  mouse clicks, checking 306, 307
  mouse clicks, handling 306, 307
GUI elements
  collection mode 301, 302
  detection mode 299-301
  drawing 297-299
  recognition mode 305, 306
  startup mode 299
  training mode 303, 304

H

hamming code 72
homography estimation
  about 102
  PatternDetector.cpp 103, 104
homography refinement
  about 104, 105
  PatternDetector.cpp 105, 106
HSV (Hue-Saturation-Brightness) 16, 20

I

ICCV conference papers
  URL 44
image
  cartoonifying 31-33
  saving, to Android gallery 33-36
image binarization 65, 66
image recognition 95
imwrite() function 33
Infrared (IR) camera 162
initWithCoder function 83
inside() function 306
iOS project
  creating 48, 49
  OpenCV framework, adding 49-51
  OpenCV headers, including 51, 52
Iterative Closest Point(ICP) procedure 147

J

JavaCV library 24
JNI (Java Native Interface) 24

K

keypoints container 96
k-nearest neighbor (kNN) radius 138

L

Laplacian filters 11
Linear Discriminant Analysis (LDA) 285
loDiff parameter 171

M

main camera processing loop
  for desktop app 10
main_desktop.cpp file 8
marker
  about 62
  limitations 94
  placing, in 3D 76
  strengths 94
marker-based approach
  versus marker-less approach 94, 95

S

saved image
Android notification message, displaying
for 36, 37
savePNGImageToGallery() function 33, 34
savingRegions variable 175
scene
reconstructing 143-146
reconstructing, from multiple view 147-150
Scharr 11
searchScaleFactor parameter 268
segmentation 167-173
setupCamera() function 43
showNotificationMessage() function 36, 37
ShowPreview() function 28, 29, 31
SIFT 97
Simple Sparse Bundle Adjustment (SSBA)
library 151
Singular Value Decomposition
(SVD) 141, 206
sketch drawing
real-life image, converting to 11
sketch image
random pepper noise, reducing from 40, 41
skin color changer
implementing 19-23
skin detection
used, for generating alien mode 16
Skin detection algorithm 16
Sobel 11
Sobel filter 167
solvePnP functions 147
solvePnPRansac function 150
Speeded-Up Robust Features (SURF)
features 133
Startup mode 299
statistical outlier removal (SOR) tool 156
Structure from Motion (SfM)
about 129
exploring 130, 131
subspaceProject() function 293
subspaceReconstruct() function 293
Support Vector Machine (SVM) 161, 166
Support Vector Machine (SVM)
algorithm 173

SURF 97
surfaceChanged() function 43
system components
relationship, diagram 190

T

threshold function 168
training mode 303, 304
TriangulatePoints function 150

U

UIGetScreenImage function 55
UIViewController interface 52
Unity 82
Unreal Engine 82
upDiff parameter 171
user face
placing, for alien mode 17, 18
utilities
about 191
data collections 193
Object-oriented design 191-193

V

videos
capturing, OpenCV used 118
VideoSource interface 57
ViewController class 52
VisualizationController 53
VisualizationControllerclass 85
Visual Studio 8

W

warpAffine function 172, 248
warpAffine() function 276
webcam
accessing 9

X

XCode 8

Thank you for buying
Mastering OpenCV with Practical Computer Vision Projects

About Packt Publishing

Packt, pronounced 'packed', published its first book "*Mastering phpMyAdmin for Effective MySQL Management*" in April 2004 and subsequently continued to specialize in publishing highly focused books on specific technologies and solutions.

Our books and publications share the experiences of your fellow IT professionals in adapting and customizing today's systems, applications, and frameworks. Our solution based books give you the knowledge and power to customize the software and technologies you're using to get the job done. Packt books are more specific and less general than the IT books you have seen in the past. Our unique business model allows us to bring you more focused information, giving you more of what you need to know, and less of what you don't.

Packt is a modern, yet unique publishing company, which focuses on producing quality, cutting-edge books for communities of developers, administrators, and newbies alike. For more information, please visit our website: www.packtpub.com.

About Packt Open Source

In 2010, Packt launched two new brands, Packt Open Source and Packt Enterprise, in order to continue its focus on specialization. This book is part of the Packt Open Source brand, home to books published on software built around Open Source licences, and offering information to anybody from advanced developers to budding web designers. The Open Source brand also runs Packt's Open Source Royalty Scheme, by which Packt gives a royalty to each Open Source project about whose software a book is sold.

Writing for Packt

We welcome all inquiries from people who are interested in authoring. Book proposals should be sent to author@packtpub.com. If your book idea is still at an early stage and you would like to discuss it first before writing a formal book proposal, contact us; one of our commissioning editors will get in touch with you.

We're not just looking for published authors; if you have strong technical skills but no writing experience, our experienced editors can help you develop a writing career, or simply get some additional reward for your expertise.

OpenCV 2 Computer Vision Application Programming Cookbook

ISBN: 978-1-84951-324-1   Paperback: 304 pages

Over 50 recipes to master this library of programming functions for real-time computer vision

1. Teaches you how to program computer vision applications in C++ using the different features of the OpenCV library

2. Demonstrates the important structures and functions of OpenCV in detail with complete working examples

3. Describes fundamental concepts in computer vision and image processing

Processing 2: Creative Programming Cookbook

ISBN: 978-1-84951-794-2   Paperback: 306 pages

Over 90 highly-effective recipes to unleash your creativity with interactive art, graphics, computer vision, 3D, and more

1. Explore the Processing language with a broad range of practical recipes for computational art and graphics

2. Wide coverage of topics including interactive art, computer vision, visualization, drawing in 3D, and much more with Processing

3. Create interactive art installations and learn to export your artwork for print, screen, Internet, and mobile devices

Please check **www.PacktPub.com** for information on our titles

open source
community experience distilled

Mastering openFrameworks:
Creative Coding Demystified

ISBN: 978-1-84951-804-8 Paperback: 300 pages

Boost your creativity and develop highly-interactive
projects for art, 3D, graphics, computer vision and
more, with this comprehensive tutorial

1. A step-by-step practical tutorial that explains
   openFrameworks through easy to understand
   examples

2. Makes use of next generation technologies and
   techniques in your projects involving OpenCV,
   Microsoft Kinect, and so on

3. Sample codes and detailed insights into the
   projects, all using object oriented programming

Blender Game Engine: Beginner's
Guide

ISBN: 978-1-84951-702-7 Paperback: 206 pages

The non programmer's guide to creating 3D video
games

1. Use Blender to create a complete 3D video
   game

2. Ideal entry level to game development without
   the need for coding

3. No programming or scripting required

Please check **www.PacktPub.com** for information on our titles

6141716R00183

Made in the USA
San Bernardino, CA
02 December 2013